GORDON RAMSAY'S

# UNCHARTED

While filming *Uncharted*, Gordon braved jungles, cliffs, and volcanoes to seek the freshest ingredients, the boldest flavors, and regional techniques.

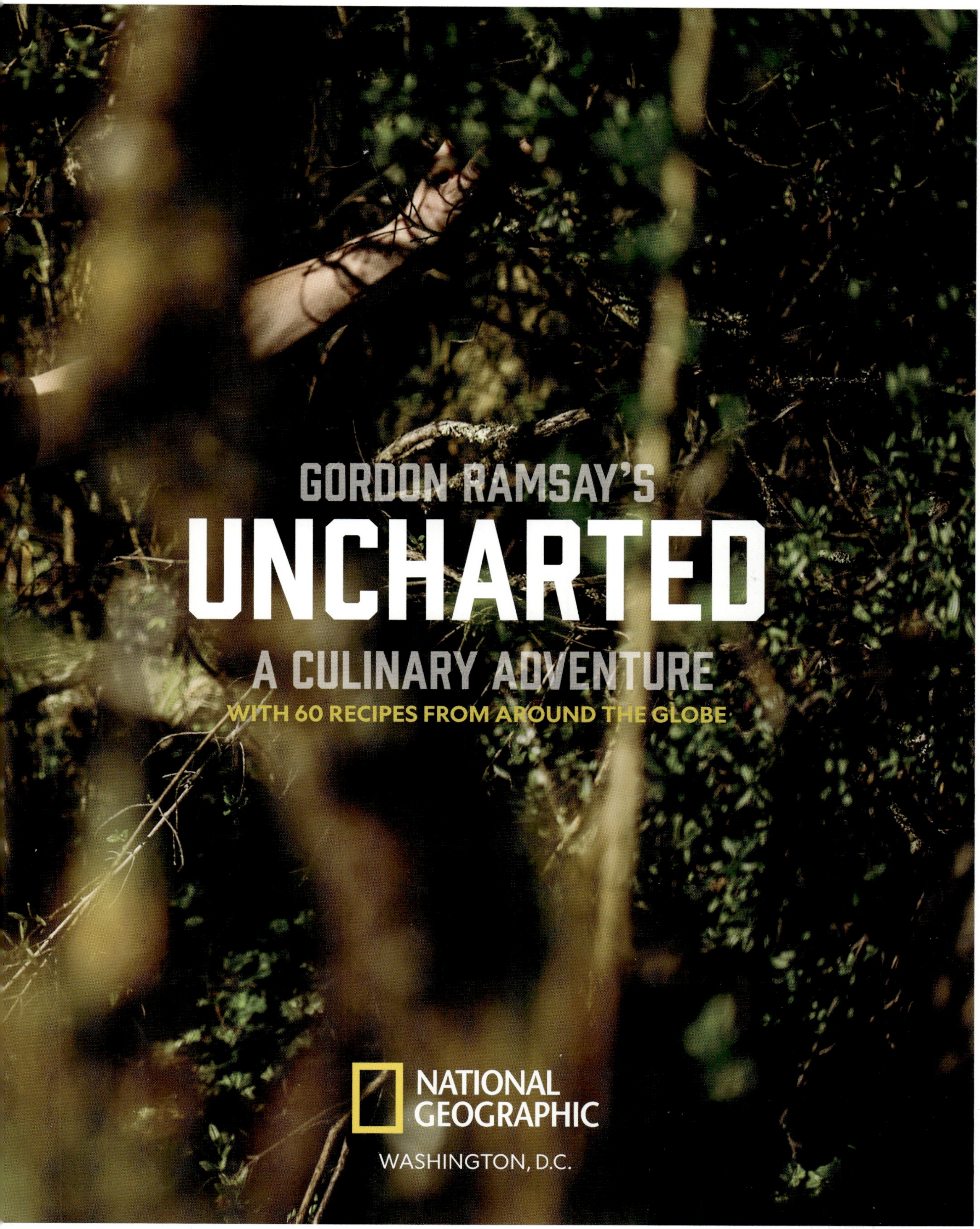

GORDON RAMSAY'S

# UNCHARTED

## A CULINARY ADVENTURE

### WITH 60 RECIPES FROM AROUND THE GLOBE

**NATIONAL GEOGRAPHIC**

WASHINGTON, D.C.

# CONTENTS

Moroccan flavors and ingredients inspired Harissa-Spiced Moroccan Carrots (page 53) and Ras El Hanout Braised Beef Short Ribs (page 50).

# INTRODUCTION

**P**ACK YOUR BAGS and your taste buds to join me on the food adventure of a lifetime, a dirt-under-your-fingernails quest to learn about the ingredients, flavors, dishes, and cultures unique to different locations around the world. In this book, you'll journey with me to 21 destinations, unlocking the secrets to each region's cuisine—just as we do on the National Geographic television series *Gordon Ramsay: Uncharted*.

When we began the show *Uncharted*, I felt that it was important for those in the United States to see me outside of the kitchen. *Uncharted* is hardly my first show about food and adventure. Indeed, my series *Gordon's Great Escape*, which aired on Channel 4 in the United Kingdom in 2010 and 2011, took a deep dive into the culinary traditions of India, Thailand, Cambodia, Malaysia, and Vietnam. In a time when people are increasingly interested in learning about the deeper history and meaning behind local dishes and ingredients on their travels, this opportunity with National Geographic felt like the right time to return to those types of adventures.

*Uncharted* brings cuisine from around the world to viewers through a chef's eyes. Diving in from a hands-on perspective and experiencing it all in person—whether I'm shoveling sheep manure to make an amazing whisky or climbing rocks in Alaska to gather lichen for tea—allows me to get a deeper

The festive conclusion of the Big Cook near Marshall Point Lighthouse on the St. George Peninsula, Maine

understanding of a culture's cuisine. For those watching at home, I like to think the show gently picks you up and sticks you in my rucksack. The audience is right there riding along with me.

The journey through the first three seasons of the show, which are featured in this collection, put me back in touch with the period in my life—between 18 and 27 years old—when I had an incredible introduction to food. My first pair of chef whites and my knife were bought by a charity when I entered catering college. Being the recipient of this kind of generosity pushed me to strive to learn quicker, to be more confident. I was focused, hungry, vulnerable, and desperate to absorb every bit of information and experience. I learned from the ground up. It's very rare that I get to reconnect with that soul-searching vulnerability—but I did just that while filming *Uncharted*.

The more successful I've become in my life, the more I want to return to the essence of my education. I love being back on the floor, as a member of the team and not the one in charge. It challenges me to rely on those who have deep experience and knowledge of local cuisine when I'm dropped into a place with only a good palate and my knife skills.

In restaurant kitchens, we complain when the white asparagus from France is a day late because it inconveniences us with our menu planning. In the locations I visited on *Uncharted*, the chefs and cooks are self-sufficient, depending on local ingredients within a 50-mile (80 km) radius.

Traveling to culinary regions around the world, I get an opportunity to approach food from a beginner's perspective, dropping my expectations and seeing things with a fresh pair of eyes. I don't overstudy

before I get to a new place; I want to go into every destination with an open mind. It makes me slightly nervous—I don't want to disappoint the chefs and experts. But the best thing I can do is let go and let them lead, to get up to speed with what they are showing and telling me. My job is to listen and absorb.

Really understanding the interconnected nature of ingredients and culture is essential. Sharing these culinary traditions with viewers and hearing they've learned something new or can't wait to taste these dishes for themselves—that's what I'm going for. There's no adventure like it. I am grateful for the opportunity to put food back on the map with National Geographic, where it deserves to be.

For me, this journey is all about food and discovering what really lies behind a destination. We've gone to 21 places and have gotten something incredibly special from each and every one of them. *Uncharted* is about being adventurous in learning about the DNA of a region's cuisine. The simplicity of flavors in locally sourced ingredients is the essential character of the show. It makes the experience deeper than just a travel checklist, allowing you to understand the culture and history of each destination so much more.

I want to reposition the foodways of a place, to show that by peeling back the layers we can get to the root of

## For me, this journey is all about food and discovering what really lies behind a destination.

**GO BIG OR GO HOME**
Flames flash over Gordon's
grill as he tackles steaks at
the Big Cook in southeast
Texas.

a region's culinary reputation. When I meet these local chefs, I really want to be mentored by them—each is a key part of discovery. At the end of each adventure, I think about how I can put respect on the table with everything I've learned.

From a chef's point of view, I've missed acquiring my own ingredients. I rely instead on restaurant purveyors. I've missed the journey to the source, which really begins the adventure of creating a dish. Some of the best foodie items, methods, and insights I've learned in my career have come from filming *Uncharted*. It has been a way to tap into the source unlike any cooking show—or experience—I've ever done in my life.

In the discovery process, challenges are as much a part of the adventure as successes are. Wildlife doesn't operate on a timetable. Remoteness and precarious locations are often part of the foraging and hunting equation. Weather may not cooperate. There are only so many hours of daylight. For each destination's experts who rely on these ingredients, the challenges have made them more knowledgeable about the most trusted methods and times to obtain them.

In some cases, these challenges resulted in missing out on getting the ingredients I wanted, forcing me to pivot, change my expectations, and forge a new path. Even if I am not going to be successful in obtaining an ingredient, I still want to have a bloody good go at it.

Even if I feel the disappointment when it doesn't come together as planned—when I don't catch the fish or get a dish perfectly right—I want to tell the story. I may feel as though I'm the only fisherman who has gone to Alaska and not caught salmon, but those moments of letdown are important elements of *Uncharted*. They show reality—that sometimes you just don't come home with that ingredient. It showcases the challenges these local chefs and experts face every single day. There are no excuses. If it wasn't my day, I'll be back first thing tomorrow.

Even when I get things right at the end of my time in a destination, when I feel I've found the right way to prepare a dish at the Big Cook, it's never a one-pot wonder where I won't change it again. For me, it's like a culinary jigsaw puzzle with 2,500 pieces. When you get to those last 10 pieces—so close to that beautiful picture—you scrap it and start piecing it back together again.

These three seasons of *Uncharted* and one season of *Uncharted Showdown* have helped me create a forward-thinking, respectful vision of where I'm going as a chef. I'm always willing to learn. I want to expand my repertoire. I still want to feel the vulnerability of my 22-year-old self in Paris on a path to discovery with a salary that barely paid my rent. There's something gratifying about getting your ass kicked when you've managed your craft after three decades behind the stove.

The depth of respect for these destinations and the true insight into cultures through their food are things that can get lost in translation when they pass from chef to chef. I've been very fortunate to understand the absolute essence of each dish because I was in the place while it was being made. I'll never again be in a

I'll never again be in a position to taste the kind of magic that
I experienced in these places around the world.

position to taste the kind of magic that I experienced in these places around the world.

In *Uncharted*, we try to highlight not only the ingredients in these destinations but also technique: how these dishes are prepared, how the chefs build their fires, how they butterfly fish or slice meat. I'm actually glad that we can't take some of these ingredients home, because their flavor and freshness—something you can only experience on-site—contribute to the sense of their origin.

One technique that really tested me was in New Zealand (page 70). A traditional Maori method of cooking uses heated rocks in an earth oven called a hangi, which required us to prepare all the food and walk away once it was buried, trusting heat and time to do the work. Letting go of control was a big part of that moment, and that's the essence of *Uncharted*—to be stripped of the comforts of what I know and to embrace the discomfort in the search for understanding.

I'm always sad to leave each *Uncharted* destination. We pack into each place an experience of a lifetime. It may sound funny, but I end up feeling homesick for each place after we've gone. That deep connection stays with me, and likely far more so than if I'd spent my time zipping around to a lot of restaurants.

That connection extends from the place itself to the people who showed me the way, from the flavors of that destination to the film crew who worked alongside me. Thankfully, I can savor those experiences and the ingredients now via the book you hold in your hands. This collection is a global feast—one that brings us all together to learn more about the world in which we live. Cheers!

Chef Shri Bala shares fresh coconut juice with Gordon in southwestern India.

*Uncharted* also took Gordon to West Sumatra, Indonesia, where he shielded himself from a sudden rain shower using a pot while preparing beef rendang.

Zane, a local New Zealand fisherman, demonstrates how to open paua, one of the ocean's greatest delicacies.

Gordon heads to Don Tan in Laos to sample Lao-Lao, a superstrong local liquor similar to moonshine.

Gordon and nine-year-old Fatima use a traditional mortar and pestle while cooking a celebratory Amazigh New Year meal for family and friends.

After an afternoon of cooking, a Peruvian family shares a meal of roasted guinea pig and lawa de chuño, an ancient Andean soup with local lamb.

CHAPTER 1

# PERU'S SACRED

# VALLEY

Ancient Inca culture, ingredients, and flavors at soaring heights

The terraces of the Inca ruins of Moray in Peru's Sacred Valley ripple out toward the Andes Mountains and city of Cusco.

**M**ORE THAN 500 YEARS AGO, Peru's 68-mile-long (109 km) Sacred Valley (known as Wilka Qhichwa in the Quechua language) was the heart of the Inca Empire. The early inhabitants of this region valued the many altitudinal layers that created a variety of microenvironments for agriculture and built agrarian terraces to multiply the space suitable for growing. Here in the Andes, with 85 of the world's 110 climate zones, elevation impacts everything from the taste of the produce to the temperature at which water boils. ¶ The traditions of Andean cuisine, established over centuries, are anything but secret in this region. The Inca site of Moray, with its amphitheater-like terraces, is believed to have been an agricultural laboratory where the Inca experimented with different crops and growing methods at each

An alpaca rests at the ruins of Ollantaytambo.

## NAVIGATOR

### THE STOP

Machu Picchu makes South America's third largest country a bucket-list staple, but there are loads of riches—Inca and otherwise—to explore, from sandy beaches to lush rainforests.

### THE GEOGRAPHY

The Amazon rainforest covers nearly half of Peru, while the coastal desert makes up 10 percent of the country. In the snowcapped Andes Mountains, Peru boasts 85 of the world's 110 climate zones.

### FOOD FACT

More than 4,000 varieties of potatoes grow in the highlands of Peru.

# These communities are experts in ancient local ingredients and food practices that might be otherwise lost to time.

level's microclimate. While many things have changed, the biodiversity of the Sacred Valley's ecosystem has remained the same. These long-trusted practices and ingredients are still an integral part of life at this altitude.

"Here, food is very pure," chef Virgilio Martínez Véliz told me as we ate dried alpaca meat on a rock shelf overlooking the Sacred Valley. "We don't have to say *organic* because it all is." Virgilio is known for his use of indigenous ingredients, putting a modern twist on high-altitude Andean cuisine at Mil, his restaurant

---

TRAVEL 101

## HIGH ON ALTITUDE

Travelers to the Peruvian Andes often mistakenly believe that Machu Picchu is at a higher altitude than Cusco and the Sacred Valley. It happens to be the opposite: Machu Picchu sits at 7,972 feet (2,430 m) above sea level, while the Sacred Valley sits at about 9,000 feet (2,743 m) and Cusco at 11,152 feet (3,399 m). Regardless, high altitude is no joke. Be sure to take it seriously, drink plenty of water, and take your time. Experts recommend taking up to six days to acclimate to the altitude and keeping alcohol consumption to a minimum.

---

in Moray, which is also a food lab and center for experiential immersion in the agricultural traditions of the region. The Indigenous communities of the Andes understand well how altitude and respect for the soil affect food and farming methods and connect them to the natural environment. These communities are experts in ancient local ingredients and food practices that might be otherwise lost to time. The opportunity to use these age-old traditions and foods in modern ways helps introduce them to new generations and keeps them alive.

Later, in a field surrounded by the stunning Andes range, I met "mad potato scientist" and fourth-generation potato farmer Manuel Choqque Bravo, who works on cross-pollinating high-altitude potato strains once used by the Inca. More than 4,000 varieties of native potatoes grow in these highlands, and Andean peoples were the first to cultivate them. Because potatoes are self-pollinated, with both the male and female flowers in one plant, crossbreeding is done through meticulous hand pollination. Manuel has created more than 70 pigmented hybrids, the most spectacular versions of which have deep purple and red on the inside. Their hue deepens with altitude to protect them from the intense ultraviolet light that comes with high elevations.

Even Manuel's beer pursuits—fermented chicha de jora (an ancient corn beer)—come from the natural landscape. The first known version of this drink appeared long ago during the 15th-century government of Topa Inca Yupanqui. Manuel makes a version of chicha de jora called frutillada, adding strawberries

## MARKET TO MARKET

From verdant wild herbs to heirloom varietals and rainbow-hued markets, daily life in Peru provides an abundance of colors and flavors to savor.

# CHEF AND RESTAURATEUR VIRGILIO MARTÍNEZ VÉLIZ

Growing up in Lima with a burning desire to cook, chef Virgilio Martínez Véliz enrolled in Le Cordon Bleu in London and then worked his way through kitchens around much of the world, including at Lutèce in New York. After 10 years, Virgilio returned home to helm Gastón Acurio's flagship Astrid y Gastón, eventually exporting the restaurant and the flavors of Peru to Madrid and Bogotá. In 2008, Virgilio opened his own restaurant, Central, in Lima, offering cuisine inspired by the Pacific and the Peruvian Andes. Another restaurant, Lima, followed in London, along with two additional Lima restaurants in London (Lima Floral) and Dubai.

"The Andean region in Peru is quite biodiverse, but the real story about sourcing ingredients here is more about respect of the traditions and connecting with the local growers or foragers to get food closer to the source," said Virgilio. He helped form Mater Iniciativa, a group dedicated to preserving agrobiodiversity and designing the implementation of academic, culinary, and cultural projects. His restaurant Mil in the Sacred Valley focuses on ancestral cuisines and also operates as a culinary research laboratory. Its location in Moray, the ancient Inca agricultural experimentation site, is an important connection to the past.

**Gordon and chef Virgilio Martínez Véliz prep a Peruvian meal to be cooked on the open coals of a traditional *huatia* (outdoor oven).**

# Peru's Sacred Valley is like a rich, verdant oasis at high altitude.

Rivers and villages alike skirt the Sacred Valley at the base of the towering Andes Mountains.

for a lighter, sweeter taste. Manuel's work has even advanced to potato-fermented "wine" using oca, a type of potato with high sugar levels. The result is a four-line range called Miskioca (Quechua for "sweet oca") with white, orange, rosé, and red varieties, the alcohol levels and appearance of which are similar to traditional grape wine.

In one of the highest parts of the Sacred Valley, I was invited to dinner with a family who farms using techniques that date back to the Inca. Their simple kitchen included a stove fueled by burning cow manure, and

*cuy* (guinea pigs) were running underfoot—they'd be used for meals in the future. We made lawa de chuño, a thick soup made with freeze-dried chuño—potatoes left out in the high plateaus during successive freezing nights and warm days to repeatedly freeze then thaw. These potatoes are gently crushed underfoot to remove the skin and push out any remaining liquids. The chuño is then ground into flour and added to lamb, rice, green beans, and cut potatoes. It's like a traditional British stew but with much more depth.

Beyond potatoes, surviving in a remote region

requires diverse ingredients, and the *suksakuro* worms found in spiny-leaved *achupalla* plants that grow wild on rocky ridgelines are an excellent source of protein. A quick stir-fry in olive oil and they're ready to eat. The worm is supposed to taste like a combination of shrimp and calamari, but it was more like a crispy cockroach to me. Although I imagine if I lived here—and foraging was part of my daily life—I might develop a taste for them.

At 11,000 feet (3,350 m), the stunning crystal clear Huaypo Lake, set between Cusco and the Sacred Valley, has vistas that beat Scotland hands down. The lake is home to Peruvian silverside, a fish that's a local staple. While I caught only one small fish, my fishing guide, Domingo, and I treated it like a proper meal. We stuffed it with a paste of cumin, garlic, huacatay (an aromatic herb), and salt, and cooked it in a pan with (what else?) potatoes. The aromatic paste elevated the sweet, flaky meat and was a delicious post-fishing snack.

Fruit grown at high altitude can contain a higher level of concentrated sugars, and in the Cuyabamba I found a family farm with the most incredible, juicy mangoes. Along with the altitude, the strong sun and low humidity enhance the fruit's sweetness and make it burst with flavor. I considered these mangoes my secret weapon for the Big Cook, where I made a glaze of mango and chili pepper for an alpaca loin that was ultimately voted the best dish. Cooking using a *huatia*, an earthen oven dating to the Inca Empire, wasn't quite what I'd planned for the Big Cook. But since it was my goal to highlight Andean ingredients and cooking techniques, it was the perfect challenge.

Peru's Sacred Valley is like a rich, verdant oasis at high altitude. Using long-practiced Inca and Andean ingenuity made this trip a mind-blowing culinary adventure. After a week tasting this wonderful food— made from some of the best ingredients I've ever encountered—I realized that it kicks the arse off the food of any fancy restaurant anywhere. It was breathtaking in more ways than one.

# WRANGLING FOR WORMS

An excellent source of protein for foragers here are *suksakuro* worms, which live in the wild *achupalla* plants on the ridgelines above Peru's Sacred Valley. Achupallas look like small agave plants but are most closely related to bromeliads. Achupallas aren't always found in easy-to-reach places; I had to harvest one by lasso while dangling off the edge of a cliff. While I'd hoped that the worms—said to taste of shrimp crossed with calamari—would be a rich culinary reward, I couldn't quite develop a taste for them, unfortunately.

Gordon learns about Peruvian cactus worms.

# MANUEL'S POTATOES FRIED IN DUCK FAT

## WITH HONEY AND QUESO FRESCO

*Recipe provided by Manuel Choqque Bravo*

**YIELDS:** 4 SERVINGS

**25  mixed baby potatoes, scrubbed and washed**

**2  tablespoons kosher salt**

**3  tablespoons duck fat**

**1  teaspoon smoked flaky sea salt**

**1  teaspoon freshly ground black pepper**

**1  teaspoon fresh thyme leaves**

**1  tablespoon high-quality honey**

**½  cup crumbled queso fresco**

### DIRECTIONS

**1.** Place the potatoes in a medium pot and cover with water. Season with the kosher salt. Bring the potatoes to a boil, then reduce to a simmer and continue cooking until the potatoes are tender, about 20 minutes.

**2.** Immediately drain the potatoes from the cooking liquid and let cool.

**3.** When the potatoes are cool enough to handle, carefully press on each of them with the palm of your hand until they are slightly smashed, making sure not to break them apart.

**4.** Heat a large cast-iron pan over medium-high heat and add the duck fat.

**5.** Once the fat is shimmering, carefully place each potato in the pan in a single layer. You may need to work in batches.

**6.** Let the potatoes cook until they are golden on the bottom and then flip them to crisp the opposite side, about 5 minutes per side.

**7.** Season to taste with the smoked salt, pepper, and thyme leaves.

**8.** Move the crispy potatoes to a platter, and then drizzle with the honey and sprinkle with the crumbled queso fresco.

# AJI AMARILLO–MARINATED GRILLED PORK LOIN

## WITH PISCO AND MANGO GASTRIQUE AND SMOKED CHAMOMILE SALT

**YIELDS:** 4 SERVINGS

1 whole pork tenderloin (about 1½ pounds), trimmed of silverskin

PORK MARINADE

½ cup aji amarillo paste

2 tablespoons flaxseed oil

1 tablespoon minced garlic

1 large orange, zested and juiced

2 teaspoons kosher salt

1 teaspoon freshly ground black pepper

1 tablespoon dried chamomile flowers, crushed

1 teaspoon fennel pollen

1 teaspoon fennel seed, toasted and ground

MANGO GASTRIQUE

1 ripe mango, peeled, pitted, and chopped

1 habanero pepper, stem and seeds removed

1 teaspoon cane sugar

¼ cup pisco

3 tablespoons honey

2 tablespoons Chinese black vinegar

½ teaspoon kosher salt

HERB FINISHING SALT

2 tablespoons smoked flaky sea salt

1 teaspoon dried chamomile flowers, crushed

½ teaspoon fennel pollen

## | DIRECTIONS

**1.** Make the **pork marinade:** In a large mixing bowl, whisk together all of the pork marinade ingredients.

**2.** Place the pork loin in a 2-inch-deep baking dish and pour the marinade on top. Cover and let marinate in the refrigerator for at least 6 hours.

**3.** Make the **mango gastrique:** Place the mango and habanero in a blender and puree until smooth. In a small saucepan over medium-high heat, add the mango-pepper puree and the cane sugar and cook until the sauce is thickened and beginning to caramelize, about 10 minutes.

**4.** Add the pisco to the pan and let reduce for 1 minute. Finish the sauce by whisking in the honey, black vinegar, and salt. Reserve half of the gastrique for basting and set aside the remaining half to serve with the pork loin.

**5.** Make the **finishing salt:** In a small mixing bowl, whisk together all the finishing salt ingredients.

**6.** Cook the pork: Preheat a grill to 400°F.

**7.** Grill the pork loin until nicely seared on all sides.

**8.** Brush the pork loin with the mango gastrique and continue basting until it is sticky and golden. Cook the pork until a thermometer reads 145°F for medium doneness, about 20 minutes.

**9.** Let the pork loin rest for 10 minutes and then slice it into medallions.

**10.** Garnish with the finishing salt and spoon over the reserved gastrique.

# BEEF TENDERLOIN ANTICUCHOS
## WITH QUINOA

*Recipe provided by*
*Virgilio Martínez Véliz*

**YIELDS:** 4 SERVINGS

**2 pounds beef tenderloin, cut into 2-inch cubes**

ANTICUCHERA SAUCE

**¾ cup aji panca chili paste***

**¾ cup red wine vinegar**

**¾ cup vegetable oil**

**¼ cup garlic paste**

**2 teaspoons ground cumin**

**2 teaspoons dried oregano**

**2 teaspoons kosher salt**

**1 teaspoon freshly ground black pepper**

QUINOA

**1 cup chicha de jora* or light beer**

**1 cup water**

**1 cup quinoa, rinsed**

**2 tablespoons sacha inchi oil or sesame oil**

**Flaky sea salt**

### DIRECTIONS

**1.** Make the **anticuchera sauce:** In a large mixing bowl, add all of the anticuchera sauce ingredients and whisk to combine.

**2.** Add the cubed beef to the sauce and toss to coat completely. Cover and refrigerate for at least 4 hours.

**3.** Make the **quinoa:** In a medium saucepan over medium-high heat, combine the chicha de jora and water. Bring the mixture to a boil.

**4.** Add the quinoa to the boiling mixture and cook until tender, about 10 minutes.

**5.** Strain the quinoa and toss with the sacha inchi oil. Sprinkle sea salt over top to finish.

**6.** Grill the anticuchos: Preheat a large grill pan over medium-high heat.

**7.** Thread the cubes of beef onto 6-inch skewers.

**8.** Once the grill pan is almost smoking, place the skewers on the grill and cook until the outside of the beef is crispy, about 3 minutes. Rotate the skewers and continue cooking until the beef is crispy on all sides, about 6 minutes total.

**9.** Serve the skewers over the quinoa and finish with more sea salt, if desired.

*\* Aji panca chili paste and chicha de jora can be found at many Latin grocery stores.*

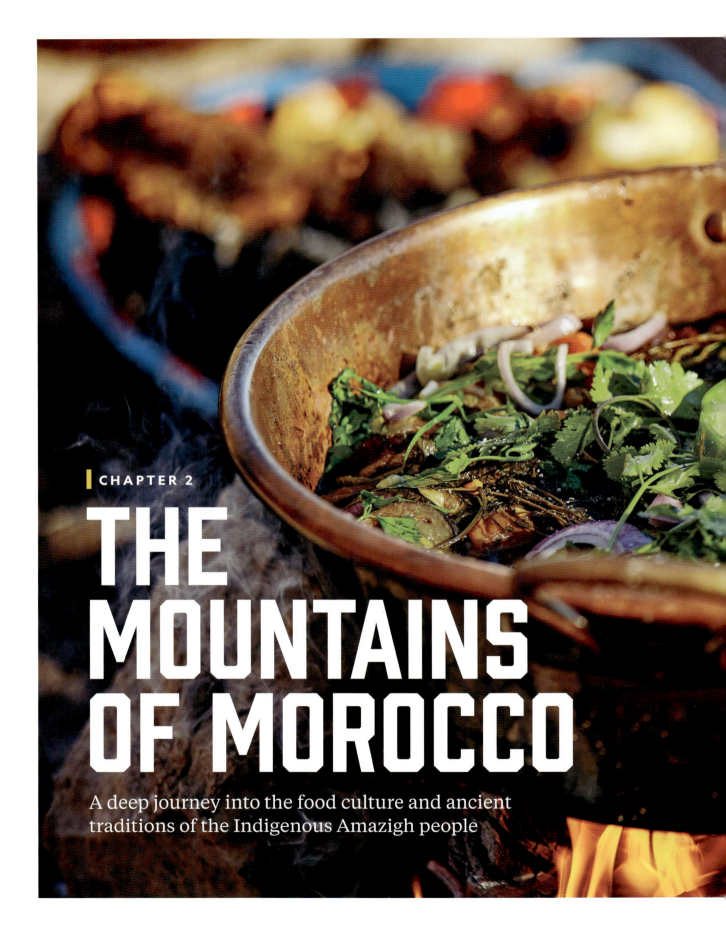

# CHAPTER 2

# THE MOUNTAINS OF MOROCCO

A deep journey into the food culture and ancient traditions of the Indigenous Amazigh people

Fresh flat-leaf parsley and sliced jalapeños add pops of color and zest to traditional Amazigh cuisine.

The mountainside
near Fès in
northwest Morocco

**M**OROCCO HAS BEEN at the crossroads of different civilizations, which has influenced the incredible blend of spices, sweet-and-savory flavors, and beautifully textured dishes that are indicative of Moroccan food. Over the centuries, Arab, Ottoman, Spanish, and French cultures have left their mark on the cuisine of the Indigenous Amazigh (also known as Berber) people—the name Amazigh (plural Imazighen) translates to "free people." Traditional Amazigh cuisine draws from Morocco's Atlas Mountains and from other heavily populated Berber cities and regions but differs regionally from one area to another across North Africa. Here, every bite is steeped in history. ¶ In rural life, attachment to the land is key, and Moroccans gather what grows wild around them, lending native flavors to any dish—no matter its origins. For newcomers who gaze across the Moroccan landscape,

**NAVIGATOR**

**THE STOP**

Morocco is known for its diversity of traditions and landscapes—largely influenced by the Indigenous Amazigh people and the various cultures that have been at the crossroads of the country.

**THE GEOGRAPHY**

The Atlas Mountains run through northwest Africa; the highest peak, Toubkal, is in Morocco and stands at 13,671 feet (4,167 m).

**FOOD FACT**

Traditional Amazigh cuisine draws from Morocco's Atlas Mountains and from heavily populated Berber cities.

Gordon and chef Najat Kaanache prepare their celebratory Moroccan New Year meals for the Big Cook.

it's difficult to immediately understand how much grows here. Morocco has one of the highest levels of biodiversity in the Mediterranean, and the knowledge of the wild herbs, plants, and shrubs that can be used in the country's cuisine has been handed down over many lifetimes. I learned to forage for heart of palm with some Amazigh men and boys who knew the mountains like the back of their hand.

While the Atlas Mountains and Amazigh culture form the backbone of Moroccan food, along with the other cultures that have added flavors over time, contemporary chefs like Najat Kaanache are changing the face of the country's cuisine. After earning her stripes at a string of Michelin-starred establishments across Europe and the United States, Najat is getting a lot of attention for her focus on the flavors of the Middle Atlas region at her restaurant, Nur. It's located in the

Fès medina, a food market that dates back to the ninth century. "Berber land is where the people still have the traditions and the way of cooking," Najat told me after we wandered through the medina.

In that very medina is where I tried making warka, a paper-thin pastry dough that's a little like phyllo. It's a lot harder than it looks. Making warka is a time-consuming process that starts with a ball of the simple dough that you delicately stretch and pull to make thin sheets, which are then cooked briefly in what looks like an inverted copper pan. Warka is used to make a number of savory and sweet dishes and pastries, such as bastilla (a savory meat pie) and briouat (dough stuffed with a variety of fillings and then fried).

The forests of Morocco conceal a wide variety of edible wild mushrooms. After a couple of days foraging in the Middle Atlas, mushroom hunter Abdallah handed me a basket he'd packed with the bounty of the area: chanterelles, morels, and porcini. He and his crew showed me how to incorporate those mushrooms into medfouna, a stuffed flatbread referred to as "Berber pizza." The word *medfouna* means "buried," referring to the delectable blend of ingredients (ranging from meats to nuts to vegetables) and spices hidden within the bread-like crust, as well as the traditional method of cooking it in the eastern Sahara—set atop hot stones and buried in the desert sand. As we were in the mountains, we cooked ours over a campfire (many families bake medfouna in mud ovens). When it's done, it's sliced into pieces to be shared by everyone. It seemed an added luxury to incorporate those expensive mushrooms in everyday cuisine.

Some say that if certain spices are missing in a par-

---

**TRAVEL 101**

# THE MARKETS OF THE MEDINA

The Fès medina has been a food market since the ninth century. Walking among the labyrinth of alleys, lanes, and streets made me feel as if I'd been transported back in time. Imagine how wonderful it would be to have a restaurant here with the wealth of products on your doorstep. To take it all in, embrace the pleasure of exploring and getting lost in the medina. It's almost guaranteed you will, anyway. Among the sounds, smells, and riot of colors, you'll see everything from raw ingredients to complete dishes to the most amazing local carpets.

Some say that if certain spices are missing in a particular dish, that dish isn't Amazigh.

ticular dish, that dish isn't Amazigh. Ras el hanout, an earthy spice blend whose name means "head of the shop," is truly top-shelf. It incorporates a variety of spices—from as few as 10 to as many as 80—that can change from recipe to recipe and region to region. Most recipes include anise, cardamom, chili pepper, cinnamon, ginger, nutmeg, and turmeric. It's the perfect example of how a mix of diverse spices can be blended to create something bigger and better. Morocco is also the fourth largest producer of saffron, a spice that dates back at least 500 years to when it was carried here by Arab and Jewish traders from the eastern Mediterranean and Persia. The luxurious and expensive spice is used extensively in tagines, as well as in chermoula, a spicy green sauce traditionally served with grilled fish.

Speaking of luxury, the low-cholesterol and high-protein meat from a camel is more expensive than beef or lamb in Morocco. When I tasted it for the first time after it was baked in a terra-cotta pot called

# FORAGING WITH THE KING OF THE MUSHROOMS

**C**hef Najat Kaanache connected me with Abdallah, a local mushroom hunter who is secretive about his forage locations to both preserve the environment where the fungi grow and protect his self-proclaimed status as "king of the mushrooms." He deserves his title: Abdallah provides Najat with the best mushrooms found in the Atlas Mountains, including black trumpets, chanterelles, matsutake, morels, porcini, and truffles. They're delivered in straw baskets to her restaurant in the Fès medina late at night when the temperature is cool. Abdallah delivers his mushrooms by donkey or mule because cars can't fit into the maze of narrow alleys in the medina.

Living close to the land, many Amazigh people know it intimately through changing seasons and shifting weather conditions. Goat herders out in forests with the flock sometimes pick up mushrooms for home kitchens or to sell in local markets. Women out gathering firewood collect mushrooms too. Some foragers, like Abdallah, collect excellent specimens for restaurants in Morocco's largest cities or for European markets. From a chef's point of view, the basket of mushrooms we put into the medfouna was magical. Sandwiched between two slices of dough, the mushrooms were luxurious and absolutely delicious.

Wild mushrooms including chanterelles, morels, and porcini

Abdallah (far left), foraging guide Berrin, and Gordon discuss the collection of wild mushrooms Abdallah has foraged from the remote forest outside Fès.

**COLORFUL AND SPICY**
Clockwise from top: Dried chilies and spices at a market-place in Fès; garlic and chickpeas, staples of the Moroccan diet; intricate tilework adorning a doorway

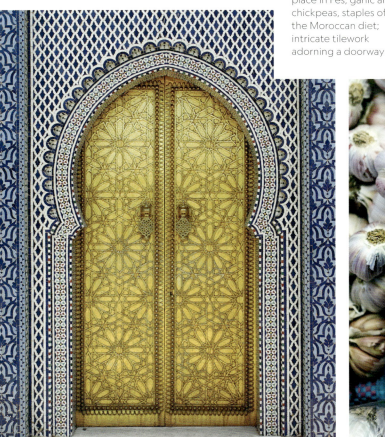

**I'd never tasted** olive oil straight from the press before—the sample I tried was incredibly flavorful and delicious.

a *tangia* (like tagine—the name of the pot and the dish that results are the same), I was surprised at the deep richness of the meat combined with the citrus, onions, and spices in the dish. Tender and fattier than the rest of the camel, the hump is the most prized part and is often grilled or added to meat tagines or in small pieces to a kefta mince that's essential in sausages.

Olive oil is another central ingredient in Moroccan cuisine, as it is throughout the Mediterranean. The mild winters and warm, dry summers of Morocco's climate are ideal for olive oil production, and olives have been growing here since as early as the ninth century. In the village where one of Abdallah's mushroom hunters, Karda, lives, they use a traditional stone grinding wheel pulled by a mule to crush the olives before putting them in a woven bag to place in the press. I'd never tasted olive oil straight from the press before—the sample I tried was incredibly flavorful and delicious.

In Morocco, I learned techniques that go back centuries, and I wanted to honor those traditions in the Big Cook. We prepared our dishes outdoors, grilling or slow cooking over hot coals. It was a good reminder that you don't need a fancy kitchen to produce truly outstanding cuisine. Combined with time-tested practices that bring out the best in each element, multilayered flavors emerged from the rich bounty of ingredients that date back to ancient times—all of which added to the whole delicious experience.

## TASTING THE TRADITIONS

**K**arda, one of Abdallah's mushroom hunters, invited me to a lunch of lentils, flatbread, and olives in the village where he lives with his family. He and his daughter, Fatima, showed me their traditional way of life—from carpet making to olive oil pressing. Like other Amazigh villages, theirs was preparing for the Yennayer (New Year) celebration. Food is a very important element of the festivities. Fatima led me to her grandmother's house, where I dove deeper into Berber traditions: I traded some of my foraged heart of palm for the local honey I needed for my Wild Mushroom Medfouna (page 54).

Carpet-weaving techniques in the region date back to the 12th century.

# RAS EL HANOUT–BRAISED
# BEEF SHORT RIBS

## WITH CHICKPEAS, OLIVES, AND GREEN HARISSA

**YIELDS:** 6 SERVINGS

### BRAISED SHORT RIBS

2 tablespoons grapeseed oil

6 2-inch pieces bone-in beef short ribs, about 2 pounds

1 tablespoon kosher salt

2 teaspoons freshly ground black pepper

2 yellow onions, sliced

1 tablespoon minced garlic

2 tablespoons ras el hanout

1 teaspoon ground white pepper

1 tablespoon paprika

1 tablespoon cumin seed, crushed

1 teaspoon coriander seed, crushed

2 cups beef stock

1 cup water

1 15-ounce can chickpeas, drained

1 cup green olives, pitted and sliced in half

1 teaspoon preserved lemon, finely diced

¼ cup chopped fresh parsley

### GREEN HARISSA

3 green chilies, finely chopped

2 Meyer lemons, zested

1 bunch cilantro, finely chopped

½ teaspoon dried red chili flakes

½ cup extra-virgin olive oil

1 teaspoon kosher salt

Toasted bread, for serving

## DIRECTIONS

**1.** Start the **short ribs:** Heat a large Dutch oven with the grapeseed oil over medium-high heat until the oil begins to shimmer.

**2.** Season the short ribs liberally with the salt and black pepper. Sear the short ribs on all sides until golden brown, working in batches if necessary.

**3.** Remove the short ribs from the pot and set aside. Remove all but 2 tablespoons of the fat from the pot.

**4.** Reduce the heat to medium and add the onions. Cook until they begin to caramelize, about 8 minutes.

**5.** Add the garlic, ras el hanout, white pepper, paprika, cumin, and coriander and continue cooking until the spices begin to toast and the garlic becomes fragrant, about 2 minutes.

**6.** Add the beef stock and water to deglaze the pot, making sure to scrape up all of the brown bits at the bottom of the pot. Return the short ribs to the pot and bring the mixture to a boil.

**7.** Cover the pot with a lid and reduce the heat to low. Continue cooking until the short ribs are fork-tender, about 2½ to 3 hours.

**8.** Make the **green harissa:** In a small mixing bowl, combine all the harissa ingredients. Let the mixture stand for 30 minutes to allow the flavors to bloom.

**9.** Finish the short ribs: After 1 hour of cooking, add the chickpeas, green olives, and preserved lemon to the pot. Continue cooking until the short ribs begin to fall off the bone.

**10.** Add the parsley and stir to combine.

**11.** To serve, place one short rib in a bowl and ladle over the chickpea stew.

**12.** Garnish with a spoonful of the green harissa and serve with toasted bread.

# HARISSA-SPICED MOROCCAN CARROTS

**YIELDS:** 4 SERVINGS

CARROTS

**4  teaspoons lemon juice**

**1  tablespoon kosher salt**

**1  teaspoon sugar**

**8  carrots, peeled and sliced on a bias into 1-inch pieces**

HARISSA SAUCE

**½  cup olive oil**

**6  garlic cloves, finely chopped**

**2  teaspoons green chili pepper, finely chopped**

**1  teaspoon ground cumin**

**1  teaspoon ground white pepper**

**1  cup cilantro, chopped, plus more for garnish**

**10  teaspoons lemon juice**

**2  teaspoons preserved lemon, finely chopped**

**2  teaspoons harissa spice**

**1  teaspoon kosher salt**

**DIRECTIONS**

**1.** Blanch the **carrots:** Fill a large pot about halfway full with water. Add the lemon juice, salt, and sugar and bring to a boil over medium-high heat.

**2.** Add the carrots to the liquid and blanch until tender, about 2 to 3 minutes. Quickly strain the carrots and place in an ice bath to stop the cooking process.

**3.** Drain the carrots from the ice bath and dry on a paper towel–lined tray.

**4.** Make the **harissa sauce:** In a medium sauté pan over medium heat, add the olive oil, garlic, and chilies and sauté until softened but not browned.

**5.** To the pan, add the cumin and white pepper and toast until aromatic, about 1 minute.

**6.** Remove from the heat and add the cilantro, lemon juice, preserved lemon, harissa, and salt.

**7.** To serve, toss the carrots in the harissa sauce and let marinate for 3 hours.

**8.** Garnish the marinated carrots with cilantro and serve at room temperature.

# WILD MUSHROOM MEDFOUNA

*Recipe provided by foragers Abdallah and Berrin*

**YIELDS:** 6 SERVINGS

## DOUGH

4½ cups bread flour, plus more for dusting

1 tablespoon dry active yeast

3 teaspoons kosher salt

2 cups warm water

1 teaspoon honey

## MUSHROOM FILLING

2 tablespoons olive oil, plus more for finishing

2 pounds wild mushrooms, cleaned and roughly chopped

1 white onion, thinly sliced

3 garlic cloves, minced

1 teaspoon kosher salt

1 tablespoon ras el hanout

1 teaspoon paprika

10 ounces goat cheese, crumbled

1 tablespoon chopped fresh parsley

1 tablespoon za'atar

1 small black truffle, thinly sliced

## SPICE MIX

1 tablespoon caraway seeds

1 tablespoon fennel seeds

1 tablespoon za'atar

1 teaspoon chili flakes

1 teaspoon flaky sea salt

## DIRECTIONS

**1.** Make the **dough:** In the bowl of a stand mixer fitted with the dough hook attachment, combine the bread flour, yeast, and salt and mix to combine.

**2.** In a small mixing bowl, whisk together the water and honey until the honey dissolves completely.

**3.** Turn the stand mixer on to the lowest kneading setting and slowly pour in the honey water.

**4.** Let the dough mix in the machine for 4 to 5 minutes, until it starts to easily pull away from the surface of the bowl.

**5.** Remove the dough to a floured surface and knead by hand until it is glossy and smooth.

**6.** Place the dough in a large bowl, cover with plastic wrap, and place in a warm space to let it proof until it has nearly doubled in volume, about 2 hours.

**7.** Make the **mushroom filling:** Preheat a large skillet over medium-high heat until it is searing hot.

**8.** Add the olive oil and wild mushrooms, sautéing in batches if necessary to prevent overcrowding.

**9.** Once the mushrooms are lightly golden, add the onion and garlic and season with the salt. Continue cooking until the onion has softened and started to brown, about 4 minutes.

**10.** Add the ras el hanout and paprika and cook until the moisture is gone and the spices have started to toast, about 3 minutes.

**11.** Remove from the heat and add the goat cheese, parsley, za'atar, and black truffle and toss to combine. Taste the filling for seasoning and adjust if necessary.

**12.** Make the **spice mix:** In a small skillet, toast the caraway seeds and fennel seeds until bright and fragrant.

**13.** In a small bowl, combine the toasted seeds, za'atar, chili flakes, and salt.

**14.** Make the medfouna: Preheat your oven to 400°F.

**15.** Divide the dough into two pieces and roll out each piece on a lightly floured surface until they are each about 12 inches in diameter.

**16.** Lightly oil a large cast-iron skillet and place one piece of dough along the bottom of the pan, making sure the dough comes up the walls to the lip.

**17.** Carefully spread the mushroom filling evenly on the dough.

**18.** Cover the filling with the second round of dough, folding it over the filling and sealing it to the bottom layer of dough. Use your fingers to pinch the seal closed.

**19.** Bake the medfouna until the dough is golden brown and crispy, about 15 to 20 minutes.

**20.** Finish the medfouna under a broiler if it appears to be lacking color.

**21.** Drizzle the medfouna with olive oil and sprinkle it with the spice mix.

**22.** Cut the medfouna into wedges and serve.

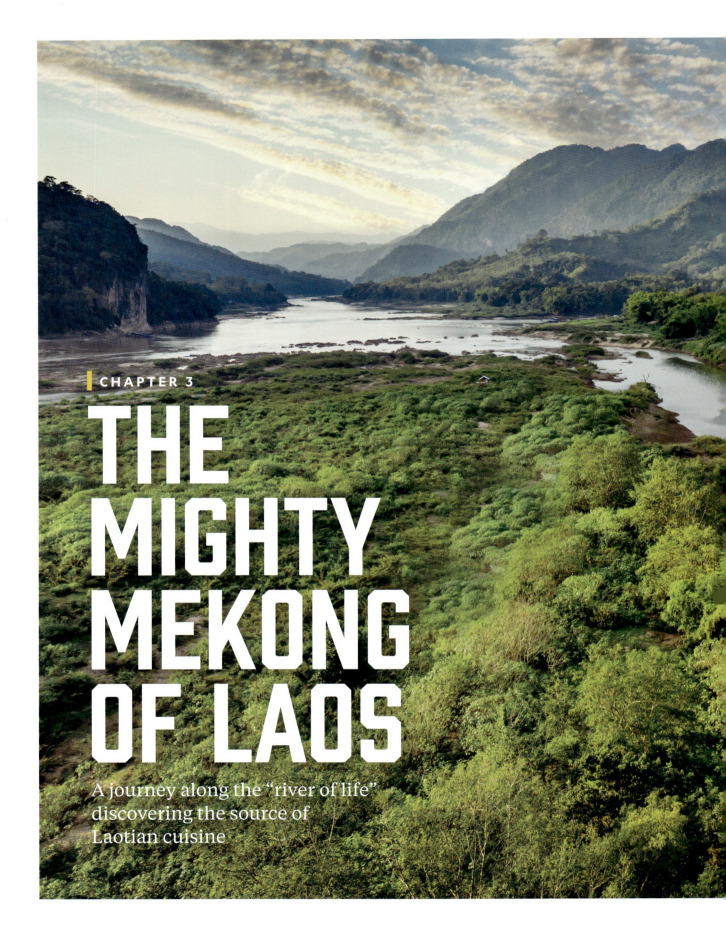

# CHAPTER 3

# THE MIGHTY MEKONG OF LAOS

A journey along the "river of life" discovering the source of Laotian cuisine

Running from north to south on its way to the South China Sea, the Mekong River pours through the lush Si Phan Don (also called the 4,000 Islands) region of southern Laos.

Gordon makes his way over a precarious section of the Mekong River to cast-net fish just beyond the Khone Falls rapids.

**T**HE MEKONG RIVER, one of the longest in the world, travels through six countries on its way to the East Vietnam Sea—and it is landlocked Laos's river of life. Running from north to south, the Mekong River is the country's backbone. It's part highway, part water supply, and a vital source of food. The river can also unleash Mother Nature's fury upon its shoreline residents. But even in the worst of times, there's a strong connection between the people of Laos and the mighty Mekong River, especially in the Si Phan Don (also known as 4,000 Islands) region that I visited.

Laos is a lesser known destination compared with its neighbors Thailand, Cambodia, and Vietnam—and Laotian cuisine is often confused with Thai cuisine. While Laotian and Thai food may share some similarities, there are ingredients particular to Laos, especially plant-based herbs, ferns, and leaves. Nearly everything

## NAVIGATOR

### THE STOP

I take to the Mekong River, a vital source of life for the people of Laos. It serves as a transportation route and source of electricity, water, and food.

### THE GEOGRAPHY

Laos is the only landlocked country in Southeast Asia. Mountains and forested hills cover nearly three-quarters of the country.

### FOOD FACT

More than 60 percent of agricultural land in Laos is dedicated to rice growing.

Gordon embraces the Laotian saying "please don't rush" while on a passenger boat to the island of Don Tan.

is harvested from personal gardens, the Mekong River, local farms, and the country's forests. And while the food can be spicy, it's a mindful balancing of flavors: not too sweet, not too sour, and spiced just right.

"The fish that fight against the current are more tasty," chef Joy Ngeuamboupha argued when he suggested that I try my hand at cast-net fishing at Khone Falls, considered the widest waterfall in the world. The great volume of the falls—with 2.5 million gallons (9.5 million L) rushing per second—is nearly double the volume of Niagara Falls. Joy was inspired to become a chef after spending seven years as a monk. Now he focuses on celebrating Laos's culinary heritage at one of the top-rated restaurants in the country, Tamarind Restaurant and Cooking School in Luang Prabang. He wants to ensure there's a place for his country's cuisine on the global food map.

Laotians go to extreme lengths to source their ingre-

dients, be it casting a net into Khone Falls or perching precariously on the rugged shoreline of the Mekong River. The river is home to about 1,200 fish species including freshwater, marine, and coastal fish. Fish markets in larger villages along the river abound, some with behemoth catfish and carp. Along the riverbank, Joy and I sampled our catch, wrapped in a banana leaf, stuffed with lemongrass, and cooked slowly over a fire. Steaming fish in banana leaves like this is a popular preparation here, as is grilling seasoned fish on bamboo skewers.

The Mekong River is the second most biodiverse river in the world and hosts much more than fish. Before jumping in to gather snails from the base of underwater plants, I assumed that they were prey slow enough for me to catch. But it was much harder than I thought. In the river's strong current, it was challenging to maintain a position for even 30 seconds without falling backward. My local guide, Mr. Ten, his family, and I took the snail meat from the shell and wrapped it in lettuce with spring onion. After a quick dip in spicy sauce, it was like a little snail spring roll.

## TRAVEL 101
# R&R BY THE RIVER

Covering more than 3,000 miles (4,800 km) from its source on the Tibetan Plateau to the Mekong Delta in the Gulf of Thailand, the Mekong River flows through China, Myanmar, Thailand, Laos, Cambodia, and Vietnam. Too frequently, travelers feel the urgency to rush from place to place, but you shouldn't miss opportunities to slow down and savor the experience. In Laos, one of my favorite things to do at the end of the day was to relax while sitting by the Mekong and watching the sunset with a local beer or other cold drink. It's one of the most beautiful things you'll see.

This river of life continues to give … a rich culture that thrills the taste buds and feeds the soul.

Food scarcity in areas where the river is less generous means that villagers must seek protein resources beyond river fish. The lush rice paddy fields yield smaller animals, such as frogs and giant water bugs known as toe-biters. They get their nickname because they can deliver a painful (but not toxic) bite when you're walking through their habitat. The brown, flat toe-biters are put on traditional bamboo skewers and roasted over a flame before being dissected to extract the small amount of meat. They don't look appetizing, but they're delicious and very sweet, like a cross between lobster and crab meat. The effort it takes to create just one meal from them was humbling.

Sticky rice is the staple food of Laotian meals, and green rice paddies seem to spread to the horizon. Lao-Lao, a rice whiskey, requires sticky rice to be steamed, then fermented with yeast for a few days. The result can produce a moonshine topping out at 120 proof—a simple replacement for more expensive imported liquors. Lao-Lao distilleries are a social hub from early in the morning to late in the evening, with customers dropping by in their boats and buying a container to go.

Even ant larvae from nests in the forest contribute to the Laotian diet. While getting the larvae required me to use an ingeniously made woven basket attached

**SITES AND TREASURES**
Clockwise from top left: Toe-biters (giant water bugs) are grilled on bamboo skewers over hot charcoal; Laos is home to many Buddhist monasteries; Gordon and his guides forage for toe-biters, which are a good source of protein in the Laotian diet.

Cooking in the morning near the temple with the Mekong River meandering slowly past on its long journey felt like a scene from many generations ago.

to the end of a long bamboo stalk, having to shake the nest resulted in a hailstorm of aggressive fighting ants falling on my head. In the small village where I was a guest, larvae were served along with some fresh herbs, picked from the jungle, in a soup. The larvae had the citrus flavor of tiny particles of lemon or lime; the herbs added a zesty freshness to the final flavor.

On the way to the Big Cook, Joy and I stopped at an outdoor market to get our last ingredients. Just like at the riverbank, there was plenty of freshly caught fish, but the market also had fermented fish. Joy pointed out padaek, a fermented fish sauce. The traditional Laotian condiment is made from fermented or pickled fish that have been cured, and it contains fish, salt, sticky rice husk, galangal (a spice closely related to ginger and turmeric), and hot chili peppers.

For the Big Cook, we had the additional challenge of serving the monks at Wat Khon Tai at 11 a.m.; it's against the rules for monks to eat after midday. Cooking in the morning near the temple with the Mekong River meandering slowly past on its long journey felt like a scene from many generations ago. This river of life continues to give the people who live along its banks something very valuable—a rich culture that thrills the taste buds and feeds the soul. That's priceless.

ADRENALINE RUSH

## KAYAKING THE RIVER

Australian adventurer Mick O'Shea has been exploring this region for decades and was the first person to kayak the length of the Mekong River from source to sea. I had two choices to get to a remote village: drive for hours on a dirt road or take a shortcut. The shortcut was the river. Mick promised to get me through in one piece. We paddled our inflatable kayaks through an area of waterfalls known locally as Li Phi ("spirit trap"), named after demons believed to be caught beneath the rapids. We bounced through the whitewater but luckily emerged unscathed.

**Strong whirlpools and rapids are a few of the challenges Gordon and Australian adventurer Mick O'Shea navigate on a stretch of the Mekong River locals call the "spirit trap."**

# MR. SING'S LAO-LAO WHISKEY

**M**r. Sing has been making Lao-Lao (Laotian rice whiskey) for more than 20 years. His distillery on the island of Don Tan operates like a Mekong River drive-through: Customers drop by as early as 7 a.m. to get their Lao-Lao at the start of the day. I can't imagine how they do it, as the spirit can top out at around 120 proof. But imported liquor is far too expensive for most Laotian people, so moonshine is the preferred solution. After my first sip, Mr. Sing told me that the first batch is always a little stronger. I wish he'd mentioned that before the packs-a-punch Lao-Lao turned my lips numb.

Sticky rice has a high starch content, which makes it the perfect base for whiskey. After it's steamed and washed, yeast is added, and it's fermented in a bucket for several days. (Diageo would not approve of this process.) If my first sip wasn't enough, I tasted some Lao-Lao infused with geckos and "secret herbs." While it was hard to get past feeling sad for the poor geckos, the sweet flavor was extraordinary. I brought some for the Big Cook, but monks don't do moonshine, even if the alcohol is burned off.

**Whiskey distiller Mr. Sing (left) and Nang, a local café owner and guide, show Gordon the process of making Laotian moonshine.**

# CRISPY WHOLE RED SNAPPER

## WITH SQUASH BLOSSOM TEMPURA, STICKY RICE, AND CHILI DIPPING SAUCE

**YIELDS:** 2 SERVINGS

### DIPPING SAUCE

**6 tablespoons water**

**2 tablespoons fish sauce**

**1 tablespoon lemon juice**

**1 bird's eye chili or other small hot chili, thinly sliced**

**1 teaspoon minced garlic**

**Kosher salt, if needed**

### CRISPY FISH

**2 quarts canola oil**

**1 large whole red snapper or any other meaty whole fish, scaled and gutted**

**1 tablespoon kosher salt**

**2 garlic cloves, sliced**

**2 makrut lime leaves**

**1 2-inch piece ginger, peeled and thinly sliced**

**1 stalk lemongrass, smashed**

**¼ cup Lao basil or Thai basil, julienned**

### SQUASH BLOSSOM TEMPURA

**12 ounces ice cold soda water**

**1½ cups rice flour, plus more for dusting**

**10–15 squash blossoms**

**1 teaspoon kosher salt**

**1 banana leaf and steamed sticky rice, for serving**

## DIRECTIONS

**1.** Make the **dipping sauce:** In a small mixing bowl, combine all the dipping sauce ingredients. Taste and adjust seasoning, adding more lemon juice and salt, if needed.

**2.** Make the **crispy fish:** Heat a large pot filled with the canola oil over medium heat to 325°F.

**3.** Score each side of the fish by making shallow incisions along each fillet side, about 1 inch apart. Season generously with the salt, making sure to season the inside cavity of the fish as well.

**4.** Stuff the cavity with the garlic, lime leaves, ginger, lemongrass, and basil. Use a skewer or long toothpick to thread the cavity closed.

**5.** Carefully place the fish in the oil. The fish will likely pop with any moisture, so be cautious and do not stand too close to the pot when you begin frying.

**6.** Continue frying until the fish is crispy and cooked through, about 10 minutes. Remove the fish from the pot and place it on a wire rack.

**7.** Make the **squash blossom tempura:** Increase the temperature of the oil to 350°F.

**8.** In a large mixing bowl, combine the soda water and rice flour to make the tempura batter. Use chopsticks to mix gently. The batter should be made right before preparation and used immediately.

**9.** Lightly dust the squash blossoms with rice flour and quickly dip them in the batter.

**10.** Place the battered blossoms in the heated oil and fry until crisp, about 2 minutes.

**11.** Remove the blossoms from the oil and place on a cooling rack set over a sheet tray. Season with the salt.

**12.** To serve, lay out a banana leaf on a large platter and place the fish on top.

**13.** Garnish with the squash blossom tempura and steamed sticky rice and serve with the dipping sauce.

# SWEET AND SOUR CATFISH SOUP

**YIELDS:** 4–6 SERVINGS

2  baby eggplants

2  bird's eye chilies or other small hot chili pepper

1  shallot, peeled and trimmed

1  2-inch piece ginger, peeled

5  cups water

1  2-inch piece galangal, thinly sliced

2  lemongrass stalks, smashed

2  fresh tamarind pods or ¼ cup tamarind paste if fresh is not available

2  tablespoons fish sauce

1  teaspoon kosher salt

2  bone-in catfish fillets, cut into 2-inch pieces (about 1¾ pounds)

3  makrut lime leaves

2  spring onions, thinly sliced

¼  cup cilantro, chopped

**DIRECTIONS**

**1.** Preheat a grill to 400°F. Once hot, place the eggplants, chilies, shallot, and ginger on the grill, whole, and grill until charred on all sides, about 5 minutes.

**2.** In a large pot, combine the water, galangal, lemongrass, tamarind, fish sauce, and salt and bring to a boil over medium-high heat.

**3.** Add the catfish and simmer the broth until it begins to thicken from the collagen in the catfish bones, about 8 to 10 minutes.

**4.** Add the lime leaves and continue reducing until the broth is rich and flavorful, about 20 minutes.

**5.** Using a mortar and pestle, mash the charred baby eggplant, chilies, shallot, and ginger until they are broken apart but not so much so that they turn into paste. You should have a chunky mixture of very fragrant charred aromatics.

**6.** Mix the grilled aromatics into the broth. Taste and adjust seasoning as needed.

**7.** To serve, ladle the soup into small bowls and garnish with the spring onions and cilantro.

Chef Monique Fiso helps Gordon spot edible wild plants, including peppery horopito, asparagus-tasting pirita (supplejack), and sweet purple fuchsia berries, tucked amid the trees, vines, and ferns.

# CHAPTER 4

# NEW ZEALAND'S

European, Asian, and Polynesian flavors come together in contemporary

# RUGGED SOUTH

cuisine inspired by Maori traditions

Turquoise streams snake across the sandy beaches of the Matukituki River as distant snowmelt makes its way to the sea.

**N**EW ZEALAND MAY BE KNOWN as the adventure capital of the world, but the country flies under the radar in the culinary universe despite its wealth of influences: European, Asian, Polynesian, and Maori. And it's the customs and traditions of the Maori, especially their local ingredients and how they prepare them, that make this destination stand out from all others. ¶ According to Maori legend, the first explorer to reach Aotearoa (the Maori name for New Zealand) was the intrepid Kupe. Using stars and ocean currents to navigate across the Pacific Ocean on his *waka hourua* (voyaging canoe), he ventured from the ancestral Polynesian homeland of Hawaiki. Others followed him in the 13th century, bringing some crops on the journey, but much of their diet relied on hunting and harvesting food from the mountains, forests, rivers, and ocean—the four main ecosystems. The mountains and forests

## NAVIGATOR

### THE STOP

New Zealand, known as Aotearoa to the Indigenous Maori, is a remote, mountainous group of islands in the southeastern Pacific. I explore the country's South Island and Stewart Island.

### THE GEOGRAPHY

The islands were created 23 million years ago by volcanic forces. There are still more than 50 volcanoes, some still active, in New Zealand.

### FOOD FACT

Maori have been cooking with ingredients from New Zealand's native forests, combined with Polynesian techniques and flavors, for more than 1,000 years.

Gordon prepares a meal for Maori elders using local ingredients and traditional cooking techniques on New Zealand's Stewart Island.

were the domain of Papatuanuku, the earth mother. Tangaroa (god of the ocean) ruled over the ocean and rivers.

From the traditional hangi (earth oven) to foraging for ingredients harvested from the land and water, Indigenous Maori possess a tradition of food that is uniquely their own and boasts flavors found nowhere else in the world. Chef Monique Fiso aims to shine a light on Maori cuisine at her restaurant Hiakai, proving that there's a modern home for the food of her ancestors in the world of fine dining.

When we met on Stewart Island, Monique handed me a machete. We were off to forage in the New Zealand forest in search of edible wild plants. "Foraging is big on the menu," she said. As it turns out, all the chefs at her restaurant in Wellington own machetes so they can forage for ingredients that go into her boundary-pushing menus. These ingredients and dishes play a leading role in keeping Maori and Polynesian food culture alive.

The foraging tradition here stretches back to the earliest Polynesian settlers. Aotearoa has a lot of old,

**ESSENTIAL ELEMENTS**
The forests, mountains, and water are all integral to Maori cuisine.

dense native bush, and its ferns, vines, palms, fungi, berries, fruit, and seeds became important foods. Much of the forest has been around for hundreds of years and was used by those ancestral settlers for *kai* (food) and Rongoa Maori (herbal medicine); the forest is sacred to the Maori people. Thoughtful foraging practices prioritize respect for the forest, because the bush and native plants are also considered Maori ancestors.

Our haul included peppery horopito, asparagus-tasting pirita (supplejack), and sweet purple fuchsia berries, which required me to scale a tree to acquire. Without Monique along as my guide, I probably would have gotten lost in the tangled vines and emerald ferns and missed some of the fascinating flavors and contrasts that were right in front of me.

**BEHIND THE SCENES**

## FISHING WITH FLUFF

Gordon shares steamed blue cod by a beach bonfire with fishermen Fluff (far right) and Zane.

Salty old sea dog Fluff shares something in common with me—his first name, Gordon. While I went diving for paua (and luckily avoided sharks), he caught some blue cod and showed me the old Maori method of cooking fish in kelp. "Like we did when we were kids," he said. He cut a blade of kelp and opened it to make a pocket for the fish, then put that package inside another blade of kelp. The packet went directly on the embers of a beach bonfire. When I tore open the kelp envelope, the blue cod was steamed to perfection.

Indigenous Maori possess a tradition of food that is uniquely their own and boasts flavors found nowhere else in the world.

Other land-based bounty includes non-native mountain goats called tahr, introduced to New Zealand's Southern Alps from the Himalaya in the early 20th century. With no predators, they've caused untold damage to native vegetation. Because Maori have always sought to live in harmony with their environment, hunting invasive species may be one way for modern-day Kiwis to help redress the balance.

Huhu grubs, the larvae of the longhorn beetle, are an ingredient I could have done without. The grubs can be found in rotting pine logs on the forest floor and likely saved lives of those who got lost in the bush. Today, they're still popular in Maori cuisine. They have more protein packed into their small bodies than beef, lamb, chicken, or chickpeas. Monique said they taste like peanut butter, and once they're ground up into a creamy sauce, they really do. But eating them raw and wriggling was a step too far for me.

From the domain of Tangaroa, paua are highly prized New Zealand abalone. Regarded by the Maori as a gift from the gods, they are extremely challenging to secure. It took me a few tries while free diving,

# CHEF MONIQUE FISO SHOWCASES MAORI CUISINE

**M**odern-day food warrior chef Monique Fiso is an inspiration to many for bringing the ancient knowledge of her Maori and Samoan cultures to the world at large. Her Samoan grandmother had a huge influence on her cooking. From a very young age, Monique helped her prep Sunday lunches for their extended family. With early training in the kitchen of renowned New Zealand chef Martin Bosley, as well as in top Michelin-starred kitchens in New York City (the Musket Room and the now shuttered restaurants Public and A Voce), she returned to New Zealand in 2016 determined to take Maori cuisine to a new level of sophistication.

After testing her idea of celebrating Maori foodways with indigenous ingredients in a series of pop-ups around the country, she opened her own restaurant, Hiakai (the Maori word for "hungry"), in Wellington. "Maori cuisine has been here for centuries and is a deeply fascinating cuisine to explore," she said. "The entirety of New Zealand has a rich culinary heritage that goes far beyond pies and pavlovas." Her book, *Hiakai*, is a deep dive into Maori history, mythology, customs, and ingredients—and includes more than 30 recipes that give new life to the knowledge that's been handed down for generations.

**Chef Monique Fiso demonstrates how to prep local ingredients as she and Gordon cook a traditional meal.**

"Maori cuisine has been here for centuries and is a **deeply fascinating** cuisine to explore."

—Chef Monique Fiso

Gordon presents a platter of goat that was wrapped in puka leaves and smoked in a hangi (earth oven) to Maori elders on Stewart Island.

scanning the surrounding water for sharks, looking for paua in thick kelp, and finally prying them off the rocks. In Maori legend, paua were compared to mighty warriors, able to overcome their opponents with stubborn strength. Sea dogs Zane and Fluff showed me how they tenderize paua meat in the field by wrapping it in a cloth and giving it a smack with a rock.

Eels are another highly valued food in Maori cuisine and were harvested through a variety of techniques. But it has also always been important to the Maori to protect the eels and their environment since all living things are interconnected—what affects one element affects all the rest. Eel fisherman Jeromy van Riel showed me how to stand in a stream, get my hands under a shortfin eel's slippery belly, and flick it up onto the bank. Eels are pretty sneaky, and their mouths are filled with teeth, so I couldn't help but imagine what a bite might feel like. Thank goodness I didn't find out.

I didn't realize how important a hangi is in Maori culture until I had to dig a hole and cook in a pit at the end of my week in New Zealand. Fire-heated stones are placed into the pit and topped with wet sacks. Then, *kaimoana* (seafood) and *kaiwhenua* (food from the land) are wrapped in puka leaves, placed in the pit, covered with more wet sacks, and then covered again with earth to trap the heat. It's not the easiest practice for a chef who's used to checking the oven frequently: Once that pit is closed, you can't open it again until it's all over—maybe three to four hours later. This was a practice in releasing control, which is not always easy for me. But when you do it right, the result of the long cooking process is tender, fall-off-the-bone meat and delicious vegetables—all of which are infused with a smoky, earthy fragrance.

With an ideal Maori meal comprising the harmony and balance of the four different ecosystems, the connection Maori people have with their ingredients from the land and ocean seems sacred. I'll carry their inspiration with me wherever I go.

## MAORI TRADITIONS

Jeromy van Riel taught me the skill of hand-fishing for shortfin eel in New Zealand's Matukituki Valley, but he also told me that the connection between Maori people and their food is "all about the *puku* [stomach], the source of emotion and feeling." Over the past 25 years, Jeromy has taught *te reo* Maori (the Maori language) from early childhood level to diploma level and everything in between. He's also a skilled artist, creating stunningly beautiful designs in New Zealand nephrite pounamu, an endemic stone. Pounamu, also known as green-

Gordon and Jeromy van Riel proudly hold their catch.

stone, is believed to have its own life force and carries special meaning for its wearer.

# BRAISED GOAT LEG AND SHOULDER

## WITH FUCHSIA BERRY CHUTNEY

### BRAISED GOAT

1 bone-in goat leg

1 bone-in goat shoulder

¼ cup olive oil

¼ cup rosemary leaves, finely chopped

2 tablespoons thyme leaves, chopped

2 tablespoons flaxseed oil

2 tablespoons minced garlic

1½ tablespoons kosher salt

1 tablespoon smoked paprika

1 tablespoon ground coriander

1 teaspoon lemon zest

1 teaspoon freshly ground black pepper

15–20 grape leaves or banana leaves

2 quarts chicken stock

### FUCHSIA BERRY CHUTNEY

1 tablespoon unsalted butter

1 shallot, finely diced

1 teaspoon minced garlic

1 teaspoon minced ginger

Kosher salt

Freshly ground black pepper

2 cups fuchsia berries or sweet red currants

1 tablespoon brown sugar

¼ cup orange juice

2 tablespoons red wine vinegar

1 tablespoon extra-virgin olive oil

Sweet potato flatbread, for serving (page 85)

## DIRECTIONS

**1.** Prepare the **braised goat:** Place the goat leg and shoulder on a large tray.

**2.** In a small mixing bowl, combine the olive oil, rosemary, thyme, flaxseed oil, garlic, salt, paprika, coriander, lemon zest, and black pepper.

**3.** Rub the marinade all over the goat leg and shoulder and refrigerate for at least 6 hours but preferably overnight.

**4.** Preheat a grill to 400°F.

**5.** Place the goat leg and shoulder on the grill and cook until the meat is charred and golden all over. Remove the goat from the grill and set aside.

**6.** Arrange the grape leaves on a cutting board so that each leaf is overlapping. Place the goat leg and shoulder in the center of the leaves and wrap them tightly. Use kitchen twine to tie up the leaves.

**7.** Preheat your oven to 285°F.

**8.** Place the goat in a large roasting pan and add enough chicken stock to cover halfway up the leaves. Cover the pan with aluminum foil and place in the oven.

**9.** Braise the goat until it is fork-tender, about 3 hours.

**10.** Make the **fuchsia berry chutney:** In a large sauté pan over medium heat, melt the butter. Add the shallot, garlic, and ginger and sweat until translucent, about 3 minutes. Season with a pinch of salt and pepper.

**11.** Add the berries and brown sugar and cook down until the berries start to burst and release their liquid.

**12.** Reduce the heat to low and add the orange juice and red wine vinegar and continue to cook until the chutney has thickened slightly. Finish with olive oil and taste for seasoning.

**13.** To serve, once the goat meat is falling off the bone, remove it from the pan and carefully shred the meat.

**14.** Serve the braised goat with the chutney and sweet potato flatbread.

# BURNT SUGAR STEAMED PUDDING

*Recipe inspired by Monique Fiso*

**YIELDS:** 2 LOAVES

---

⅓ cup, plus 1¼ cups granulated sugar

1 cup boiling water

2½ cups all-purpose flour

2 teaspoons ground mixed spice or pumpkin pie spice

1 teaspoon baking soda

¼ teaspoon kosher salt

1 cup (2 sticks) unsalted butter, chilled and cubed

3 large eggs, beaten

## ▌DIRECTIONS

---

**1.** Preheat your oven to 300°F.

**2.** Fill a roasting pan with 1 inch of water and place in the center of the oven to heat. Lightly coat two 1-pound loaf pans with nonstick spray.

**3.** In a medium heavy-bottom saucepan over medium heat, add ⅓ cup sugar and cook, stirring gently and constantly, until it completely melts and turns a deep amber color, about 10 minutes.

**4.** Remove the saucepan from the heat and carefully pour in the boiling water. Stir the mixture until it thickens and becomes a syrup. Set aside.

**5.** In a large mixing bowl, combine the flour, 1¼ cups sugar, mixed spice, baking soda, and salt. Add the butter and use your fingertips to press the dry ingredients into the butter. Continue pressing and mixing until the mixture resembles coarse sand. Add the eggs and stir with a wooden spoon to combine.

**6.** Slowly add syrup to the pudding mixture and continue stirring until a thick batter forms. Divide the batter between the two prepared loaf pans and cover each with aluminum foil.

**7.** Place the loaf pans in the roasting pan with water in the oven and cook for about 2 hours, until a toothpick inserted in the middle of the loaves comes out clean.

**8.** Remove the pudding from the pan and let cool on a rack.

**9.** To serve, cut into individual slices and serve warm or at room temperature.

# SWEET POTATO FLATBREAD

## WITH CILANTRO

*Recipe provided by*
*Monique Fiso*

**YIELDS:** 6–8 SERVINGS

2 large sweet potatoes, skin on

2 tablespoons, plus 2 teaspoons kosher salt

¼ cup (½ stick) unsalted butter

1 tablespoon minced garlic

2 tablespoons cilantro, finely chopped, divided

¼ cup all-purpose flour, plus more for dusting

1 teaspoon freshly ground black pepper

Flaky sea salt

## ▮ DIRECTIONS

**1.** In a medium saucepan over medium-high heat, combine the potatoes with about 2 quarts of water and 2 tablespoons of the salt and bring to a boil.

**2.** Reduce the heat to a simmer and continue cooking until the potatoes are fork-tender, about 20 minutes.

**3.** Preheat a grill to 400°F.

**4.** In a small saucepan over low heat, combine the butter and garlic and warm gently.

**5.** Remove the potatoes from the heat, drain, and peel immediately. Use a potato masher to quickly mash the potatoes until they are nice and smooth.

**6.** Add 1 tablespoon of the cilantro and enough all-purpose flour to make a malleable dough.

**7.** Season the dough with the black pepper and remaining 2 teaspoons of salt.

**8.** On a lightly floured work surface, carefully knead the dough until it comes together, being careful not to overwork it.

**9.** Separate the dough into four equal-size balls and roll each one out with a rolling pin into ¼-inch-thick circles.

**10.** Place the rolled-out dough on the grill and cook until charred. Use a pastry brush to coat the flatbreads evenly with the garlic butter.

**11.** Finish each flatbread with sea salt and sprinkle with the remaining cilantro.

Maui's rugged Hana Coast is home to rich and diverse culinary traditions as well as breathtaking scenery.

# CHAPTER 5

# HAWAII'S HANA COAST

An epic array of indigenous ingredients
and the fascinating effects of trade winds
on Hawaii's culinary traditions

Gordon practices the karate-kick method of harvesting kalo (taro).

R EPRESENTING FAR MORE than Spam and poke bowls, the cuisine of the Hawaiian Islands has been developed with the influence of migrants. Polynesian voyagers, who navigated by the stars and by observing birds, ocean swells, and wind patterns, traveled in outrigger and double-hulled canoes between the Hawaiian Islands and the rest of the Polynesian Triangle. Groups who came later to the archipelago also helped to diversify Hawaiian cuisine. ¶ Canoe plants, so named for the life-sustaining plants carried on those voyaging vessels, were important for all life's vital needs: food, medicine, fabric, containers, and cordage. These canoe plants—kalo (taro), 'awa (kava), kukui (candlenut), mai'a (banana), niu (coconut), 'uala (sweet potato), and 'ulu (breadfruit)—that were so much a part of Hawaii's history are now an integral part of Hawaiian culture today.

White-capped waves meet volcanic cliffs along the Hana coastline.

## NAVIGATOR

### THE STOP

Polynesian voyagers came ashore in Hawaii about 1,500 years ago. They, along with other Pacific migrants, informed the traditions and cuisine of the islands.

### THE GEOGRAPHY

The volcanic islands of Hawaii make up the world's largest island chain, but only seven of its 132 islands are inhabited. I spent my time on the Hana coast of Maui.

### FOOD FACT

The canoe plants— crops originally brought to the islands by voyaging canoes— are essential ingredients of traditional Hawaiian cuisine.

Among the canoe plants, kalo is especially important. According to the Hawaiian creation chant, the Kumulipo, the plant is a sacred connection to the ancestors, and all Hawaiians trace their roots back to the kalo. While many visitors know the plant only through the Hawaiian staple poi, it's only one of the many uses for kalo, which is used in everything from flour to greens to chips to pudding. Traditional knowledge of its preparation is important, as raw kalo contains calcium oxalate crystals, which can cause intense pain in the mouth and are associated with gout and kidney stones. These crystals break down when the plant is cooked.

Adding his own story to Hawaii's cuisine is Hilo-born chef Sheldon Simeon. The menu at his restaurant Tin Roof is a representation of the migrant groups that have come to the archipelago and forged a new cuisine, like his own Filipino grandparents. As the *piko* (navel) of the Pacific, Hawaii is the central place where flavors from the entire region come together.

**DEEP DIVE**
Spearfishing off the
Hana coast of Maui

"The trade winds bring all these different cultures, and they just seamlessly meld together," Sheldon told me when I met him on Maui. "Every time somebody leaves their mark, it's one layer of deliciousness that's added to the whole."

On the Hana coast, the land curves upward from the beach past hillside homes, through alternating emerald gulches and ridges carved by streams and waterfalls. The view from the water is as important to the Hawaiian culture as having feet planted firmly on land. It's an ideal vantage point from which you can see the land as it was originally divided by *ahupua'a*, a subdivision of land similar in appearance to a slice of pie that is traced from top to bottom, from the uplands

# FREE DIVING

**F**ree diving, despite popular belief, isn't about holding your breath as much as it is about staying calm in discomfort. It's like underwater meditation. To Kimi Werner, a world-record-holding spearfisher and United States National Spearfishing Champion, free diving brings peacefulness and the need to be fully present. "It's about relaxing into whatever discomfort is there," she said. "You have to get down into your gut and let something deeper than the thought process guide you." Kimi is also a trained chef, acclaimed artist, inspirational

**Kimi Werner prepares Gordon for a free dive.**

speaker, and environmental activist. Like many others in Hawaii, the ocean plays a central role in her life.

to the ocean. The ancient Hawaiian system ensured a variety of essential resources for the residents of each area.

To be immersed in a wealth of natural resources is not only part of the heritage of the original Polynesian settlers, but it's also an essential element of modern Hawaiian culture. Surrounded by ocean, the people of the archipelago rely heavily on fishing and a successful angler is a valued asset in the Hawaiian community. I got a good look at two ways of gathering seafood on Maui. First, snorkeling to forage sea urchins, spiny lobster, and *'opihi*—a limpet that's often called "the fish of death" due to the risk that 'opihi pickers face in harvesting them from dangerous shores. But it's no

wonder people gamble with their lives for its sweet, creamy flavor and natural saltiness. Free diving with Kimi Werner was a little intimidating. Aside from the fact that she's one of the best divers in the world, I couldn't help but constantly scan the water for sharks. But under the surface, I could see why it's so easy for Hawaiians to value their ocean community.

In 1868, King Kamehameha V introduced eight axis deer to Molokai. Today, there are more than 100,000 on the islands of Molokai, Lanai, and Maui. Along with other non-native ungulates such as goats and pigs, they are responsible for widespread destruction of lowland ecosystems, including critical forested watershed. Hunting them and introducing venison

# CHEF SHELDON SIMEON'S REAL HAWAII

**B**orn in the town of Hilo on Hawaii, chef Sheldon Simeon inherited his love for cooking from his Filipino parents. Apart from an internship at Walt Disney World, most of his culinary education has taken place in Hawaii. The two-time finalist on Bravo's *Top Chef* operates his popular restaurant Tin Roof on Maui. One of the driving forces of modern Hawaiian cuisine, Sheldon dedicated his book, *Cook Real Hawai'i*, to the local food that feeds his *'ohana*—the Hawaiian word for "family," which also encompasses other close relationships—and tells the history of the archipelago through food and experience. In Hawaii, the power of food brings people together to share stories of heritage.

That history evolves as food traditions change with time and the people who keep them. Each culture's culinary creations interact with each other, rather than stay in separate lanes. "The food of Hawaii has always been here standing tall," Sheldon said. "As more people begin to look at the world through a lens of diversity and the culinary world becomes more inclusive, cuisine like the food of Hawaii is finally getting the spotlight it deserves. I see Hawaii local food as a shining example of the greatness that can happen when cultures begin to truly intertwine."

**Chef Sheldon Simeon holds a freshly caught spiny lobster as he and Gordon discuss the nuances of Hawaiian seafood.**

"The food of Hawaii has always been here standing tall."

—Chef Sheldon Simeon

### NATIVE ROOTS
From roadside signage to local produce and majestic hidden waterfalls, Hawaii is a land of vibrant colors and spirit.

products gives Hawaiians an opportunity to improve food security, the local economy, and the health of the islands' ecosystems. Balance is critical to Hawaiian ecology, as the archipelago's extreme isolation makes it the world capital of endemic species. The introduction of non-native plants and animals has caused many of the endemic species to become endangered.

One of the largest tropical fruit farms in the state of Hawaii, ONO Organic Farms, grows and sells a wealth of exotic fruits, cacao, and Arabica estate-grown coffee. I joined Chuck Boerner, ONO's owner, who has been farming here since he was a kid, for a mad dash to find something I'd never seen or tasted before. Right away, we pulled red bananas with sweet orange flesh from a tree and sampled the incredibly sour bilimbi—a relative of the star fruit that's used as a lime substitute. Like many foods in Hawaii, the bilimbi is from elsewhere (tropical Asia) and is just another excellent example of the combination of cultures and cuisines that thrives here.

Driving to Hana on Maui is challenging in even the best weather. The narrow Hana Highway, also known as the Road to Hana, has 620 curves and 59 bridges along a route with rainforests and waterfalls. With visitors stopping frequently to enjoy the dramatic seascapes, the journey can take anywhere from two to four hours. It's a good thing that there are fantastic food stops along the way. Uncle Russell's Huli Huli Chicken stand is a must stop. Russell and his family members constantly turn the sweet and smoky chicken on the barbecue as it cooks (it's called huli because *huli* is the Hawaiian word for "turn"). Another delicious stop is Aunty Sandy's Banana Bread, where the hot fresh loaves take me back to my childhood.

Maybe that's why so many people love Hawaii. Aloha is more than merely a greeting—it's a sentiment of mutual regard and living in harmony with the people and land. The trade winds have stirred the culinary pot and have come up with a remarkable cuisine that's a blend of everyone's history.

# KALO ROOTS

Poi is a staple food made from the tuber of the kalo (taro) plant, which was brought to these islands by the Polynesians around 1,000 years ago. In ancient times, Hawaiian planters cultivated nearly 300 varieties of kalo, both wet and dryland varieties. Wade Latham, a kalo farmer in Maui, showed me how to harvest the plant from his *lo'i* (kalo patch), which was so full of slippery mud that I had trouble keeping my balance. After steaming and peeling the kalo tubers, we ground them up with water to get perfect poi consistency—smooth and sticky.

The kalo (taro) plant is a staple of the Native Hawaiian diet and a core part of Hawaiian culture.

# POI PANNA COTTA

## WITH COCONUT WHIPPED CREAM
## AND KUKUI NUT CRUMBLE

**YIELDS:** 8 SERVINGS

### POI

**1 taro root or 1 small sweet potato (about 2 ounces)**

**3 tablespoons boiling water**

### PUDDING

**2 cups whole milk**

**½ cup granulated sugar**

**2 tablespoons cornstarch**

**2 eggs**

**1 vanilla bean, scraped**

### WHIPPED CREAM

**1 cup coconut cream**

**1 cup heavy cream**

**¼ cup powdered sugar**

**1 lime, zested**

**Kukui nuts, chopped**

### DIRECTIONS

**1.** Make the **poi:** Place the taro in a small sauce pan and cover it with water. Bring to a boil and cook until tender, about 30 minutes. Remove the taro from the water and let cool for 10 minutes. Peel the taro and place it in a medium mixing bowl with the boiling water. Mash the mixture together until it resembles a smooth paste.

**2.** Make the **pudding:** In a large saucepan, whisk together the milk, sugar, and cornstarch. Bring the mixture to a boil over medium-high heat and immediately reduce to a simmer.

**3.** In a medium mixing bowl, whisk together the eggs. Use a ladle to slowly drizzle the simmering milk mixture into the eggs, making sure to whisk constantly so that the eggs do not curdle.

**4.** Slowly pour the tempered eggs back into the saucepan and continue whisking over medium-high heat until the mixture is thickened, about 15 minutes. Remove the pudding from the heat and stir in the vanilla bean and poi.

**5.** Strain the pudding through a fine mesh sieve. Pour the pudding into individual serving dishes or coconut shells. Refrigerate until set, about 1 hour.

**6.** Make the **whipped cream:** In a large mixing bowl, combine the coconut cream, heavy cream, and powdered sugar. Using an electric hand mixer, whip the mixture until medium peaks form.

**7.** To serve, top the pudding cups with the whipped cream and lime zest and sprinkle with kukui nuts.

# GRILLED SPINY LOBSTER

## WITH SPICY BLACK BEAN SAUCE, POHOLE, AND UNI

*Recipe provided by*
*Sheldon Simeon*

**YIELDS:** 2–3 SERVINGS

**1 whole 2-pound spiny lobster**

BLACK BEAN SAUCE

**1 cup salted cooked or canned black beans**

**2 large garlic cloves, sliced**

**1 2-inch piece ginger, peeled and thinly sliced**

**2 tablespoons sambal oelek**

**2 tablespoons soy sauce**

**1 14-ounce can coconut milk**

**1 pound fresh pohole, or fiddle-head ferns, washed and rinsed, woody stems removed**

**1 bunch cilantro, thicker stems removed, roughly chopped**

**1 bunch scallions, sliced**

**1 bunch watercress, chopped**

**3 ounces uni**

### DIRECTIONS

**1.** Break down the lobster: Press the tip of a large chef's knife in the crack set slightly behind the eyes on the head. Press down firmly and quickly, splitting the head completely in half. Remove any waste and rinse.

**2.** Twist off the arms and then twist the tail away from the body to separate it. Cut the tail in half lengthwise, exposing the meat.

**3.** Make the **black bean sauce:** In a large stockpot over medium heat, add the black beans and mash into a coarse paste. Add the garlic, ginger, sambal oelek, and soy sauce and mix to combine. Cook until fragrant and the mixture begins to simmer.

**4.** Add the coconut milk and continue cooking until thickened, about 10 minutes.

**5.** Grill the lobster: Preheat a grill to 400°F.

**6.** Place the lobster pieces meat side down on the grill and cook until opaque and cooked through, about 10 minutes.

**7.** Grill the pohole: Place the pohole on the grill and cook until just charred, about 3 minutes.

**8.** Add the cooked lobster and grilled pohole to the pot with the black bean sauce and top with the cilantro, scallions, watercress, and uni. Serve family style.

# VENISON SHEPHERD'S PIE

## WITH BREADFRUIT MASH AND BEER GRAVY

**YIELDS:** 4 SERVINGS

BREADFRUIT MASH

**4 cups breadfruit, peeled and cut into 1-inch cubes (can also substitute Yukon Gold potatoes, parsnips, or celeriac)**

**2 tablespoons kosher salt, plus more as needed**

**¼ cup milk**

**½ cup (1 stick) unsalted butter, cubed and chilled**

**½ teaspoon ground white pepper**

VENISON SHEPHERD'S PIE

**1 tablespoon unsalted butter**

**½ cup carrot, diced**

**½ cup yellow onion, diced**

**½ cup celery, diced**

**3 tablespoons minced garlic**

**1 tablespoon fresh thyme leaves**

**3 teaspoons kosher salt, divided**

**1½ teaspoons freshly ground black pepper, divided**

**2 cups venison trimmings, cut into 1-inch pieces (we used trimmings from the legs, shoulder, ribs, and loin)**

**¼ cup Wondra flour**

**1 cup lager**

**2 cups venison, beef, or chicken stock**

**Hawaiian volcanic salt**

**1 tablespoon chopped fresh parsley**

## | DIRECTIONS

**1.** Make the **breadfruit mash:** In a large pot over medium-high heat, add the breadfruit, about 2 quarts of water, and the salt. Bring to a boil and cook until the breadfruit is tender but not falling apart, about 20 minutes.

**2.** Strain the breadfruit and pass through a ricer.

**3.** Return the breadfruit puree back to the pot and place over low heat.

**4.** Add the milk and stir until the liquid has dissolved and the breadfruit starts to stick to the bottom of the pot, about 5 minutes.

**5.** Slowly add the cubed butter, stirring constantly, until all the butter has been incorporated.

**6.** Season the mash with the white pepper and additional salt if needed, to taste.

**7.** Make the **shepherd's pie:** In a large cast-iron pan over medium heat, add the butter. Once the butter has melted, add the carrot, onion, celery, garlic, and thyme. Cook until the vegetables have softened and begun to caramelize. Season the vegetables with 2 teaspoons of salt and 1 teaspoon of black pepper. Remove the sautéed vegetables to a bowl and set aside.

**8.** Season the venison with the remaining 1 teaspoon of salt and ½ teaspoon of pepper. Dredge the seasoned venison in the Wondra flour and then place in the hot skillet. Cook the venison until it browns on all sides.

**9.** Add the lager to deglaze the pan, making sure to scrape up all the brown bits at the bottom of the pan.

**10.** Add the stock and the sautéed vegetables to the pan and bring to a simmer. Continue cooking on low heat until the gravy has thickened, about 15 minutes.

**11.** Preheat your oven to 375°F.

**12.** Pour the stew into a 9-by-13-inch baking dish. Top the stew with the breadfruit mash and bake until the top is golden brown, about 20 minutes. Finish cooking under the broiler if the breadfruit mash needs more color.

**13.** Finish with a pinch of Hawaiian salt and the parsley.

# GRILLED VENISON STRIP LOIN

## WITH CHARRED PINEAPPLE
## AND HAWAIIAN CHILI GLAZE

**YIELDS:** 4 SERVINGS

CHARRED PINEAPPLE AND HAWAIIAN
CHILI GLAZE

1 pineapple, cored, peeled,
and quartered

½ cup soy sauce

⅓ cup rice wine vinegar

3 tablespoons honey

2 small Hawaiian chili peppers or
habaneros, finely diced

1 lime, zested and juiced

½ teaspoon kosher salt

VENISON

2 venison strip loins, about 1½
pounds total, silverskin removed

2 tablespoons grapeseed oil

2 teaspoons kosher salt

1 teaspoon freshly ground
black pepper

Hawaiian volcanic salt

**DIRECTIONS**

**1.** Make the **glaze:** Preheat a grill to 400°F.

**2.** Place the pineapple quarters on the grill and cook until charred all over, about 5 minutes. Cut the grilled pineapple into small dice. Keep the grill hot while you finish the glaze.

**3.** In a small saucepan over medium heat, combine the diced pineapple, soy sauce, rice wine vinegar, and honey. Bring the mixture to a boil and cook until it reduces to a thick glaze, about 10 minutes.

**4.** Once the sauce is reduced, add the peppers, lime zest and juice, and salt. Taste for seasoning and adjust if needed. Reserve half of the glaze for basting and set aside the remaining half to serve with the finished venison loin.

**5.** Grill the **venison:** Brush the venison loins with the oil and season with the salt and pepper all over.

**6.** Place the seasoned venison on the grill and sear quickly on all sides.

**7.** Once some color has developed, begin brushing the venison with the pineapple chili glaze.

**8.** Continue rotating the venison while basting until the loins have begun to caramelize and the internal temperature of the venison is about 135°F, about 5 minutes. Be careful not to overcook the venison, as it tends to become gamey and tough because the meat is so lean.

**9.** Remove the venison from the grill and let it rest for at least 5 minutes.

**10**. To serve, slice the venison into medallions and garnish with the reserved pineapple chili glaze. Sprinkle with Hawaiian volcanic salt.

Sunset paints a herd of antelope with a fiery palette in KwaZulu-Natal (KZN), a province in southeastern South Africa.

# CHAPTER 6

# THE WILDS OF SOUTH AFRICA

In the ancestral land of the Zulu, the simplicity of South African cuisine is inspired by a wealth of cultures

Gordon is all smiles while fishing in KwaZulu-Natal.

T

**THE PROVINCE OF** KwaZulu-Natal (often referred to as KZN) occupies the southeastern portion of South Africa. It's the country's second largest and most ecologically diverse province, stretching from the subtropical Indian Ocean coastline to uKhahlamba-Drakensberg Park's sandstone cliffs and gigantic peaks. It's also the ancestral land of the Zulu people, the largest ethnic group in South Africa. The challenging history of the Zulu people—who battled man, animal, and incredible terrain to survive—helped shape an incredible cuisine. ¶ Agriculture has played a principal role in Zulu culture. Zulu cuisine has revolved around grains, wild plants, and meat due to the Zulu people's history as nomadic farmers. Because of their historical agricultural practices, many foods in their cuisine are organic and don't require extensive processing, letting the ingredients speak for themselves.

## NAVIGATOR

### THE STOP

In South Africa's KwaZulu-Natal, I explore ancient food traditions with the Zulu community, ancestral farmers, and cattle farmers who rely on what the land provides.

### THE GEOGRAPHY

KwaZulu-Natal is a mountainous region of South Africa that rises from the coast to more than 11,000 feet (3,350 m) high.

### FOOD FACT

Traditional braai is cooked over local wood, but throughout South Africa you may find braai cooked over charcoal.

Elephants, giraffes, and leopards inhabit the grasslands of iSimangaliso Wetland Park.

Zulu people are traditionally cattle farmers, too, and place a great amount of value in their livestock, considering it an element of wealth. Meat—such as beef, goat, and lamb—cooked over an open flame in the outdoors is the quintessential South African way of eating.

"*Braai*, or cooking over an open fire, is how Zulu people used to cook traditionally in ancient times, and still today," chef Zola Nene told me as she gave me a braai tutorial while informing me that I'd have to cook for a Zulu chief who is the direct descendant of the king Shaka Zulu, founder of the Zulu Empire. But braai is more than just a cooking technique—it's the centerpiece of family and community gatherings. While *braai* is Afrikaans for "barbecue" or "roast," the deeper practice started long before Dutch settlers arrived in the 17th and 18th centuries.

Modern-day braai uses marinades and rubs, a result of Afrikaans influence, but Zulu traditional braai doesn't add a lot of external flavors to the meat or fish. Zola showed me how to keep things uncomplicated in Zulu fashion. "The cuisine is simple, but very important, and it's one of the things that unifies all our different cultures because cooking outdoors is something that all the cultures in South Africa do in some way," she said. Zola has made it her mission to bring the flavors of her ancestors to the rest of the world.

The metaphorical mixing pot of influences, due to the country's political and colonized past, includes Zulu warriors, Dutch settlers, British colonists, and Indian laborers. KZN has the largest population of Indians outside of India, and the strong ties that these South Africans have to their traditional Indian roots have brought added diversity to the regional cuisine. A salsa dish such as ushatini (with chopped onions, tomatoes, and chili) and a township classic such as chakalaka (with onion, peppers, carrots, tomatoes, baked beans, and curry powder) illustrate the incorporation of Indian spices with local dishes.

I searched a township in Durban to find the spice blend called pelepele ("chili" or "pepper" in the Zulu language) from a woman whose family has been perfecting it for generations. They're so dedicated that she told me they use it on everything they eat. Although the ingredients vary depending on who's making it, pelepele often includes chili, onion, garlic, tomato, basil, parsley, and salt. The dependence on chili peppers in pelepele is another example of how integral Indian ingredients are in this region of South Africa.

## TRAVEL 101

# GAME FOR SOMETHING NEW

Local markets are some of the easiest ways to dive into a destination and not only learn about regional ingredients and food, but also get to know the culture in a deeper way. In KwaZulu-Natal, the mix of influences comes especially from the Zulu community, Dutch settlers, British colonists, and Indian laborers, which makes for a diverse South African culture. Sampling a little bit of everything helps get beyond the expectations of a place and may very well introduce you to something you've never tried before. Don't worry, not all the spices are blisteringly hot.

Braai is more than just a cooking technique—it's the centerpiece of family and community gatherings.

Walking through the market in Durban gave me an even better sense of the importance of spices here. Chili pepper doesn't just show up in one way but through seemingly countless permutations of spice blends, from curry masala to the creatively named "Mother-in-Law Exterminator." Curries in this region are considered much hotter than those around the world and will often incorporate spicy cayenne pepper or curry masala, sweet spices, and curry leaves. The premixed blends for home cooking can make things easier, and spice merchants are more than happy to help you find the ideal one. They'll guide you to a blend that has plenty of traditional flavor but doesn't feel like licking a flamethrower.

And then there are the treasures in the water. Fishing for bass in a lake in South Africa is a little different from doing it at home, partly because there might be behemoth hippos to watch out for. While I learned to find bait in the dung of rhinos for my fishing excursion, the stress of watching out for angry rhinos made me wish for a nearby bait shop. It may have been worth the stress, as I had a successful haul for the Big Cook.

# CHEF ZOLA NENE SHARES HER ZULU PRIDE

Chef, TV personality, and cookbook author Zola Nene was born in Durban, South Africa. Her passion for Zulu cuisine was instilled at a young age by her mother and grandmother. Today, she is a champion of traditional South African cuisine. Shunning a career in law, she chased her dreams of becoming a chef to England, working in a brasserie in Cheshire before returning to South Africa to attend the Institute of Culinary Arts in Stellenbosch.

Her passion and love for food landed her a job as a TV morning-show culinary host, where she shares her simple, down-to-earth cooking style with a large audience. The show quickly became the most famous breakfast program in South Africa. Zola's enthusiasm is infectious, as is her pride in her Zulu heritage. Her two cookbooks, *Simply Delicious* and *Simply Zola*, have won numerous accolades.

Our special guest star at the Big Cook, aside from the Zulu chief, of course, was a hippo that scared both of us. "That hippo was a distraction for me, too," she said. "I don't think people realize how scary it actually was. We had escape routes planned, and I'm glad we didn't have to use them."

**As Gordon looks on, chef Zola Nene garnishes a freshly caught fish with ushatini, a chopped salsa of onion, tomatoes, and chilies.**

## ANIMAL BEHAVIOR

**L**onely Masiane has been a local guide and wildlife expert at the Tala Game Reserve for about 17 years. The reserve in KwaZulu-Natal is a wildlife sanctuary of nearly 7,400 acres (2,995 ha) across many diverse natural environments. "I was my mother's first child," he told me. "Because my father wasn't around, my mother was a little lonely while she was pregnant, and that's how I got my name." Lonely has spent so much time among rhinos and hippos that they've become his friends, and his knowledge of the animals' habits was incredibly helpful while I was in his company.

**Local wildlife expert Lonely Masiane**

> Peeling back the layers of simplicity in Zulu cuisine was instrumental to understanding the level of respect for produce and cooking with such humble ingredients.

Even fish on the braai requires very little seasoning—just some salt and then straight on the grill, letting the flavor of the fish come through along with an accompaniment, such as ushatini, sprinkled on the top.

Traditional Zulu breads such as uJeqe and dombolo are staples in many South African homes. They both use the same dough but are prepared differently. With uJeqe, the dough is steamed in a pot and served with various dishes like chakalaka, meat, soups, or stews. For dombolo, the dough is cooked on top of a stew, already integrated into the dish it is accompanying. Another staple food—due to its versatility and low cost—is pap, a porridge made from maize meal that can be cooked runny, soft, or stiff, depending on your preference. It can be eaten with milk and sugar for breakfast or served alongside meat or vegetables for lunch or dinner.

Peeling back the layers of simplicity in Zulu cuisine was instrumental to understanding the level of respect for produce and cooking with such humble ingredients. That vibrant freshness is super religious for me. It opened my eyes to Zulu heritage in wasting nothing, eating incredibly modestly, and appreciating the wealth of flavors in everything on the table. I'm especially happy that I don't have to cook regularly near a watering hole packed with hippos.

### SIGHTS AND BITES
Large mammals, such as rhinoceroses and giraffes, roam the KwaZulu-Natal province. The province is home to the largest population of Indians outside of India, and its cuisine has strong ties to the country, with Indian spices and chilies featuring prominently in traditional dishes.

# BRAAIED T-BONE STEAKS
## RUBBED WITH PELEPELE RELISH

**YIELDS:** 4 SERVINGS

4  T-bone steaks,
about 14 ounces each

BRAAI SPICE

1  tablespoon garlic powder

1  tablespoon smoked paprika

1  teaspoon cayenne

1  teaspoon ground coriander

1  teaspoon ground cumin

1  teaspoon freshly ground black
pepper

1  teaspoon kosher salt

PELEPELE RELISH

2  large red onions, cut in half

4  tomatoes, cut in half

1  2-inch piece ginger, peeled

1  head garlic, peeled

6  red chilies

2  tablespoons olive oil

8  curry leaves

Flaky sea salt

## DIRECTIONS

**1.** Make the **braai spice:** In a medium mixing bowl, combine all the braai spice ingredients.

**2.** Season the steaks with half of the braai spice and let marinate in the refrigerator for 1 to 2 hours. Reserve the rest of the spice mix.

**3.** Make the **pelepele relish:** Preheat a grill to 400°F.

**4.** Toss the onions and tomatoes with the reserved braai spice.

**5.** Place the onions, tomatoes, and ginger on the grill and cook until charred, about 3 minutes.

**6.** Finely dice the charred vegetables, garlic, and chilies.

**7.** In a medium saucepan over medium heat, add the oil. Once the oil is shimmering, add the curry leaves and toast for 3 seconds. Add the diced vegetables and continue cooking until fragrant and soft, about 10 to 12 minutes. Reserve half of the relish for grilling and set aside the remaining half to serve with the steaks.

**8.** Grill the steaks: Place the steaks on the grill and cook until nicely seared on both sides, about 3 minutes per side.

**9.** Spoon over about half of the pelepele relish and continue grilling until the steaks are cooked to an internal temperature of 130–140°F and the pelepele relish has caramelized, about 5 minutes more.

**10.** Let the steaks rest for 5 minutes to prevent them from bleeding and becoming dry.

**11.** Slice the steaks, season with sea salt, and serve with the remaining pelepele relish on the side.

# CHAKALAKA

Recipe provided by
*Zola Nene*

**YIELDS:** 4 SERVINGS

3 tablespoons olive oil

3 yellow onions, diced

3 green bell peppers, diced

2 garlic cloves, minced

1 teaspoon kosher salt

4 tomatoes, diced

3 carrots, peeled and shredded

½ cup brown sugar

½ cup apple cider vinegar

2 tablespoons curry powder

4 curry leaves

2 cups tomato sauce

1 14-ounce can English baked beans

## DIRECTIONS

**1.** In a medium saucepan over medium heat, add the oil. Once the oil is shimmering, add the onions and sauté until translucent, about 3 minutes.

**2.** Add the bell peppers and garlic and continue cooking until fragrant, about 2 minutes. Season with the salt.

**3.** Add the tomatoes, carrots, brown sugar, apple cider vinegar, curry powder, and curry leaves. Reduce the heat to low and continue cooking until the vegetables are tender and caramelized, about 10 minutes.

**4.** Add the tomato sauce and continue cooking until the mixture thickens, about 5 minutes.

**5.** Add the baked beans. Taste for seasoning and adjust as needed.

# BRAAIED WHOLE RED SNAPPER
## WITH GREEN MONKEY ORANGE CHUTNEY

**YIELDS:** 6 SERVINGS

### BRAAI SPICE

**1 tablespoon garlic powder**

**1 tablespoon smoked paprika**

**1 teaspoon cayenne**

**1 teaspoon ground coriander**

**1 teaspoon ground cumin**

**1 teaspoon freshly ground black pepper**

**1 teaspoon kosher salt**

### USHATINI SALSA

**2 serrano chilies, finely diced**

**2 tomatoes, finely diced**

**1 red onion, finely diced**

**1 bunch cilantro, chopped**

**1 lime, zested and juiced**

**1 teaspoon kosher salt**

### GREEN MONKEY ORANGE CHUTNEY

**2 tablespoons olive oil**

**1 onion, finely diced**

**1 teaspoon kosher salt**

**1 2-inch piece ginger, peeled**

**1 tablespoon brown sugar**

**1 tablespoon honey**

**¼ cup red wine vinegar**

**6 green monkey orange fruit, seeds removed**

### RED SNAPPER

**3 whole red snappers, gutted, scaled, and gills removed**

**2 tablespoons grapeseed oil**

**2 limes, halved**

## DIRECTIONS

**1.** Make the **braai spice:** In a medium mixing bowl, combine all the braai spice ingredients.

**2.** Make the **ushatini salsa:** In a small mixing bowl, combine all the salsa ingredients.

**3.** Make the **chutney:** In a large skillet over medium heat, combine the oil and onion and cook until translucent. Season with the salt.

**4.** Grate the ginger into the pan and continue cooking until the ginger and onion are fragrant, about 2 minutes.

**5.** Add the brown sugar and honey and stir to combine.

**6.** Add the red wine vinegar to deglaze the pan, making sure to scrape up any brown bits stuck to the bottom of the pan.

**7.** Reduce the heat to low and add the green monkey orange fruit and continue cooking until thickened, about 5 minutes.

**8.** Grill the **snapper:** Preheat a grill to 400°F.

**9.** Brush the fish with the oil and transfer to the braai spice bowl. Coat the fish generously with the braai spice, making sure to season inside the cavity as well.

**10.** Place the fish on the hot grill and do not move it until the skin has started to crisp and form a crust, about 4 to 5 minutes, or until it releases easily from the grill.

**11.** Carefully flip the fish and continue cooking until the meat is flaky and opaque, about 5 minutes.

**12.** Place the limes on the grill to char, about 1 minute. Remove and set aside.

**13.** Once the fish is nicely charred and cooked through, place it on a large wooden cutting board.

**14.** Spoon the salsa over the fish and serve with the green monkey orange chutney and grilled lime halves.

Gentle waters and rugged cliffs welcome visitors to this cozy spot on the Norwegian coastline.

# CHAPTER 7

# NORWAY'S VIKING COUNTRY

A thrilling quest—from herding reindeer to scuba diving in wintry waters—to the heart of Norwegian cuisine

The mountainside
of Voss, Norway

**N**ORWAY'S CUISINE HAS BEEN SHAPED by its 63,000-mile (101,000 km) coastline, its long winters and brief summers, the forests that cover a third of its surface, and the mountains that cut off west from east. The spectacular scenery among the fjords and mountains of southern Norway regularly makes the covers of magazines and shows up in Instagram posts, and for good reason. In winter, it's especially spectacular: The crystal clear fjords are enveloped in mist, mountain peaks are covered with snow, the nights are long and dark, and the temperatures are freezing. ¶ To live through the harsh conditions of "Viking season"—the bitter winter months—Norwegians rely on their creative methods of preservation and fermentation. Despite the cold and darkness, there's an abundance of culinary riches at this time of year. Seafood is at

The second largest city in Norway, Bergen is located near several fjords.

## NAVIGATOR

### THE STOP

In western Norway, I seek out the foods and traditional methods locals use to make surviving harsh winter conditions flavorful and easy.

### THE GEOGRAPHY

Norway's cuisine has been shaped by its 63,000-mile (101,000 km) coastline, along with its mountainous terrain and fjords, forged by glaciers thousands of years ago.

### FOOD FACT

Fermentation is a key method Norwegians use to preserve the robust flavors of earlier seasons.

its tastiest, reindeer herding is underway, and rakfisk (fillets of freshwater trout salted and layered in wooden barrels to ferment) that's been fermenting for months is finally ready to serve.

"If someone wants to discover the food of my region, they have to look at how people settled hundreds of years ago along the fjords and up in the mountains and how they hunted and fished and tried not to starve to death in winter," chef Christopher Haatuft said when we met at his favorite foraging spot on a small island outside Bergen, off Norway's southwestern coast. At the cutting edge of western Norway's food scene, he focuses on fresh local seafood and gives a modern twist to traditional Nordic cuisine. "Here, it's mainly about salting, smoking, drying, and fermenting food. It's hardcore survivalist food for dirt-poor farmers," he said. Aside from essential survival, all those methods of preservation are about trying to prolong summer and making the fresh, sunlit taste of the season last.

While old-school Viking-style foods aren't as necessary in a modern society, traditional Norwegian dishes like rakfisk, smalahove (salted and smoked sheep's head), and pinnekjøtt (salted, air-dried lamb ribs) are such an essential part of the culture that they're often enjoyed at celebratory and holiday meals. Char or trout packed with salt and sugar, stored in a cool place under pressure, and fermented for at least three months results in the aroma-packed rakfisk—which is eaten raw as a special Christmas tradition. I tried the "not very strong" three-month batch that tasted like a salty-sweet cross between cured salmon and Vacherin cheese. As I took a bite, I was told not to think about the smell but about the flavor. However, it's pretty hard to ignore the nose-numbing smell of rakfisk that's been fermented for a year or more.

Originating as a sustainable effort to use the whole animal and not let anything go to waste, smalahove is another appetizing Christmas delicacy—a sheep's head that has been salt-cured, smoked, and steamed. It can be disconcerting when the food stares back at you, but it really is delicious. Smalahove is served with potatoes and turnips, and the fattiest parts (jaw, ear, eye, tongue) are eaten first because they taste better when they're hot. Pinnekjøtt is a dish made from lamb ribs that are salted, smoked, and dried. Before the meat is smoked, it needs to be soaked in water, sometimes for more than a day, to remove most of the salt. The result is an intensely delicious and savory piece of lamb.

Farther north live the Sami, Europe's oldest living Indigenous culture. Inhabiting Sapmi—a homeland spread across the northern reaches of Norway, Swe-

## TRAVEL 101
# TO THE MARKET WE GO

Norway's northern latitude means that nights are long and dark, and temperatures are cold. But there's a bright light around the winter holidays when little villages pop up in big cities, selling traditional food and holiday knickknacks. On Norway's southwestern coast, Bergen is known as the capital of the fjords and for being a cosmopolitan city with small-town charm. Seafood holds a special place in the city's gastronomy, and you can get some of the freshest fish in the Nordic countries at Bergen's fish market, which has provided the best locally caught seafood since 1276.

den, Finland, and a corner of Russia—the different cultural groups of Indigenous Sami number about 75,000 together, and their traditional livelihoods are fishing, gathering, handicrafts, hunting, and, most significant, reindeer herding. Families herd the reindeer as a community, but each animal is individually owned, and the relationship between herder and reindeer is symbiotic. Nearly everything from the reindeer is used, from skin and fur in clothing to blood in sausages and pancakes to meat in a variety of ways, including hearty stews like bidos, made with reindeer meat, carrots, and potatoes.

Norway's long history of fishing adds fresh seafood to its wealth of ingredients. The clear and cold waters allow fish and shellfish to grow slower here, while the

## To live through "Viking season," Norwegians rely on preservation and fermentation.

cold winter weather preserves the freshness of the catch. Many of the shellfish are harvested by hand, which is a gentler way of interacting with the ocean and the ingredients we love. Oysters, langoustines, crabs, urchins, and even mahogany clams—marine mollusks that can live for as long as 500 years—are all part of the essential gastronomy of Norway. And ingredients that weren't historically part of the daily

# CHRISTOPHER HAATUFT GOES LOCAL

Former punk rocker chef Christopher Haatuft grew up in Bergen and spent time as a food writer before apprenticing as a cook. He went on to work in the kitchens of institutions Alinea, Per Se, and Blue Hill at Stone Barns. "When I started cooking here, it was hard to find great examples through which I could learn how to run a restaurant," he told me. "I downloaded old episodes of your shows, like *Boiling Point* and *Ramsay's Kitchen Nightmares*, to get some of the best advice I still

use today for ordinary people running restaurants. It was a crash course—Restaurant 101."

When Christopher returned to Bergen, he jokingly coined the term "neo-fjordic" to describe food that's locally sourced from the surrounding fjord lands, and it stuck. He focused on looking at western Norway as a culinary region. At Lysverket,

his Bergen restaurant, he's built an identity that's natural and organic. "My goal is to have a restaurant that the people who live here are proud to have in the city," he said. I think he has achieved it.

**Gordon and chef Christopher Haatuft (right) cook a Christmas meal outdoors for their guests.**

**NORWEGIAN WAYS**
Gordon's journey in Norway took him to the company of a rakfisk master, to the frigid waters off the coast, and to the Christmas dinner table—to enjoy the most important meal of the year for Norwegians.

Norwegian diet have been added thanks to technological advances, such as scallops that became accessible with the advent of scuba diving. I dared to breathe at greater depths for a good harvest. Despite wearing a dry suit, I could still feel the icy water temperature as I dove for scallops. But after tasting the sweetness of the fresh scallops, I would have gone in again for more.

There's a history to the beverages here, too. Akevitt, Norwegian aquavit, is a neutral spirit distilled from fermented potato or grain mash that dates back to the 15th century. Its distinct flavor comes from spices and herbs—the main note is either caraway or dill—but it can also include floral notes, citrus, and summer berries. In Norway, aquavit is made from potatoes, 95 percent of which must be grown in the country. After distilling, the aquavit is put in oak barrels to age for at least six months, giving it a golden hue. Traditionally, the spirit was enjoyed ice cold at Christmas time, but today there's an aquavit for any occasion. In his Bergen distillery, Stig Bareksten helped me flavor my own aquavit, which tasted like the bottled essence of Norwegian nature.

It was truly inspiring to see authentic Viking cooking and preservation methods and to experience the wealth of what western Norway has to offer. The ingredients are second to none and evoke an incredibly strong sense of place in this beautiful region.

> Despite wearing a dry suit, I could still feel the icy water temperature as I dove for scallops. But after *tasting the sweetness of the fresh scallops,* I would have gone in again for more.

# DIVING FOR SCALLOPS

Knut Magnus Persson and his sister, Mariann Persson, grew up in Litle-sotra, one of the islands in the archipelago west of Bergen. They were raised in a family that cherishes the ocean and frequently went on adventures together. Knut Magnus has been diving since he was 15, and his business Scalmarin is a Norwegian shellfish producer that's a regular supplier to the most exclusive restaurants in the Nordic countries and Europe, including Lysverket. Mariann is the founder of Bergen Fjord Adventures, which introduces visitors to gastronomic experiences by preparing food in the wild with the freshest Norwegian seafood caught on their journey.

Knut Magnus Persson has been diving for shellfish for more than 15 years.

# GRILLED LANGOUSTINES
## WITH SPRING SHOOT BUTTER AND CAVIAR

*Recipe provided by*
*Christopher Haatuft*

**YIELDS:** 4 SERVINGS

PICKLED SPRING SHOOTS

**4 tablespoons soft pine needles or 2–3 rosemary sprigs**

**4 tablespoons flowering pine cones or 4 sprigs thyme**

**4 tablespoons ramson seeds**

**½ cup distilled vinegar**

**¾ cup sugar**

**1½ cups water**

SPRING PICKLE BUTTER

**½ cup pickling juice (from pickled spring shoots, above)**

**1 cup (2 sticks), plus 2 tablespoons unsalted butter, cut in small dice**

**Fresh lemon juice**

**Kosher salt**

**2 tablespoons chopped pickled spring shoots (from above)**

GRILLED LANGOUSTINES

**10 fresh langoustines (about 2 pounds)**

**Kosher salt**

**Extra-virgin olive oil**

**Caviar, for serving, optional**

### DIRECTIONS

**1.** Make the **pickled spring shoots:** Pack the pine needles, pine cones, and ramson seeds in a large mason jar. In a medium saucepan over medium heat, combine the vinegar, sugar, and water and bring to a boil. Pour the liquid over the shoots to cover, reserving ½ cup of the pickling liquid. Let cool completely.

**2.** Make the **spring pickle butter:** Place the reserved pickling liquid in a medium pan over medium-high heat and boil until the liquid is reduced by half. Reduce the heat to low and whisk in the butter until you have a thick sauce. Season with a squeeze of lemon juice and a pinch of salt. Stir in the pickled spring shoots last.

**3.** Make the **grilled langoustines:** Preheat a grill to 400°F. If not already cleaned, cut the langoustines in half lengthwise and remove the intestines. Season the flesh with salt and let sit for 10 minutes. Pat the langoustines dry and brush the flesh lightly with oil.

**4.** Place the langoustines on the grill cut side down. Grill them for about 1 minute and flip. Cook for about 1 minute more—by the time you've flipped the last one, the first one is done.

**5.** To serve, pile the spring shoots and langoustines on a serving platter and spoon over the spring pickle butter. Top the langoustines with caviar, if using.

# SMOKED COD CHOWDER

## WITH FRESH COD, MUSSELS, AND SCALLOPS

**YIELDS:** 4 SERVINGS

1 pound bacon, cut into lardons

4 shallots, julienned

3 celery stalks, finely diced

2 leeks, washed and cut into
½-inch pieces

2 tablespoons all-purpose flour

3 quarts fish stock

1 quart clam juice

1 Yukon Gold potato, peeled and
finely diced

1 teaspoon kosher salt, plus more
as needed

1 cup heavy cream

18 mussels, cleaned and scrubbed

1 8-ounce cod fillet, diced into
1-inch pieces

1 8-ounce smoked cod fillet, diced
into 1-inch pieces

6 sea scallops, diced into ½-inch
pieces

1 lemon, zested and juiced

1 tablespoon fresh dill fronds,
chopped

1 tablespoon celery leaves,
chopped

1 tablespoon fresh parsley leaves,
chopped

### DIRECTIONS

**1.** In a large pot over medium-low heat, cook the bacon lardons until the fat has rendered and the bacon is crispy, about 5 minutes.

**2.** Using a slotted spoon, remove the bacon to a paper towel–lined plate, leaving the rendered fat in the pot.

**3.** Increase the heat to medium and add the shallots, celery, and leeks. Continue cooking until soft, about 5 to 7 minutes.

**4.** Add the flour and stir until a thick paste is created to make a roux. Cook the roux until it becomes a light golden color, about 2 minutes.

**5.** Add the fish stock and clam juice and bring to a simmer.

**6.** Add the potato and salt and continue cooking until the potato is tender, about 10 minutes.

**7.** Add the cream and reserved bacon and bring to a simmer.

**8.** Add the mussels and cover the pot with a lid. Continue cooking until the mussels begin to open, about 3 minutes.

**9.** Add the cod, smoked cod, and scallops and continue cooking just to heat through, about 3 to 4 minutes. Be careful not to overcook the seafood.

**10.** Add the lemon zest and juice. Taste and adjust seasoning as needed.

**11.** In a small mixing bowl, combine the dill fronds, celery leaves, and parsley leaves. Season the mixture with salt.

**12.** Ladle the chowder into bowls and garnish with the fresh herb mixture.

# HAND–DIVED SEA SCALLOPS

## WITH AQUAVIT–SEAWEED BEURRE BLANC AND PICKLED SHALLOTS

### SEAWEED BUTTER

1 piece kombu seaweed

1 cup (2 sticks) unsalted butter, softened

½ teaspoon kosher salt

### PICKLED SHALLOTS

4 shallots, peeled and thinly sliced

1 cup water

1 cup champagne vinegar

½ cup granulated sugar

1 tablespoon kosher salt

4 juniper berries, toasted

1 teaspoon yellow mustard seeds

### BEURRE BLANC

1 teaspoon grapeseed oil

2 shallots, finely diced

¼ teaspoon kosher salt

½ cup aquavit or white wine

1 cup seaweed butter (from above), cubed and chilled

1 lemon, zested and juiced

### SCALLOPS

12 hand-dived sea scallops, shells cleaned and reserved for plating

1 teaspoon kosher salt

1 tablespoon grapeseed oil

Ground pink peppercorns

Fresh dill, roughly chopped

## ▍ DIRECTIONS

**1.** Make the **seaweed butter:** Place the kombu in a mixing bowl and cover with hot water. Let the seaweed sit until it is fully hydrated, about 10 to 15 minutes.

**2.** Finely chop the seaweed and combine with the softened butter in a mixing bowl. Season with the salt and mix until fully incorporated.

**3.** Wrap the butter in parchment paper or plastic wrap and roll into a cylinder. Place the butter in the refrigerator until it is firm, about 30 minutes.

**4.** Make the **pickled shallots:** Place the sliced shallots in a heatproof jar.

**5.** In a small saucepan over medium-high heat, combine the water, vinegar, sugar, salt, juniper berries, and mustard seeds. Bring the mixture to a boil until the sugar has dissolved and then pour over the shallots to completely submerge.

**6.** Cover the jar with plastic wrap and let the shallots sit for 20 minutes.

**7.** Remove the plastic wrap and place the shallots in the refrigerator to cool.

**8.** Make the **beurre blanc:** In a shallow saucepan over medium heat, add the oil and diced shallots and sauté until translucent, about 2 minutes. Season with the salt.

**9.** Add the aquavit and continue cooking until the liquor reduces by half, about 3 minutes.

**10.** Reduce the heat to low and slowly add the cubed seaweed butter a few pieces at a time, constantly swirling the pan to ensure the sauce doesn't get too hot and break.

**11.** Once all the butter has been incorporated, remove from the heat and add the lemon zest and a splash of lemon juice. Keep warm until ready to serve.

**12.** Make the **scallops:** Pat the scallops dry and season all over with the salt. Set a large skillet over medium-high heat. Add the oil to the skillet. Quickly but carefully place each scallop in the skillet, being careful not to overcrowd them, and cook for about 30 seconds, until the scallops begin to brown on the bottom. Flip to sear the other side. Cook for about 30 to 60 seconds more before removing them from the pan.

**13.** To serve, place the seared scallops inside the shells and spoon over the seaweed beurre blanc. Garnish with a pinch of ground pink peppercorns, a sprinkle of dill, and the pickled shallots.

This remote landscape has been home to Aboriginal peoples for more than 30,000 years.

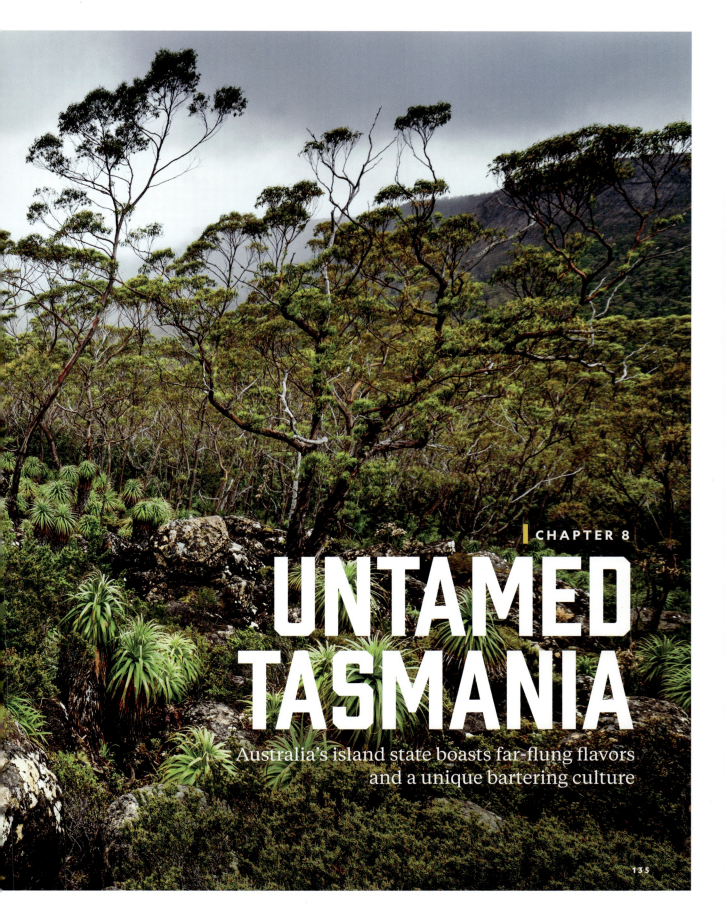

# CHAPTER 8

# UNTAMED TASMANIA

Australia's island state boasts far-flung flavors
and a unique bartering culture

A thrilling view from the Neck Lookout awaits those who ascend the beachside staircase on Bruny Island, Tasmania.

**T**HE REMOTE ENVIRONMENT OF TASMANIA—famous for rich soil, pure air, and clean water—is home to some of the freshest ingredients in the world. That wealth has been enjoyed for more than 30,000 years by Aboriginal peoples, but it's now becoming more recognized beyond its island shores. Artisanal, small-batch, and farm-to-table ingredients and dishes have all become expected culinary requirements for many producers and destinations. In Tasmania, with a population reaching slightly more than 500,000, these terms accurately describe the way things have always been done. ¶ While the cuisine here is shaped by its quality ingredients, Tasmania's remoteness has created a need for self-sufficiency. That, coupled with strict import laws that protect the island's biodiversity, has influenced a strong barter culture among producers, and the tradition of small-scale production here

## NAVIGATOR

### THE STOP

In western Tasmania, I discover native ingredients from land and sea—found in the country's nutrient-rich environment.

### THE GEOGRAPHY

Tasmania lies 150 miles (240 km) south of Victoria, Australia, separated from the mainland by the Bass Strait.

### FOOD FACT

Aboriginal peoples have lived in Tasmania for more than 30,000 years and have maintained a diet of local ingredients including pepperberry, leatherwood honey, and wallaby.

A red-necked wallaby makes eye contact in the Tasmanian wild.

## LOCAL FLAVOR

# ECO-FOOD TOURISM

When Shane Wilson was eight years old, his father, who dove for abalone commercially, introduced him to diving. He's been hooked ever since. With fellow diver Nick Daft, Shane champions environmentally responsible eco-food tourism in Tasmania so that visitors can sample fresh seafood at the source. Their company, Tasmanian Wild Seafood Adventures, shines a light on the abundant seafood—such as urchins, periwinkles, blacklip abalone, and rock lobster—that lives in the clean waters off the coast. Shane also works with the fishing and tourism industries on sustainable initiatives so that Tasmania's pristine waterways continue to be home to seafood and people for generations to come.

Shane Wilson cooks a freshly caught crayfish.

supports the allure of Tasmania's local gourmet economy. Residents have discovered that it's easier to rely on their own resources than to wait for ingredients to come from the mainland of Australia, 150 miles (240 km) away.

I learned about this barter culture straight off the bat while meeting chef Analiese Gregory on the beach in the wild and sparsely populated Forestier Peninsula. She nicked my diving watch in exchange for a bag of sea urchins that I could use to start my week off in Tasmania working and bartering for ingredients that I used at the end of my stay. (I got the watch back, eventually, when she needed to use some honey in the Big Cook.)

Analiese, a culinary nomad and forager who has trained with some of the world's best chefs in France and the United Kingdom, moved to the Huon Valley in Tasmania and started cooking in an entirely different way. "Since I've moved to Tassie, I've pretty much only been cooking with produce from the island," she said. "There's such a bounty of stuff here, so it seems silly to be flying in things from other places when you can just use what's here."

Tasmania is sometimes eclipsed by mainland Australia for attention, and its distance from its neighbors has presented the challenges of isolation and the need for resourcefulness. Tassie's lack of dense population means that fresh food doesn't have to travel far from where it's raised or foraged to where it's eaten. Because small batches are made directly for the island's businesses and restaurants, most of the region's signature food is enjoyed only in Tasmania.

Those fresh ingredients apply to the waters of

Tasmania's coast, too. Offshore from Cape Frederick Hendrick, I went SNUBA diving (a hybrid of snorkeling and scuba) for southern rock lobster, known as crayfish in Tasmania. Living in water that circulates directly from the Southern Ocean and Antarctica, they're some of the best in the world. While I've done a lot of diving in my life, I've never quite experienced anything as majestic, or more rewarding, as catching a Tassie cray. Whether enjoyed as freshly caught sashimi or simply steamed, the crayfish is translucent, delicious, meaty, and super firm.

Despite Tasmania being surrounded by the ocean, it's the island state's interior lakes that are largely responsible for the region's growing reputation as an angler's paradise. Lake St. Clair, the deepest freshwater lake in Australia, is a place of rugged beauty surrounded by Mount Olympus, Mount Rufus, Mount Hugel, Mount Ida, and the Traveller Range. Fly-fishing for brown and rainbow trout in this crystal clear lake is some of the best in the world. My fishing guides, Robbie Aitkenhead and his daughter, Esther,

told me that the best fishing is along the shoreline where the fish hang out just near the deep drop-offs. When we brined and smoked our catch using some of the native pepperberry and leatherwood honey, it was incredible.

That leatherwood honey, a creamy, buttery honey that's produced from the nectar of the endemic leatherwood plant, is one example of how Tasmanian flavor tastes like the wilderness in which it's found. Native to Tasmania, leatherwood trees are often found in the wet, marshy parts of western Tasmania. They take nearly 70 years before they reach nectar-producing maturity and the dense, spicy flavor is in high demand. Plus, the honey is considered antibacterial and an immune-system booster, much like manuka honey from neighboring New Zealand.

Tasmania also has a long history of brewing and distilling, combining traditional craft with sustainable practices. The island's temperate climate, pure water, and abundance of barley and peat have resulted in more than 30 sought-after whisky distilleries—more

# PETER BIGNELL'S WHISKY BUSINESS

After growing rye for years, the sixth-generation Tasmanian farmer Peter Bignell had an outstanding crop in 2008 for which he couldn't find a buyer. He thought the obvious thing to do was to start Belgrove, Australia's first bespoke rye distillery, to make whisky. The products he makes get rave reviews, from peppery and smoky white-rye whisky to smooth, earthy rye whisky. The Belgrove Wholly Shit Rye Whisky uses dried sheep dung in the smoking process instead of peat. The taste is rustic and herbal, with notes of hickory.

Nearly everything Peter uses to make Belgrove Distillery's whisky is on his farm. "To me, craft distilling means a person or a small team using their senses and hands to manipulate every step in the process," he said. Peter grows the rye, which is then malted, mashed, fermented, and double distilled in stills built by hand on-site. He collects rainwater from his roof, digs peat from one of his family farms, and takes used cooking oil from a roadhouse next to his farm to fire the stills, heat the water, and fuel the tractors. The bio-fueled, closed-loop system results in bottles of whisky and spent mash to feed the farm's sheep.

**Peter Bignell of Belgrove Distillery awaits Gordon's verdict as he samples Peter's rye whisky, grown and distilled completely on-site.**

A FIRE SHOW
Always a showstopper:
Flames dance during
the Big Cook.

# CHEF ANALIESE GREGORY

After a career working as a chef in fine-dining restaurants such as Michelin-starred Le Meurice in Paris and Quay in Sydney, Auckland-born Analiese Gregory moved to a farmhouse in the Huon Valley in Tasmania in search of a simpler, more sustainable life. Living on the wild, biodiverse island, she started cooking in an entirely different way—enchanted with how the locals live and cook off the land. Her cookbook, *How Wild Things Are*, celebrates her slowed-down life filled with cooking, hunting, fishing, and foraging in Tasmania, closely connected with the people whose life work it is to grow and harvest food.

Chef Analiese Gregory serves her dish at the Big Cook.

than in any other state in Australia. Considering that there was a ban on distilling alcohol until 1992, that's quite an impressive feat. Distillers here flew under the radar until recently, when Sullivan's Cove won the World's Best Single Cask Single Malt distinction in the World Whiskies Awards in 2018 and 2019. My visit to the bio-fueled Belgrove Distillery opened my eyes to the unique process behind Australia's first bespoke rye distillery, which operates on a closed-loop system and feeds spent mash to the Belgrove sheep.

And then there are the wallabies. A source of sustenance for Aboriginal peoples for thousands of years, wallabies look similar to the kangaroos Australia is famous for; however, they produce a much milder and sweeter meat. It's also a more environmentally friendly source of meat than beef and lamb and is incredibly lean. Tasmania is the only place in Australia where it is legal to harvest wallabies. With nature chef Sarah Glover, I tasted wallaby prepared with foraged ingredients such as sweet native cherries, spicy pepperberry leaves, and samphire (sea beans)—a coastal succulent that's crunchy and tastes a little like asparagus. It seemed only appropriate to combine all those native ingredients together to get a true sense of place through the palate.

Tasmania has such a gift. Its landscape is majestic, pure, and uncrowded. The wealth of native ingredients gives locals little need to want for anything outside of the island and its waters. The self-sufficiency and small-scale production keep resources from being overused and keep focus on quality and sustainability. It's the combination of the food elements and quality of life that makes it shine.

# WALLABY TARTARE

## WITH CHARRED BREAD, NATIVE CHERRIES, AND PEPPERBERRY

**YIELDS:** 6 SERVINGS

SAUCE

**2 egg yolks**

**¼ cup ketchup**

**2 tablespoons mustard**

**2 tablespoons Worcestershire sauce**

**Tabasco**

**¾ cup grapeseed oil**

**1 teaspoon kosher salt**

TARTARE

**3 8-ounce wallaby topside fillets or beef tenderloin**

**2 tablespoons capers, chopped**

**2 tablespoons shallots, finely diced**

**2 tablespoons cornichons, chopped**

**1 tablespoon parsley, finely chopped**

**1 tablespoon chives, chopped**

**1 tablespoon ground pepperberries or any ground peppercorns**

FOR SERVING

**6 slices thick country bread**

**3 tablespoons extra-virgin olive oil**

**1 teaspoon kosher salt**

**½ teaspoon freshly ground black pepper**

**2 garlic cloves, smashed**

**Native cherries or currants, optional**

**Fleur de sel**

## DIRECTIONS

**1.** Make the **sauce:** In a large mixing bowl, combine the egg yolks, ketchup, mustard, Worcestershire sauce, and a few dashes of Tabasco. Gradually whisk in the grapeseed oil and season with the salt.

**2.** Make the **tartare:** Chop the wallaby or beef tenderloin fillets into a very fine dice. Make sure to keep the meat in a chilled bowl to prevent it from becoming warm and soft.

**3.** To the meat, add the capers, shallots, cornichons, parsley, chives, and pepperberries. Toss to combine evenly.

**4.** Add 1 to 2 tablespoons of the sauce and mix with a fork to combine. Taste and adjust seasoning or sauce as needed. Refrigerate until ready to serve.

**5.** To serve, heat a cast-iron pan or grill over medium-high heat. Drizzle the bread with the olive oil and season with the salt and pepper. Grill the bread until charred. Rub the smashed garlic cloves across each piece of grilled bread.

**6.** Spoon the tartare onto the bread and garnish with native cherries and fleur de sel.

# GRILLED ROCK LOBSTER

## WITH SEA URCHIN BUTTER, SAMPHIRE, AND CHARRED LIME

**YIELDS:** 2 SERVINGS

### SEA URCHIN BUTTER

1 cup (2 sticks) high-quality butter, softened

1 cup uni

2 tablespoons chives, chopped

2 tablespoons scallions, chopped, divided

2 tablespoons parsley, chopped, divided

1 tablespoon fresh dill fronds, chopped

1 tablespoon ground pepperberries, optional

1 tablespoon ground black peppercorns

1 lime, zested and juiced

1 teaspoon kosher salt

### ROCK LOBSTER

2 whole 2-pound rock lobsters (spiny lobsters) or Maine lobsters

2 limes, halved

### SAMPHIRE

2 tablespoons brown butter*

¼ cup samphire (sea beans)

### DIRECTIONS

**1.** Make the **sea urchin butter:** In a medium mixing bowl, combine the butter, uni, chives, 1 tablespoon of the scallions, 1 tablespoon of the parsley, the dill, pepperberries, peppercorns, and lime juice. Season with the salt and set aside. Reserve half of the butter for basting and set aside the remaining half to serve with the lobster.

**2.** Cook the **rock lobster:** Preheat a grill to 400°F. Heat a large pot of water over high heat until it is boiling. Add the lobsters to the boiling water and blanch, about 2 to 3 minutes. Remove the lobsters from the water and use a sharp knife to split each lobster in half.

**3.** Place the lobster halves on the grill, flesh side down, and cook until the meat is lightly charred and has turned opaque, about 3 minutes.

**4.** Cut the remaining 2 limes in half and place on the grill, flesh side down, until charred. Set aside.

**5.** Flip the lobster halves so that the shell side is down and brush the flesh with the sea urchin butter. Once the meat is firm, remove from the grill and place on a platter. Brush with more butter.

**6.** Cook the **samphire:** Place a medium skillet over medium heat and add the brown butter. Once shimmering, add the samphire and cook until tender, about 2 minutes.

**7.** Arrange the lobster on a platter and garnish with the remaining scallions and parsley, the samphire, and lime zest.

**8.** Serve with the remaining sea urchin butter on the side.

*\* To make brown butter: Heat butter in a heavy-bottomed pan over medium heat. Whisk frequently until butter has a nutty aroma, then remove from heat.*

# CHAPTER 9

# INDIA'S SPICE HUB

An enriching dive into the mastery of complex culinary layers on a tour through southwestern India

"Nature has given us more spices because of the climatic conditions. You're in the spice hub," said chef Shri Bala.

Gordon helps
Fancy prepare
coffee liqueur.

**F**ROM THE TROPICAL BEACHES and port cities of Kerala and Karnataka along the coast of the Arabian Sea to the interior hills of Kodagu, southwestern India has served as one of the world's leading exporters of spices—including pepper, chili, and cardamom—for more than 5,000 years. Referred to as the Malabar Coast by spice traders, this region saw the beginning of globalization as goods traveled first to Egypt and ancient Babylonia, then to the Middle East, Asia, and Europe. Spices became another measure to define what it meant to be wealthy and powerful. ¶ Despite being a global spice capital, southwestern India has a cuisine that's more than simply "hot." In fact, it has delicate nuances in how complex flavors are balanced. The tropical climate of Kerala and Karnataka allows spices and the complementary ingredients that balance them to not only grow well but flourish—from loamy, waterlogged

The beautiful multihued coast of Kerala has served as one of India's main hubs of the spice trade for thousands of years.

## NAVIGATOR

### THE STOP

I taste the spices that make southwestern India rich in flavor—and heat.

### THE GEOGRAPHY

The Western Ghats are a mountain chain in southwestern India that is home to unique sky islands—tops of tall mountains that have become environmentally isolated from each other even though they are close together.

### FOOD FACT

Pork is rare to find in India, but in Kodagu, pork-based pandi curry is hugely popular, with roots that date back to tribal ancestors in the region.

soil for growing cardamom to a hot and humid climate that supports black pepper, clove, cinnamon, ginger, turmeric, nutmeg, and star anise. The combination has resulted in this region having some of the most spectacular tastes in the country.

"Nature has given us more spices because of the climatic conditions," chef Shri Bala told me after she served a welcome mystery drink full of the native chili pepper called kanthari. The TV host and food historian's culinary calling started at an early age learning recipes from the groundbreaking Indian cookbook *Samaithu Paar*, written by her great-aunt. Luckily, shortly after she made my mouth catch fire, Shri gave me some coconut water to temper the heat of the chili. It was my first lesson in how people in southwestern India blend spices with other ingredients to change the flavor of a dish. Or, in my case, to quench the five-alarm fire in my mouth.

# MONKEY BUSINESS

The tropical climate of Kerala and Karnataka is an essential element of the region's ideal growing conditions for the incredible ingredients that have made it one of the world's leading exporters of spices. But the heat combined with humidity is no joke, and cooler temperatures in the early morning and late evening are best for exploring. If you stop by the side of the road to take a break on the way up to the mountains, you'll likely be approached by curious monkeys. You'll be tempted to look them in the eyes, but don't—they consider eye contact to be a sign of aggression.

**VERDANT HILLS**
The tea plantations of the lush Western Ghats mountain range

Spicy curries using those same kanthari chili peppers (also known as bird's eye chili) make people sweat, which in turn makes them cool down faster. That's helpful in hot climates, but it can be a challenge for folks who are hesitant to eat spicy foods. Coconut is one of the best ways to balance an extremely spicy dish without taking away from the overall taste of the other ingredients, and it is used to lighten and sweeten spicy dishes like curries. The name of the state of Kerala translates to "land of coconut trees" in the region's Malayalam language, and it is the top producer of coconuts in the country. Coconut is regarded as a source of healthy fat, its meat containing protein, fiber, copper, iron, magnesium, and manganese.

Seafood is also an integral part of the cuisine of Kerala, with a 360-mile (580 km) coastline and a wealth of inland waterways. Fresh seafood—especially mackerel, prawns, shrimp, squid, and tuna—is served everywhere at food stalls on the coast. Despite my disappointing fishing attempt at the tail end of high season, there were enough successful anglers to

> The name of the state of Kerala translates to "land of coconut trees" in the region's Malayalam language, and it is the top producer of coconuts in the country.

# THINGS GET A LITTLE HEATED

In Kerala, *uppilittathu* is a popular preservation method in which fruits and vegetables are soaked in a saltwater brine. Anything from guava to mangoes, pineapple to tamarind, and cucumbers to gooseberries can be preserved. Spices and aromatics like chilies, pepper, garlic, and ginger are often included for flavor. My guide, Harish, took me to his favorite local fruit stand and handed me a slice of pineapple soaked in chili water to taste. The ginger-bearded vendor told me that the pineapple had been soaked in the chilies for only 15 minutes, but it immediately numbed my lips and set my throat on fire.

When it's hot outside and you eat something hot or spicy, your esophagus and stomach trigger your body to start sweating to release some of the heat. All those little droplets of sweat are just energy leaving the body; when it evaporates off your skin, it leaves you a little bit cooler. In this case, spice serves a purpose greater than flavoring a dish. I have to say that I could have gone without that lesson and just started with the cold watermelon juice with no added chilies, but I certainly learned something.

**Harish (right) and Gordon sample a vendor's assortment of spicy pickled fruits and vegetables.**

## It's a little like food roulette . . .
## wondering which ones will set my mouth ablaze.

supply me with an incredible catch for my Big Cook fish curry dish, which was inspired by Shakeela, the wife of my local guide, Moidu. The picky spice ladies I served seemed to be pleased with the combination of grilled fish (marinated in chili powder, coriander, salt, and turmeric) and curry sauce (containing curry, fenugreek leaves, fish sauce, garlic, ginger, green chili, mustard seeds, onion, and salt).

The food stalls in Kerala have everything from essential ingredients to prepared food. On a hot day, popular snacks such as sliced pineapple in a saltwater brine loaded with chilies create a refreshing spicy-sweet nibble. It's a little like food roulette, to look at all the containers of brined fruits and vegetables,

wondering which ones will set my mouth ablaze. It turned out that for me, the best cooling agent was a simple cup of watermelon juice.

Inland, among the Western Ghats' misty landscape, acres of coffee, tea, and spice are grown in the forested hills of Kodagu (also known by its anglicized name, Coorg) in the state of Karnataka. While pork isn't widely eaten in India for religious reasons, here in Kodagu, pork-based pandi curry is legendary, dating back to the Kodava people (tribal ancestors of the region), who hunted wild boar to survive. The dish gets its rich, dark color from Kachampuli vinegar, the concentrated juice of the *Garcinia gummi-gutta* fruit, which has a sour taste. Instead of coconut, bitter limes are the cooling

**FRESH INGREDIENTS**
Left: Gordon and a guide
attempt to catch a nest of
weaver ants as it falls from
a tree branch above.
Right: A lively market

agent. Combining the lime juice to balance the sour and spicy notes is akin to composing music.

Local legend credits the first coffee in India to a Muslim pilgrim smuggling a handful of coffee beans aboard a ship to India and planting them in the hills of Karnataka. Coffee now flourishes in the state, which is the largest producer of both Arabica and Robusta varieties in India. Of course, coffee is used in a variety of ways beyond a traditional morning ritual. The coffee liqueur that my host, Fancy, made on her plantation was absolutely delicious, and at 40 percent alcohol by volume, it only takes a few sips to really feel it. I added it to a rice pudding for the Big Cook, but it would also be perfect over ice cream or in a cocktail.

Chigli is a chutney made with weaver ants and their larvae. A local delicacy here, the ants have a spicy and salty taste. When mixed with chili powder, coconut, coriander seeds, garlic, salt, and water, the resulting chutney is fresh, vibrant, and slightly tangy. But getting a weaver ant nest out of a tree and obtaining the ants and their larvae without getting bitten is a feat that few humans can manage. I must have been bitten 50 or 60 times, but it was worth it to taste that chutney.

Spending time in southwestern India helped me understand the abundant ingredients the region has to offer, from the coast to the mountains. It was also an invaluable lesson to experience how single ingredients help people handle the heat, providing spices that help cool the body, as well as other cooling agents that magically balance that fire.

**INSIDER KNOWLEDGE**

## AS THE LOCALS DO

've done a lot of fishing in my lifetime, but nothing like the traditional dragnet fishing that Moidu practices, which involves using a weighted net to trawl the bottom of the sea. After all the work of swimming to set the net and then pulling it in to the beach, I was hungry for some authentic Kerala cuisine. Moidu's wife, Shakeela, made an incredibly spicy fish curry and used a traditional coconut grater—with her feet— to grate coconut meat. She squeezed a handful of the meat over my bowl of curry to add the right amount of coconut milk to make the dish sweeter and more fragrant.

Shakeela awaits Gordon's reaction as he tastes fresh coconut water.

# COORG-STYLE PANDI CURRY

## WITH BITTER LIME–PICKLED ONION

## PORK BELLY

2 tablespoons ground turmeric

2 tablespoons Kashmiri chili powder

3 teaspoons kosher salt

2 pounds pork belly, skin removed and cut into 2-inch cubes

3 cups pork stock

## WET MASALA

15 fresh curry leaves

12 shallots, minced

8 garlic cloves, peeled

4 serrano chilies, seeds removed, minced

2 tablespoons cumin seeds, toasted

1 2-inch piece ginger, peeled, roughly chopped

1 bunch cilantro with stems, roughly chopped

## DRY MASALA

1 tablespoon coriander seed

1 tablespoon cumin seed

1 tablespoon black peppercorns

1 1-inch piece cinnamon stick

2 bay leaves

6 cloves

## PICKLED RED ONION

1 large red onion, thinly sliced

1 bitter lime, juiced

1 teaspoon kosher salt

1 tablespoon jaggery or light brown sugar

1 tablespoon Kachampuli vinegar or vinegar of your choice

2 tablespoons cilantro, chopped

1 bitter lime, cut into wedges

## DIRECTIONS

**1.** Make the **pork belly:** In a large mixing bowl, combine the turmeric, Kashmiri chili powder, and salt. Add the pork to the seasoning blend and toss to coat completely.

**2.** In a large pot over medium-low heat, sear the pork until some fat has rendered and the pieces are lightly golden.

**3.** Add the pork stock to the pot and bring to a boil. Reduce the heat to low and simmer until the pork becomes tender, about 40 minutes.

**4.** Make the **wet masala:** In a large mortar, combine all of the wet masala ingredients. Use the pestle to create a coarse, wet masala. Alternatively, you can blend all ingredients in a blender or food processor.

**5.** Add the wet paste to the pot of pork and continue cooking, stirring constantly until the mixture begins to thicken.

**6.** Make the **dry masala:** In a small skillet over medium heat, toast each spice individually until dark golden brown but not burnt. Grind the spices together using a mortar and pestle or a spice grinder until completely pulverized into a powder.

**7.** Make the **pickled red onion:** Place the onion slices in a small mixing bowl and cover with the bitter lime juice, salt, and jaggery and toss to combine. Set aside.

**8.** Finish the pork belly: Once the pork is cooked through and tender, and the sauce has started to thicken, add a few spoonfuls of the dry masala. Taste for seasoning and adjust as needed.

**9.** Continue simmering to give the spices time to fully season the pork, about 20 to 25 minutes.

**10.** Remove from the heat and finish with the Kachampuli vinegar.

**11.** Garnish the curry with the cilantro and serve with the pickled red onion and bitter lime wedges on the side.

# CARDAMOM AND BAY LEAF–SPICED RICE PUDDING

## WITH FANCY'S COFFEE LIQUEUR

**YIELDS:** 6 SERVINGS

1 cup basmati rice

2 tablespoons ghee

6 green cardamom pods, crushed

2 bay leaves

Kosher salt

4 tablespoons coffee liqueur, divided

3 cups milk

1 cup heavy cream

⅓ cup jaggery or brown sugar, plus more if needed

**▌ DIRECTIONS**

**1.** Rinse the rice in several changes of water, then cover with cold water and let soak for 20 minutes. Strain and set aside.

**2.** In a medium pot over medium heat, add the ghee and then toast the cardamom pods, bay leaves, and a pinch of salt.

**3.** Add the soaked rice and lightly toast until fragrant, about 2 minutes.

**4.** Add 2 tablespoons of the coffee liqueur to deglaze the pan.

**5.** Add the milk and cream and bring to a boil, stirring constantly.

**6.** Once the rice has reached a boil, turn the heat to low and add the jaggery. Continue cooking, stirring constantly until the liquid has started to thicken, about 30 minutes.

**7.** Once the rice has cooked through, let the rice pudding cool in the refrigerator for at least 30 minutes.

**8.** Finish with a drizzle of the remaining coffee liqueur.

A wooden boardwalk meanders through the Barataria Preserve near Jean Lafitte, Louisiana.

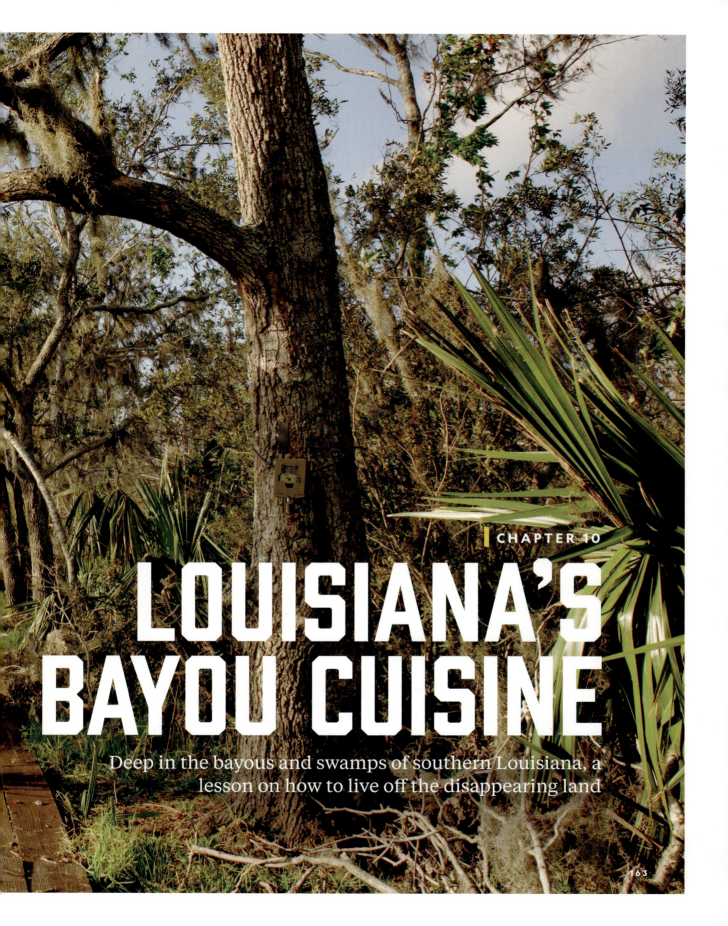

# CHAPTER 10

# LOUISIANA'S BAYOU CUISINE

Deep in the bayous and swamps of southern Louisiana, a lesson on how to live off the disappearing land

**S**CENES OF CYPRESS TREES dripping with Spanish moss in misty bayous may have inspired songs and films, but the culture of southern Louisiana has always been about survival in this wildly unpredictable environment. Survival has been the reality of many, from the region's original Indigenous inhabitants to the French Acadian settlers of the 1700s to Vietnamese immigrants today. Just a couple hours south of New Orleans, Louisiana's landscape changes significantly—from a city rich with architecture that holds tight to its French and Spanish history to some of North America's most extensive wetlands, which some locals call "the end of the world." ¶ Surviving off the land here can involve some bizarre ingredients, but with the mighty Mississippi River running right through southern Louisiana's backyard, there's also some incredibly fertile soil. The fragmented land is marked with bayous and

## NAVIGATOR

### THE SPOT

Land is disappearing fast in the bayous of southern Louisiana, but the locals here know how to make the most of the riches that live in the waterways.

### THE GEOGRAPHY

Wetlands cover the southern coastline of Louisiana, which stretches into the Gulf of Mexico. Every year, approximately 18,500 acres (75,000 ha) of wetlands are disappearing.

### FOOD FACT

Frog legs are on the menu in many of my restaurants, and they are a well-known dish in Louisiana and the American South.

Gordon learns that the bayous and swamps in southern Louisiana (opposite) are a bountiful yet fragile ecosystem.

swamps looking like Earth's lacework from the air. But closer in, much of this land is eroding at an alarming rate. The region is losing more than a football field a day of land, chef Eric Cook told me during our first meeting.

"It's a beautiful natural resource for everyone who lives here, but unfortunately, it's dwindling quickly," the Louisiana native, former marine, and executive chef and proprietor of New Orleans restaurants Gris-Gris and Saint John said. "Growing up out here, you learn that getting by is about survival, even as the land beneath your feet disappears."

Among the causes of the area's land erosion are the habits of non-native swamp rats called nutria. Just a few of the semi-aquatic rodents, with their webbed toes and orange teeth, were originally imported from South America in the 1930s by the fur industry as a potential new source of skins for hats and coats. Now millions run wild, thriving in the lush coastal marshes.

The nutria's love for the roots of marsh plants makes it difficult for the plants to grow back. When those roots are gone, the soil around the plants erodes more quickly, converting to open water and contributing to the loss of coastal areas that are already impacted by soil subsidence and saltwater intrusion from gas and oil company canals.

Like in other parts of the world facing invasive species, hunting and eating the nutria is one way for the locals to combat the damage and control populations. Yet even when called its French name, *ragondin*, nutria hasn't been widely incorporated into local menus, likely due to the swamp-rat stigma. But I found the lean meat to be delicious—akin to rabbit.

**IN THE BAYOU**
Marshes are home to birds, crawfish, frogs, and more.

# FUSION SEAFOOD

When first cousins Thien and Nhu Nguyen were children, they piled into their uncle's pickup truck to ride to the rice fields of Sacramento, California, where crawfish were plentiful. Using a wok and ingredients they had at home (apples, ginger, lemongrass—anything sweet or fruity), they whipped up crawfish dishes that were vastly different from those found in Louisiana. In 2015, when they opened Big EZ Seafood in Gretna, Louisiana, Thien and Nhu were among the first Vietnamese Americans to introduce

Louisiana crawfish

Viet-Cajun crawfish to the region. Since then, they've won the hearts of even the pickiest crawfish connoisseurs.

"It's a beautiful natural resource for everyone who lives here, but unfortunately, it's dwindling quickly."

—Chef Eric Cook

Another, more popular, source of protein here are frog legs, a delicacy that is well known in the American South and abroad. They're rich in protein, omega-3 fatty acids, vitamin A, and potassium, and their texture is similar to chicken wings. Frog hunting is best at night (especially during a new moon when the light helps reflect frogs' eyes and bellies).

Crawfish, one of the most popular ingredients in Louisiana cuisine, also comes from these waterways. The small crustaceans are the main ingredient in crawfish boils, where they're cooked with plenty of spicy seasoning, along with corn, potatoes, sausages, and lemon slices. The meat of the crawfish may be in the tail, but the moisture and flavor collect in the head—you haven't tasted the best of a crawfish until you've sucked its head. No, there aren't brains in there. It's the crawfish's hepatopancreas, which functions a little like the liver in humans, and the foie gras–like flavor is amplified by the spices that go into a crawfish boil. Those spices often include cayenne pepper, paprika, black peppercorns, coriander, cloves, allspice, salt, garlic powder, onion powder, thyme, oregano, dill, and bay leaves—but Viet-Cajun cuisine adds garlic butter and even ginger, lemongrass, and scallions. This popular fusion was created after Vietnamese refugees settled in the Gulf Coast and merged the flavors of the South with flavors of home.

And of course, with an ample supply of freshwater

# FROM THE HEART
# WITH CHEF ERIC COOK

Louisiana native, combat veteran in the United States Marine Corps, and executive chef and proprietor of two New Orleans restaurants, chef Eric Cook began his culinary career at Brennan's in New Orleans' French Quarter. "I've probably lived in every city that's a city in Louisiana," he said. "When you meet all these folks, you realize that the essence of Cajun cooking and Creole cuisine is respecting them. Because if you respect them, you understand the heritage, what it means, and the serious sense of pride."

Opened in 2018, Gris-Gris features refined Southern cuisine and New Orleans favorites, such as shrimp and grits, chicken and dumplings, and a classic redfish court bouillon. In 2021, Eric opened his second restaurant, Saint John, focusing on haute Creole cuisine and tracing its evolution in New Orleans. His love of the region comes with the recognition that resources, including the land of southern Louisiana, are becoming scarcer. "It's an amazing ecosystem; it's the mouth of the Mississippi that's been feeding into the Gulf of Mexico forever," he said. "People need to realize that it's worth preserving. If it goes away, it's not just a way of life—it's a people."

**Chef Eric Cook and Gordon go head-to-head in a gumbo cook-off for first responders.**

**WATER, WATER EVERYWHERE**
From Lake Saint Catherine to the swamps and bayous, Louisiana's waters are a seafood lover's paradise.

and salt water, there's an abundance of fish in Louisiana. I went to the easternmost point of the state—the Chandeleur Islands in the Gulf of Mexico—in search of schools of redfish and speckled trout that have made these islands home to some of the best fishing in the Gulf. Unfortunately, these barrier islands, like much of the coastline, have been battered and will likely be gone within decades.

The best dishes from southern Louisiana's bayous aren't only about protein. The swamp larder also offers oyster mushrooms that are found on decaying trees, fresh greens such as "Cajun celery," or chadron (derived from *chardon*, the French word for "thistle"), and satsumas—a variety of mandarin orange. The spiky chadrons hardly look edible, but once you peel the stalk, chop it up, and add vinegar, salt, and pepper, it's a great addition to a salad. Chadron is watery and crispy and tastes like a cross between celery and cucumber.

Eric told me that a dark roux—equal parts flour and fat—is the basis of all good Southern cooking. In France, the classic version uses butter, but Cajun and Creole roux is made with oil. Using oil allows you to get a deeper, darker color without burning the fat. Before the Big Cook, I'd never made a roux that dark. But a proper dark roux is essential for many of the well-known dishes from this region: étouffée, gumbo, and jambalaya. And according to Eric, the secret to making a great gumbo isn't what you put inside—indeed, recipes change from block to block in southern Louisiana—it's what's inside you when you're making it. You've got to feel the love.

Once you look beneath the surface of this fragile ecosystem—beyond the snakes and alligators and disappearing land—it's possible not only to survive but also to thrive on the wealth of ingredients in the marshes and swamps of Louisiana. It's no wonder that traditions here run so deep. These flavors are an essential part of what makes this region speak with its soul.

ADRENALINE RUSH

# FEELING FLY

Pilot and local fishing guide Lane Panepinto is the owner of Cajun Air, a seaplane charter business located on the Gulf Intracoastal Waterway in Lafitte, Louisiana. He's been flying since 1973, and his seaplane tours give visitors to the region a firsthand look at southern Louisiana's vast wetlands. He also offers fly-out fishing trips to the Chandeleur and Timbalier Islands to immerse anglers in some of the best fishing in the Gulf of Mexico. "We grew up fishing the Chandeleur Islands," he said. "When you get out there, it's just the water and the islands. It's a solitude, you know."

**Gordon boards the plane of pilot and local legend Lane Panepinto.**

# WHOLE REDFISH

## WITH SATSUMA BEURRE BLANC

**YIELDS:** 2 SERVINGS

### GRILLED REDFISH

1 4-pound redfish, scaled and gutted

¼ cup olive oil

2 tablespoons kosher salt

1 tablespoon freshly ground black pepper

### SATSUMA BEURRE BLANC

1 cup white wine

2 satsuma oranges, zested and juiced

2 shallots, thinly sliced

1 garlic clove, crushed

2 cups (4 sticks) unsalted butter, cubed and chilled

3 sprigs dill, finely chopped, divided

3 sprigs parsley, finely chopped, divided

2 scallions, thinly sliced, divided

1 teaspoon sugarcane vinegar or vinegar of choice

1 teaspoon kosher salt

### DIRECTIONS

**1.** Make the **grilled redfish:** Preheat a grill to 400°F.

**2.** Brush the fish with the olive oil and season it generously with the salt and pepper, making sure to season the cavity inside as well.

**3.** Place the fish on the grill and let cook until the skin is crispy and golden on both sides, about 15 minutes total.

**4.** Make the **satsuma beurre blanc:** In a small pot over medium heat, combine the white wine, satsuma zest and juice, shallots, and garlic. Bring to a boil and let reduce by half, about 10 minutes.

**5.** Reduce the heat to low and slowly add the cubed butter a few pieces at a time, constantly swirling the pan to ensure the sauce doesn't get too hot and break.

**6.** Remove from the heat and add half of the dill, half of the parsley, half of the scallions, the sugarcane vinegar, and the salt. Stir to combine.

**7.** Place the grilled redfish on a platter and pour the sauce over top. Sprinkle with the remaining herbs.

# NOLA-STYLE BBQ SHRIMP

*Recipe inspired by*
*Eric Cook*

**YIELDS:** 4 SERVINGS

1 pound jumbo shrimp or prawns, peeled and deveined, heads on

2 teaspoons Creole seasoning

1 teaspoon kosher salt

2 tablespoons olive oil

4 large garlic cloves, thinly sliced

1 shallot, peeled and thinly sliced

2 teaspoons Worcestershire sauce

1 bunch scallions, thinly sliced

3 tablespoons unsalted butter, cubed

1 ounce vodka or white wine

1 lemon, cut into wedges, seeds removed

Crusty bread, for serving

## DIRECTIONS

**1.** Season the shrimp with the Creole seasoning and salt.

**2.** Heat the olive oil in a large skillet over medium-high heat.

**3.** Once the oil is shimmering, add the shrimp to the pan in a single layer. Let the shrimp cook until they just begin to turn opaque, about 30 seconds.

**4.** Add the garlic and shallot and let cook until softened, about 1 minute.

**5.** Flip the shrimp and add the Worcestershire sauce, scallions, and butter.

**6.** Once the butter melts completely, add the vodka to the pan. Let the mixture simmer for 1 minute. Once the shrimp turns pink, remove from the heat and add a squeeze of lemon. Taste and adjust seasoning as needed.

**7.** Serve the shrimp with crusty bread and the remaining lemon wedges.

# CHICKEN ANDOUILLE GUMBO

## WITH RICE

## BRAISED CHICKEN

4 boneless, skin-on chicken breasts

4 bone-in, skin-on chicken legs, thighs attached

1 teaspoon freshly ground black pepper

2½ teaspoons kosher salt, divided

2 tablespoons grapeseed oil

4 garlic cloves, crushed

3 celery stalks, diced

2 yellow onions, diced

8 cups chicken stock

3 sprigs thyme

3 scallions, trimmed and chopped

1 lemon, cut in half, seeds removed

## GUMBO BASE

8 ounces andouille sausage, cut into ½-inch-thick slices

½ cup (1 stick) unsalted butter

1 cup all-purpose flour

2 celery stalks, finely diced

2 garlic cloves, minced

1 red bell pepper, finely diced

1 green bell pepper, finely diced

1 yellow onion, finely diced

1 teaspoon kosher salt

1 teaspoon cayenne pepper

½ teaspoon freshly ground black pepper

2 tablespoons hot sauce

## RICE

2 cups white rice

4 cups water

2 sprigs thyme, picked

2 teaspoons kosher salt

## DIRECTIONS

**1.** Make the **braised chicken:** Season the chicken with the pepper and 2 teaspoons of the salt. In a large pot over medium heat, add the oil. Once the oil is shimmering, sear the chicken on all sides until golden brown, about 10 minutes. Be careful not to overcrowd the pan, and work in batches if necessary.

**2.** Remove the chicken from the pan and add the garlic, celery, and onions. Cook in the chicken fat until the vegetables begin to caramelize. Season with the remaining salt.

**3.** Add the chicken back to the pot and cover with the chicken stock. Add the thyme, scallions, and lemon halves and bring to a simmer. Continue cooking on low heat until the chicken is tender and can easily be pulled apart, about 1 hour.

**4.** Remove the chicken from the stock and shred the meat from the bones. Cover the chicken and refrigerate until ready to use. Strain and reserve the chicken stock and discard the vegetables and thyme.

**5.** Make the **gumbo base:** In another large pot over medium heat, add the andouille sausage and cook until the fat has rendered and the sausage has crisped.

**6.** Use a slotted spoon to remove the sausage from the pot and set aside on a paper towel–lined plate.

**7.** To the fat in the pot, add the butter. Once the butter is completely melted, add the flour and mix until a thick paste forms to make a roux. Reduce the heat to medium-low and continue cooking, stirring constantly until the roux has turned a very deep brown, about 30 to 45 minutes.

**8.** Add the celery, garlic, bell peppers, and onion. Continue cooking until the vegetables are softened, about 5 minutes. Season with the salt, cayenne, and black pepper.

**9.** Add the reserved chicken stock and the hot sauce and bring to a simmer. Continue cooking on low until the gumbo base has thickened, about 30 minutes.

**10.** Make the **rice:** In a medium pot over medium heat, add the rice, water, thyme, and salt and bring to a boil. Cover and reduce to a simmer. Cook until all the moisture has evaporated, about 20 minutes. Fluff the rice with a fork just before serving.

**12.** Add the pulled chicken and andouille sausage to the gumbo and serve with the rice.

Overlooking the Adriatic Sea, Rovinj, Croatia, offers diners a dramatic view along the cliffs.

# CHAPTER 11

# CROATIA'S COASTAL TREASURES

On the Istrian Peninsula, fresh ingredients
rival the best of Italy in world-class quality

The village of Rovinj clings to the curving coast of the Istrian Peninsula.

**I**N THE NORTH ADRIATIC SEA, the Istrian Peninsula, largely in Croatia, is bordered by crystal clear water and its interior is rich with forests. The country's past has heavily influenced its culture and cuisine. Croatia has been part of Italy, the Austro-Hungarian Empire, and the former Yugoslavia. Yet Istria's diverse cuisine has flown under the radar compared with that of its neighbor Italy, despite having similar climates and terrain that host some of the same quality ingredients. The gastronomy of Istria is based heavily on seafood, olive oil, and seasonings like garlic and rosemary, typical of Mediterranean cuisine. ¶ Chef David Skoko, Croatian food celebrity and chef of his family's restaurant, Batelina, told me that the richness of Croatia's gastronomy is so big for such a small country thanks to the influence of the cultures that have left their mark on it throughout history.

## NAVIGATOR

### THE STOP

On the Istrian Peninsula in Croatia, I find food traditions that date back thousands of years and are influenced largely by the land and sea.

### THE GEOGRAPHY

The Istrian Peninsula sits at the head of the Adriatic Sea, bordered by the Gulf of Trieste and the Kvarner Gulf. Its inland is mostly forestland.

### FOOD FACT

Croatians in this region let nature call the shots: They use what's pulled in the catch and what's found in the forests to set the menu.

Gordon and chef David Skoko (center) fish for conger eels.

While Croatia is abundant with ingredients that have put it on the culinary map, it's also prosperous in the imagination it takes to incorporate lesser known local ingredients. "We have so many great ingredients, but you have to put effort into obtaining them," David said. "Our limit in the kitchen, you know, it's only in our heads."

At heart, David is a fisherman's son, born into a family of four generations of fishermen. At dawn the day he took me out fishing, his father, Danilo, set a line of baited hooks for conger eel. European congers are the largest eels in the world. On average, adults measure about 5 feet (1.5 m) long and can weigh nearly 160 pounds (73 kg), but some people have reported seeing congers as long as 9 feet (2.7 m). The tug of a conger eel on a handline is impressive. You can really feel that thing fighting you. The line we checked had nearly 100 hooks set about 10 feet (3 m) apart. Grab

**COLORFUL CROATIA**
It's worth a stroll through the kaleidoscopic streets of Rovinj.

the wrong spot, and you'll go from fisherman to catch of the day.

On our trip, David brought along some conger eel pâté that he'd made. "We try to use everything that's natural, from the land, and everything from the fisherman's net," he said. "We're not choosing our menus from our ideas, but from the catch." Despite being considered "junk fish" by many, conger eels are often found in brudet in Croatia, a stew that includes several types of fish that are plentiful along the country's coastline.

Seafood is integral to Istrian cuisine, and fishing

**INSIDER KNOWLEDGE**

## A FISHERMAN'S CATCH

With access to top-quality seafood, Croatian chef David Skoko has transformed his family's *konoba* (tavern), Batelina, into one of the best restaurants in the country. A fourth-generation fisherman, David is inspired by the daily catch and honoring Croatia's gastronomic heritage. "I enjoy being inspired by the natural bounty of the sea and using everything that the fisherman's net brings up, no matter what we get," he said. "Fishermen often sell the commercial catch, and what's left feeds their families. But to be sustainable, I challenge myself to get the most out of what our rich environment has to offer."

**David Skoko during the Big Cook**

> ## "Our limit
> ### in the kitchen, you know,
> ## it's only in our heads."
>
> —Chef David Skoko

traditions here are essential to Croatian culture. Adriatic shellfish are among the cleanest in the world, and bivalve mollusks such as Noah's Arks (known as *kunjke* in Croatia) and sea truffles add to the treasures of clams, mussels, oysters, scallops, scampi, and spider crabs. Some can be enjoyed raw, while others come to their fullest flavor grilled, prepared *buzara* style (cooked with breadcrumbs, garlic, parsley, and wine), or in pastas and risottos. Cuttlefish are featured

in the beloved dish crni rižot, a flavorful risotto that uses the black ink of these cephalopods and is found in many seaside restaurants. Just don't smile at anyone while you're eating, because you may temporarily have black teeth.

Croatia's coastline also offers opportunities to find flavor in wild herbs. Foraging here can turn up sweet and fragrant sea fennel, also known as motar and rock samphire, which grows on rocks and dunes along the shoreline where it has access to sea winds and waves. The leaves of sea fennel are often pickled or used in salads. Another herb that grows near the water is sea rosemary, which develops a natural saltiness and can be chopped up and added to sea salt for an excellent rub used on fish prior to cooking.

The fertile land of Croatia and its variety of wild plants add to the terroir of cheese, from sheep to

# FORAGING WITH VIŠNJA PRODAN JEKIĆ

T he dense forests of northern Istria are home to one of the most prized treasures in the culinary world: the divine truffle. The subterranean fungus grows close to the roots of certain types of trees, most commonly beech, hazelnut, and oak. In Buzet, Croatia's "town of truffles," Višnja Prodan Jekić is a third-generation truffle hunter who works with her family to harvest and sell truffles and truffle products for their business, Prodan Tartufi. During the season for both white and black truffle varieties, they deliver fresh truffles to restaurants and truffle lovers throughout the country and the world at large.

A trained dog's sense of smell is a key tool in truffle hunting. When I first met them, I thought Višnja's dogs, Brum and Steve, looked like little purse dogs, but I quickly realized that their noses are at the forefront of a multimillion-dollar business. Skilled truffle dogs are highly prized, and Višnja's family has bred and trained them over many generations. For centuries, pigs were used to sniff out truffles. Nowadays, dogs are preferred for truffle hunting because pigs are hard to train, difficult to transport, and tend to eat the truffles. That can be an expensive habit.

**Gordon and Višnja examine their latest truffle find among the trees.**

> Native olive trees, grown for thousands of years in the rich Istrian soil, thanks to the proximity to the sea, produce some of the best olive oil in the world.

goat to cow milk varieties. A shining example is the award-winning artisan goat cheese from Stancija Kumparička, a goat farm on the eastern side of the Istrian Peninsula. Its 250 goats graze year-round on an open buffet of more than 180 aromatic herbs and plants, making the eventual taste of the cheese dynamic and ever changing. This particular area has a long history of agriculture and food production. Donkey milk may seem like a trendy addition to the food scene, but it's been around in Croatia for thousands of years. The taste of fresh donkey milk is sweet and light.

**| TRAVEL 101**

# OLD-TOWN CHARM

At the edge of the Adriatic Sea on the west coast of the Istrian Peninsula, Rovinj is a gorgeous port city with crystal clear water. Originally, Rovinj was an island, but in 1763 it was connected to the mainland when the narrow channel separating the two was filled. The old village has lovely cobbled streets and small squares. Rovinj's port is the gateway to several local islands easily reached by water taxi. One of the closest islands, Sveta Katarina, has incredible views of Rovinj's old town and is where we filmed the Big Cook.

Premium-grade Istrian truffles, found in the peninsula's interior, rival the superstar Alba truffles from the Piedmont region of Italy. The unique soil and climate conditions here make it a perfect habitat for growing the fungi. The Istrian white truffle, with its intoxicating earthy aroma, is the most sought-after variety, fetching up to $3,000 a pound. Three kinds of black truffle grow here, the most common being the black summer truffle. There's also a black winter truffle and the Périgord black truffle, which is the most highly valued among them due to its intense flavor and aromatic scent.

Native olive trees, grown for thousands of years in the rich Istrian soil, thanks to the proximity to the sea, produce some of the best olive oil in the world. Istria's output of this liquid gold is a small drop compared with that of Spain, which is the world's largest producer, but Istria's high-quality product has placed it firmly on the gastronomic map. The prestigious Flos Olei olive oil guide has declared the Istrian Peninsula as the world's best region for extra-virgin olive oil for seven years in a row—among 55 olive-growing countries on five continents. Istria is the Mediterranean's northernmost olive-growing region, and the fruity green notes and pungent peppery effect of its olives are due to high amounts of polyphenols—chemical compounds with antioxidant qualities.

While more people are recognizing Croatia for its gastronomic excellence, it was a pleasure to experience lesser known Istria's place in the overall landscape. With such a dedication to authentic flavors and hyperlocal ingredients, it really blew me away.

**MAJESTIC MARVELS**
Truffles, majestic sunlight, extraordinary flavors, and charming views prove Croatia's magic at every turn.

# TRUFFLE PLJUKANCI

**YIELDS:** 6–8 SERVINGS

## PLJUKANCI

**2 cups all-purpose flour, plus more for dusting**

**1 teaspoon kosher salt**

**1 to 1½ cups water**

## TRUFFLE CREAM SAUCE

**¼ pound bacon, chopped**

**1 shallot, finely minced**

**2 garlic cloves, minced**

**¼ cup white wine**

**1½ cups heavy cream**

**Kosher salt**

**Freshly ground black pepper**

**1 medium black truffle (about 1 ounce), ⅓ minced and remaining ⅔ left whole for shaving**

## DIRECTIONS

**1.** Make the **pljukanci:** In a medium bowl, combine the flour and salt. Add the water, starting with 1 cup, and gradually add the remaining ½ cup, if needed, and mix until a shaggy dough comes together. Knead the dough, either in the bowl or on a lightly floured work surface, until it is smooth, about 5 minutes. Let it rest in the bowl, covered with a damp kitchen towel, for at least 20 minutes.

**2.** Once the dough has rested, dust your hands with extra flour and use your fingers to pinch off about a teaspoon. Roll this between the palms of your hands until a noodle forms that is thicker in the middle and tapers at the ends, about 1½ inches long. Repeat until all the dough has been used. Keep the noodles covered with a damp kitchen towel until you're ready to boil them. Set aside.

**3.** Make the **truffle cream sauce:** In a medium saucepan over medium-high heat, add the bacon and let the fat render so the meat crisps, about 2 to 3 minutes. Reduce the heat to medium and add the shallot, stirring every so often. Let the shallot become soft and translucent, about 2 minutes. Add the garlic and cook until fragrant, about 1 minute. Lower the heat if the garlic starts to brown. Add the wine to the pan and let deglaze, scraping up any brown bits on the bottom of the pan.

**4.** Add the heavy cream, a pinch of salt, and a few cracks of black pepper and reduce the heat to medium-low. Let the cream simmer to thicken and reduce by about half. Once reduced, turn off the heat and add the minced truffle. Let steep for a few minutes before tasting and adjust seasoning as needed.

**5.** While the cream sauce is steeping, bring a large pot of salted water to a boil. Once boiling, add the noodles and cook for a few minutes until the noodles have floated to the surface and the centers are cooked through to al dente. Drain or use a strainer to scoop the noodles directly into the cream sauce. Stir to coat them completely in the sauce, adding a splash of noodle water to thin if needed. Taste and adjust seasoning as needed.

**6.** To serve, transfer the noodles and sauce to a serving platter and shave a generous amount of black truffle over the entire dish.

# BLACK RISOTTO

## WITH GRILLED CUTTLEFISH

**YIELDS:** 4 SERVINGS

BLACK RISOTTO

**4 tablespoons unsalted butter**

**3 shallots, minced**

**2 garlic cloves, minced**

**1 cup Arborio rice**

**2 sprigs thyme, picked**

**1 tablespoon cuttlefish ink**

**1 cup dry white wine**

**6 cups fish stock, warm**

**Kosher salt**

**2 ounces grated Parmesan cheese or a hard, aged goat cheese**

**Freshly ground black pepper**

GRILLED CUTTLEFISH

**8 ounces cuttlefish, cleaned and skin removed, flesh lightly scored**

**Extra-virgin olive oil**

**Kosher salt**

**Freshly ground black pepper**

**½ bunch parsley leaves, finely chopped**

**1 lemon, juiced**

## DIRECTIONS

**1.** Make the **black risotto:** Place a large, high-walled skillet or heavy-bottomed pot over medium heat and melt the butter. Add the shallots and cook until soft and translucent, about 2 to 3 minutes.

**2.** Add the garlic, rice, and thyme and toast the rice, about 2 minutes. Add the cuttlefish ink and stir to coat the rice granules evenly. Add the wine to the pan to deglaze, scraping up any browned bits on the bottom of the pan, and let the wine reduce until only a few tablespoons remain, about 2 to 3 minutes.

**3.** Add a few ladles of warm fish stock and a pinch of salt and stir frequently until the rice has absorbed almost all the liquid. Repeat this process of gradually adding stock (but no more salt) and stirring until it evaporates, until most of the stock has been used and the rice is al dente (cooked but still firm). You may not need all the stock.

**4.** Once cooked, stir in the grated cheese and a few cracks of pepper. Taste for seasoning and adjust as needed. Remove from the heat but keep warm while you grill the cuttlefish.

**5.** Make the **grilled cuttlefish:** Heat a grill (or cast-iron grill pan) over high heat. Once hot, clean and generously oil the grill grates so the cuttlefish does not stick. Coat the scored cuttlefish in olive oil and season with kosher salt and a few cracks of black pepper.

**6.** Place the seasoned cuttlefish on the grill, letting it cook and char lightly on both sides, about 30 to 60 seconds per side.

**7.** Once cooked, remove the cuttlefish from the grill and transfer to a cutting board, letting it rest for a moment.

**8.** Slice the cuttlefish as thinly as possible. Add to a medium bowl and toss with the parsley, a generous squeeze of lemon juice, and a few glugs of olive oil. Toss to combine and taste and adjust seasoning as needed.

**9.** Transfer the risotto to a large serving bowl (or divide among individual bowls) and top with slices of the cuttlefish. Drizzle a bit more olive oil over the entire dish and serve.

Wild lupines bloom in a field in the rural and beautiful Westfjords of Iceland.

CHAPTER 12

# INCREDIBLE ICELAND

During an Icelandic summer in the land of fire and ice, a lesson in secret cooking techniques utilizing the volcanic landscape

The rugged landscape makes for picturesque scenery.

**N ICELAND, VAST GLACIERS** sit on top of the world's most active volcanoes and the cuisine is defined by the stark contrast of the formidable natural forces of fire and ice. Despite its name, this destination's landscape is extremely varied, with volcano-inspired features next to waterfalls, canyons, and deep valleys. Here, near the Arctic Circle, the most important ingredient is location. Iceland has a wealth of freshwater, clean nature, and fertile fishing grounds, and that means it abounds with culinary possibilities. ¶ I first visited this country more than a decade ago, but I'd never had a chance to focus on the breadth of delicious, sustainable ingredients available to Icelanders, even in the hidden corners of the region. There are also myriad techniques for preparation and preservation here that are connected to the region's unique geology and history.

## NAVIGATOR

### THE STOP

Near the Arctic Circle, a visit to Iceland proves the power of two dynamic forces—fire and ice. I discover the beauty of both through the country's rich and fresh ingredients.

### THE GEOGRAPHY

A volcanic island, Iceland is home to 32 active volcanic systems. About 11 percent of the country is covered by glacial ice.

### FOOD FACT

Hákarl, or fermented shark, is a national dish of Iceland made from Greenland shark or other sleeper sharks.

Frigid waters can't keep a smile off Gordon's face after diving for scallops with local master Simbi Hjálmarsson.

# "Everything we use, we have an abundance of ... They're everywhere. I can forage right in downtown Reykjavík."

*—Chef Ragnar Eiríksson*

"Everything we use, we have an abundance of," chef Ragnar Eiríksson told me as we soaked in a geothermal spring. Ragnar was awarded Iceland's first Michelin star and is now the chef and owner of Vínstúkan Tíu Sopar in Reykjavík. He loves to highlight seasonal local ingredients and obscure flavors that only this harsh landscape can provide. "Our ingredients are very fresh because we're so close to them," he said. "We don't have to climb rocks to find the 'special herb' somewhere. They're everywhere. I can forage right in downtown Reykjavík."

A variety of wild herbs—such as arctic thyme, angelica, chervil, and lovage—can be found by the country's foragers, who often need look no farther than out their back door. Because Icelandic summers are so short, wild herbs absorb energy and nutrients in a condensed amount of time to survive the harsh, dark winter months. Angelica is believed to have been used for both culinary and medicinal purposes from the beginning of settlement in Iceland, and its usage has even been reinvented in the past decade. Its flavor is slightly sweet and earthy, and all parts of the herb can be used: leaves, roots, seeds, and stalks. Fragrant arctic thyme has a distinct, stronger aroma than everyday thyme, and it elevates and adds dimension to flavors when used in cooking.

Iceland has long been a fishing nation, and the country's robust wild Atlantic salmon population is testament to dedicated fishery management. Anglers flock here in hopes of catching salmon in

INSIDER KNOWLEDGE

## A DEEP DIVE WITH SIMBI

Born and raised in Reykjavík, Sveinbjörn "Simbi" Hjálmarsson has long been drawn to the ocean and has been diving for more than 25 years. Now, living with his family in Ísafjörður in the remote Westfjords of Iceland, he sustainably harvests scallops, mussels, clams, and sea urchins that abound in the sparkling, crisp waters of the fjords. Simbi single-handedly scours the ocean floor throughout the year, no matter the weather. His desire to share his love of diving in these waters inspired him to start Dive

**Simbi Hjálmarsson and Gordon head out for the hunt.**

Westfjords, which includes a gourmet excursion to diving locations to enjoy the flavors of these decadent delights.

**WILDERNESS HERITAGE**
In addition to being an internationally important area for seabirds such as the puffin, the Westfjords peninsula is a remote wilderness area where the region's culture and heritage have been preserved.

HEITT VATN
HOT WATER

# CAPITAL CUISINE WITH CHEF RAGNAR EIRÍKSSON

Reykjavík-born chef Ragnar Eiríksson spent his youth between the capital city and his aunt's dairy farm on Iceland's south coast developing a strong connection with nature, local produce, and the culinary culture of the country. After working in restaurants and graduating from the Icelan-dic hospitality and culinary college, Ragnar moved to Copenhagen, where he briefly worked at restau-rants such as Noma and Prémisse (renamed AOC) before finding his place with chef Paul Cunningham at both his eponymous Michelin-starred restaurant, The Paul, and at Henne Kirkeby Kro.

Back in Reykjavík, Ragnar was awarded Iceland's first Michelin star and is now the chef and owner of Vínstúkan Tíu Sopar, a small wine bar where he revels in Iceland's simple ingredients found close to home in tapas-style plates, alongside natural wines from small producers and lesser known regions. Skilled at working within Iceland's natural limits, Ragnar turns simple ingredients into surprising dishes. "Early on, I wanted to focus on the ingredients and on the diversity of what we have here in Iceland," he said. "All our resources are so close that everything is literally right next to us. Even in downtown Reykjavík, it's easy to forage for many things."

**Ragnar Eiríksson (left) and Gordon prepare six dishes against a towering waterfall backdrop.**

the country's pristine glacial rivers. Every salmon I've ever caught has been with a rod, so my guide, Hakón Kjalar, decided to show me to how to catch wild salmon by net in the Þjórsá—the longest river in Iceland. It's one of the few remaining rivers here where net fishing is still practiced. The wild Atlantic salmon we caught was absolutely delicious and firm, with no fat at all. It's one of the best I've ever tasted.

Salty-sweet scallops fresh from the sea, as well as sea urchins and mahogany clams, add to Iceland's culinary bounty. Scuba diving in the chilly Denmark Strait near the Arctic Circle, I had to rely on a dry suit and an underwater scooter to stay as warm as possible while hand-harvesting some of the best scallops in the remote Westfjords of northwest Iceland, the most sparsely populated corner of the country. In Scotland, the scallops are easier to spot because of their flat tops. Here, they're rounded on both sides. Hand-harvesting shellfish is a more sustainable practice than dredging, which can damage the habitat of the ocean floor and result in considerable bycatch of nontargeted species.

Old-school preservation techniques that can be traced back to the Viking age are highlighted in the popular fermented shark dish hákarl. Greenland shark meat is toxic to humans because the shark's flesh contains high levels of uric acid and trimethylamine oxide, which act like natural antifreeze to protect the shark in the frigid waters that surround Iceland. The traditional method of fermentation includes pressing fluids from the meat while it ferments and then leaving it to dry for several months. The process neutralizes toxins, making the shark meat safe to consume. When it's ready, it smells a little like ammonia. Hákarl

Icelandic horses were introduced to the country more than 1,000 years ago.

is truly an acquired taste—one that I, personally, still haven't acquired.

On dry land, there are more sheep in Iceland than there are humans. Icelandic sheep are the largest of the short-tailed sheep and have been virtually unchanged in the past thousand years of isolation in the island country. The cold-hardy sheep roam in wild pastures, drinking from rivers and eating grass, berries, angelica, and seaweed, which makes their meat lean and tender with a fine grain and delicate taste that requires little seasoning. While Icelandic sheep aren't milked commercially, there are still some farmers who raise them for dairy on a small scale. The sweet, creamy milk is used in butter, yogurt, skyr (thicker and creamier than yogurt), and other cheeses.

Geothermal energy powers most of Iceland's electricity. Long ago, smart Icelanders learned how to harness that energy to bake rúgbrauð (rye bread) by burying the dough in the ground for 24 hours. The result is a rich, dense, sweet-and-salty bread. In the 18th century, when Iceland was still part of the Kingdom of Denmark, salt production was established using geothermal energy but was eventually discontinued. Sustainable, hand-harvested sea salt is produced again today in the Westfjords, using water from natural hot springs to heat, boil, and dry the flaky salt. The crunchy, mineral-fresh salt is used in many of the best restaurants around the world, and there are also versions made with arctic thyme, licorice, seaweed, and smoked birch.

Iceland's far-flung location in the Arctic Circle has historically made it challenging to obtain ingredients from elsewhere. The resulting reliance on locally sourced items abundant in the surrounding landscape has been far from limiting. Even though Icelanders have struggled to survive among the harsh natural circumstances for centuries, they've also been blessed with freshwater and a clean environment that let each ingredient's unique flavor come through.

| LOCAL FLAVOR

# A VOLCANIC DELIGHT

After a long professional career as a chef, Sigurður "Siggi" Rafn Hilmarsson manages the Laugarvatn Fontana geothermal spa in Lake Laugarvatn, where he grew up. The hot springs here generate enough energy to power the entire town. That energy has another purpose, too. Rye has been used in Iceland for decades and Siggi's recipe for rúgbrauð (rye bread) comes from his mother and grandmother. It's traditionally baked in a pot lined with butter that is buried in the hot sand close to thermal springs and left to cook for about 24 hours in the natural heat. The result is bread that is dark, dense, and quite sweet.

**Icelander Siggi and Gordon head to a spot to dig to make bread using geothermal heat.**

# PAN-SEARED SCALLOPS

## WITH PICKLED RHUBARB AND APPLE SALAD

**YIELDS:** 4 SERVINGS

### PICKLED RHUBARB

1 cup distilled white vinegar

½ cup water

½ cup granulated sugar

1 tablespoon kosher salt

1 teaspoon yellow mustard seeds

1 teaspoon black peppercorns

3 stalks rhubarb, red part only, cut into ¼-inch slices

### APPLE SALAD

1 small shallot, sliced thinly into half moons

2 apples, sliced thinly into strips or small dice

½ cup drained pickled rhubarb (from above)

1 lemon, zested and juiced

2 tablespoons chopped parsley, plus more for serving

2 tablespoons chopped chervil, plus more for serving

Kosher salt

1–2 tablespoons rhubarb pickling liquid

### SCALLOPS

12 fresh whole scallops, muscle detached and cleaned, shells cleaned and reserved

Kosher salt

2 tablespoons olive oil

1–2 ounces whiskey, optional

½ lemon, juiced

Flaky sea salt

### | DIRECTIONS

**1.** Make the **pickled rhubarb:** Add the vinegar, water, sugar, salt, mustard seeds, and peppercorns to a small pot and place over medium-high heat. Bring to a boil until sugar has dissolved, then remove from the heat.

**2.** Place the rhubarb in a heatproof jar and pour in the liquid mixture until rhubarb is covered. When the liquid has cooled, cover and keep in the refrigerator until ready to use, at least 20 minutes. The pickled rhubarb can be made up to a week in advance.

**3.** Make the **apple salad:** Place the shallot, apples, pickled rhubarb, lemon zest, parsley, and chervil in a medium bowl. Sprinkle with a pinch of salt, then toss to combine. Add in 1 tablespoon of pickling liquid and the lemon juice and mix. Taste for seasoning and add more pickling liquid, salt, or lemon juice as needed, then set aside.

**4.** Make the **scallops:** Pat the scallops dry and season all over with a generous pinch of salt. Set a large skillet over medium-high heat. Add the oil to the pan and quickly but carefully place each scallop in the pan, being careful not to overcrowd the pan, and cook for about 30 seconds, until the scallops begin to brown on the bottom. If using, add the whiskey to the pan to deglaze and carefully tilt the pan toward the flame to ignite the whiskey. Let it burn for a few seconds before blowing out the flame. Once the scallops are nicely browned on the bottom, about 1 minute total, flip to sear the other side. Cook for about 30 to 60 seconds more before removing them from the pan and letting them rest on a cutting board for a moment. Top with the lemon juice and a light sprinkling of sea salt.

**5.** Cut the scallops into bite-size pieces, then add to the bowl with the apple salad. Toss to combine and taste, adjusting seasoning as needed.

**6.** Arrange the 12 reserved scallop shells on a platter and divide the scallop mixture evenly among the shells. Garnish with the parsley and chervil leaves.

# GRILLED SALMON
## WITH BRENNIVÍN BEURRE BLANC

**YIELDS:** 6–8 SERVINGS

### BRENNIVÍN BEURRE BLANC

¼ cup brennivín or aquavit

¼ cup white wine vinegar

1 shallot, minced

1 garlic clove, sliced

¼ cup heavy cream

1 cup (2 sticks) unsalted butter, cold, cut into 1-inch cubes

Kosher salt

Freshly ground black pepper

### GRILLED SALMON

1 4–5 pound side of wild-caught salmon, scaled and deboned

¼ cup olive oil

Kosher salt

1 lemon, halved

Flaky sea salt

### HERB SALAD

1 bunch parsley, chopped

1 bunch chervil, chopped

1 bunch fennel fronds, chopped

1 bunch dill, chopped

## DIRECTIONS

**1.** Make the **brennivín beurre blanc:** In a small saucepan over medium-low heat, mix the brennivín, vinegar, shallot, and garlic. Bring to a low boil and reduce until only about 2 tablespoons of liquid remain. Add the heavy cream and simmer for 1 minute.

**2.** Reduce the heat to low and use a whisk to beat in a few tablespoons of butter at a time, letting the butter melt completely before adding more. Swirl the pan constantly to ensure the sauce doesn't get too hot and break. Once thickened, season with salt and pepper to taste, then pour through a fine mesh strainer and discard the shallot and garlic.

**3.** Make the **grilled salmon:** Heat a grill to high and let it heat for at least 15 minutes before cleaning and oiling the grates well.

**4.** Place the salmon on a cutting board and pat dry with paper towels. Use a sharp knife to lightly score the skin a few times. Use your hands to generously coat the salmon all over with the olive oil, then season all over with kosher salt.

**5.** Once the grill is hot and oiled, lay the salmon, skin side down, on the grill. Close the grill and let the skin sear for about 10 minutes before flipping to the other side and continuing to cook for another 8 to 10 minutes, depending on the thickness of the salmon, until it is cooked to your liking.

**6.** Carefully remove the salmon from the grill and place on a clean cutting board, crispy skin side up. Immediately squeeze the lemon halves all over and sprinkle with a bit of sea salt.

**7.** While the salmon rests, make the **herb salad:** In a medium bowl, combine all the herbs evenly.

**8.** To serve, transfer the salmon to a serving platter and scatter the herb salad on top. Serve with the brennivín beurre blanc on the side.

# HERB-CRUSTED LAMB BACKSTRAP

## WITH PAN-FRIED POTATOES AND MUSHROOMS

**YIELDS:** 2 SERVINGS

---

GREEN PEPPERCORN SAUCE

**2 tablespoons unsalted butter, divided**

**2 shallots, minced**

**1 garlic clove, minced**

**1 tablespoon green peppercorns, crushed**

**1 cup lamb or beef stock**

**½ cup lamb or beef demi-glace**

**2 tablespoons whole-grain mustard**

**2 tablespoons heavy cream**

POTATOES AND MUSHROOMS

**2 tablespoons olive oil**

**2 cups peewee potatoes or fingerlings, halved**

**Kosher salt**

**1 yellow onion, chopped**

**2 cups sliced button mushrooms**

**1 garlic clove, thinly sliced**

**Freshly ground black pepper**

**Sherry vinegar**

HERB-CRUSTED LAMB

**2 tablespoons extra-virgin olive oil**

**2 lamb backstraps or tenderloins, about 1 pound**

**Kosher salt**

**Freshly ground black pepper**

**2 tablespoons unsalted butter**

**1 garlic clove, crushed**

**4 sprigs fresh thyme, picked**

**2–3 tablespoons Dijon mustard**

**3 tablespoons chopped fresh chervil**

**3 tablespoons chopped fresh parsley**

**3 tablespoons chopped fresh dill**

**Flaky sea salt**

## DIRECTIONS

**1.** Make the **green peppercorn sauce:** In a small saucepan over medium heat, add 1 tablespoon of the butter. Once melted, add the shallots, garlic, and peppercorns and stir until soft, about 1 to 2 minutes. Add the stock, demi-glace, and mustard and whisk to combine. Let the sauce reduce by half, about 5 to 10 minutes. Stir in the heavy cream to bind.

**2.** Stir in the remaining 1 tablespoon of butter and taste for seasoning. Remove from the heat but keep on the stove to stay warm.

**3.** Make the **potatoes and mushrooms:** Set a large skillet over medium-high heat and add the oil. Once hot, add the potatoes, sprinkle with a pinch of salt, and cover with a lid. Let steam, stirring occasionally, until the potatoes are almost cooked through and tender.

**4.** Add the onion and cook until softened, about 2 to 3 minutes, lowering the heat if the onion starts to brown too quickly. Add the mushrooms and garlic, continuing to sauté until the mushrooms are cooked down and begin to brown. Season with salt and pepper, add a splash of sherry vinegar, and stir to combine. Taste and adjust seasoning as needed. Remove from the heat and keep warm.

**5.** Make the **herb-crusted lamb:** Heat a large cast-iron skillet over medium-high heat for a few minutes. Once the pan is very hot, add the oil. Pat the lamb dry and season all over with salt and pepper.

**6.** Add the lamb to the pan and sear, pressing down gently to make sure it gets a nice crust, about 30 to 60 seconds, depending on the thickness of the lamb. Once seared, flip and repeat with the other side. Add the butter, garlic, and thyme. Use the melted butter from the pan to baste the lamb.

**7.** Continue to baste until the lamb is cooked medium rare (an internal temperature of 120°F), about 1 to 2 minutes. Remove from the heat and brush all over with the Dijon mustard. Place the chervil, parsley, and dill on a plate. Let the lamb rest for about 5 minutes, and then roll it in the herbs. Move to a cutting board and slice into medallions.

**8.** To serve, transfer the warm mushrooms and potatoes to a serving platter. Transfer the sliced lamb to the platter and sprinkle lightly with sea salt and a scattering of the remaining chopped herbs. Serve the warm peppercorn sauce on the side.

The town of Nazaré
is home to some of
the biggest surfable
waves on the planet.

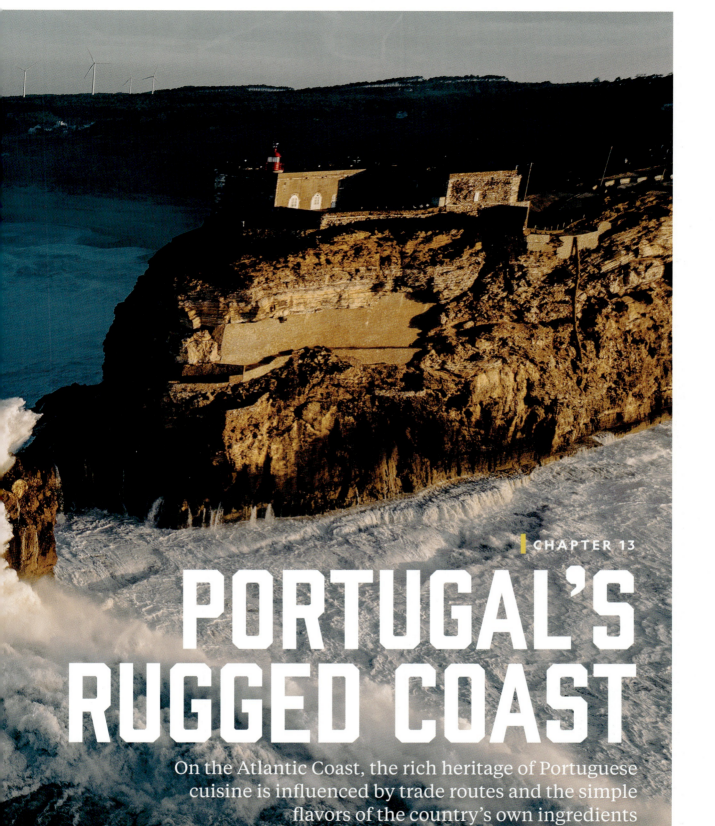

# CHAPTER 13

# PORTUGAL'S RUGGED COAST

On the Atlantic Coast, the rich heritage of Portuguese cuisine is influenced by trade routes and the simple flavors of the country's own ingredients

Gordon and chef Kiko Martins share a meal of sea barnacles.

**P**ORTUGAL, WITH ITS WIND-LASHED COASTLINE and rugged landscape, inspires an adventurous spirit that has influenced its people and food for generations. One of the most powerful seafaring countries in the world, Portugal monopolized the spice trade in the 16th century. Today, the country and its cuisine still benefit from the age of discovery and the ingredients obtained from trade routes linking Lisbon with the Maluku Islands and Malaysia by way of Kerala and Sri Lanka.¶ The roots of Portuguese gastronomy have also included a focus on ingredients' pure flavors. Quality products don't need to be overwhelmed in the process of bringing them to the table; perfectly simple dishes allow the essence of an item to shine through. And despite the country's modest size in the southwest corner of the Iberian Peninsula, it has incredibly diverse ingredients.

**NAVIGATOR**

**THE STOP**

On a tour of Portugal's rugged coast, there are treasures on land and at sea.

**THE GEOGRAPHY**

Five of the six biggest waves ever recorded have happened in Nazaré. The huge swells happen when currents rush over the largest underwater canyon in Europe, which stretches about 3 miles (5 km) deep and 120 miles (190 km) long.

**FOOD FACT**

Portuguese food is largely influenced by centuries-old trade routes, blending French, Mediterranean, and African flavors into its cuisine.

A spread from the sea: clams, sea barnacles, and sardines

"Portugal is about simplicity and the quality of its products," chef Kiko Martins told me when we met in Nazaré, a coastal town that's home to some of the biggest surfable waves on the planet, which rear up from the largest underwater canyon in Europe to reach 100 feet (30 m) high. The celebrated Portuguese chef studied at Le Cordon Bleu and honed his skills in Michelin-starred kitchens across Europe, but his culinary ties to his home country are strong. "For many generations, we have dedicated time in our families to speaking about food," he said. "When we're at lunch, we talk about what's going to be for dinner. When we're having dinner, we talk about what we'll have for lunch the next day."

With more than 1,100 miles (1,770 km) of coastline, Portugal relies heavily on seafood from the Atlantic Ocean, and the Portuguese take care to preserve the beautiful taste of the ocean in their cooking. As tasty as they are ugly, percebes (also known as gooseneck barnacles) thrive by attaching securely to rocks in the rugged intertidal zone, battered by the dangerous surf of the country's coast. They may look like tiny elephant feet, but they're incredibly easy to prepare by simply steaming or blanching in salted water. The flavor is fresh and briny, like a splash of seawater. They taste even sweeter now that I know what it takes to get them.

The challenge of harvesting percebes results in a high price—both at market and for the dedicated people who gather this prized shellfish from beneath the water line. After I watched my friend David Beckham play soccer in Madrid, David and I would always go enjoy some percebes, but I never realized that they were so difficult to get ahold of until I was getting pounded by giant waves while trying to harvest them in Portugal. When you're underwater and your ears are full of seawater, it's very hard to pay attention to anything else. Then you feel the momentum of a swell coming up, and suddenly, a wave comes crashing in and you're clinging to sharp rocks to prevent yourself

LOCAL FLAVOR

## THE SARDINE RUN

Portuguese fisherman Joaquim Zaror has been fishing since he was a young boy. While the use of sonar has improved some of the methods used for finding sardines since then, it's still humans on the ocean—the essence of the Portuguese spirit. While a typical haul can bring in 60,000 sardines, I learned that the life of a sardine fisherman isn't as easy as it may look. Sometimes nature doesn't play ball and you might wind up with very little, especially if a pod of hungry dolphins is eyeing the same school of sardines you are.

Freshly caught sardines

**FAMILY FEAST**
A bounty of local ingredients comes together for a meal served to the mayor of Nazaré (seated at the right) and his family.

# A CULTURE OF VINICULTURE

In Portugal's Sintra region, among the western-most lands of Europe, wine producers have been challenging the winds of the Atlantic Ocean for generations. But even though wine-making here is an old tradition, only about 50 acres (20 ha) of vineyards remain, compared with almost 2,500 acres (1,010 ha) that existed in the 1940s, due to suburban expansion. Winemaker Hélder Cunha, founder and co-owner of Casca Wines, partners with local growers to develop wines in more than 10 regions including Colares. His goal is to preserve Portugal's long-held wine traditions.

Only certain wines can be called Colares: They must be made from Ramisco or Malvasia grapes grown on vines on sand. Ramisco, which makes up 75 percent of the plantings in Colares, is one of those rare European grapes still grown on its own rootstock. It's nearly impossible to find outside of Colares. The aged vineyards here are national heirlooms. Vines obtain heat from the sand to mature, growing horizontally rather than verti-cally, as you'd typically see in a vineyard. Once grape bunches begin to fill out, growers gently raise the vines off the sand with wooden posts to enable air to circulate and develop further. But the Atlantic wind brings salt, which can burn the leaves, so those who tend the vines must be vigi-lant to protect the leaves.

**Señor Gonzalo (left) and Hélder Cunha explain the unique growing process of their vines.**

# HARVESTING THE WAVES

**P**ercebeiro (percebes harvester) Ricardo Cosme forages year-round for gooseneck barnacles that attach themselves to the rocks in the intertidal zone along the rugged Portuguese coastline. He said that the harder the waves and the deeper the percebes are found, the bigger and better they are. Chiseling away at the barnacle with an *arrilhada* (a wedge-like blade) before the next wave hits is a valuable and essential skill. Even though the best time to get the barnacles is at low tide, Ricardo told me that a harvester needs to be constantly watching and can never turn their back to the ocean.

Percebes hunter Ricardo Cosme shows Gordon his find.

from being drawn out to sea with the strong current.

On the tamer side of things, the sardine is an essential part of the cultural and economic fabric of Portugal, a staple of the area's diet and trade ever since the Romans found abundant schools off the coast. The irresistible scent of coarsely salted grilled sardines fills the air in summertime, especially during the June festivals dedicated to Santo António and São João. In Portugal, sardines used to be considered a poor man's food. Today, they're in such high demand that they've become more expensive—and because of climate change they're not always easy to procure as the fish seek out colder waters off northern Europe.

Sweets, known as *doces* in Portugal, are an essential part of any meal. Dating to the 1700s, the pão de ló is a sponge cake that's removed from the oven early to retain a slightly undercooked, gooey center. That means steady hands and great care are needed when transferring the cake from its copper baking pan to a cake box and ultimately to a dessert plate. Convent cakes and desserts, like this one, were developed by nuns with skill and patience. The ingredients of the cake are as humble as its origin—a combination of eggs, sugar, flour, and lemon peel, with a shot of Portuguese liquor for good measure.

The Phoenicians brought pigs to the region, and Iberian black pigs and local wild boar are direct descendants of that lot. The free-ranging pigs live outside year-round, roaming the oak forests of the country's Alentejo region for acorns. The wide-open space and rich oleic acid of the acorns are instrumental in the resulting succulent porco preto being marbled with fat. I've had some of the most extraordinary Wagyu, but the taste of the secreto cut of porco preto (akin to the skirt) is amazing—a melt-in-the-mouth experience. It's the best pork I've tasted in my career.

The vineyards of Colares, with some of the oldest vines in Portugal, wind along the sand like emerald serpents, influenced by the Atlantic just as they have been for centuries. The vines are trained to grow low

# The Portuguese take care to preserve the beautiful taste of the ocean in their cooking.

along the ground to avoid the ocean wind, and the sandy topsoil underpinned by heavy clay is fundamental to the crop. The topsoil is credited for saving the Colares vines from the 19th century phylloxera epidemic that decimated other European vineyards because the phylloxera, an aphid-like bug, can't live in sandy soil. The tiny vineyard I visited produced magnificent wine that tasted just like some of the most expensive Burgundies.

Portugal was an eye-opener for me, tapping into the bold spirit of local cuisine and the preference for less-is-more preparation. It's a lesson in keeping things simple, serving the flavors of the ingredients themselves. The knowledge has given me another string in my bow and opened my mind to larders of ingredients that I hadn't thought to use before. The gastronomy of Portugal has been eclipsed by that of its Spanish neighbor, but it truly stands on its own.

The cliffs of Sítio overlook the majestic coast of Nazaré.

# GRILLED SARDINES STUFFED WITH BELL PEPPERS

## AND LEMON-HERB BREADCRUMBS

**YIELDS:** 4–6 SERVINGS

2 tablespoons extra-virgin olive oil, plus more for drizzling

1 yellow onion, diced small (about 1 cup)

2 red bell peppers, seeded and diced small (about 2 cups)

Kosher salt

2 Fresno chili peppers, seeded and minced

1 garlic clove, finely minced

4 cups breadcrumbs

1 lemon, zested

⅓ cup parsley leaves, finely chopped

Freshly ground black pepper

6 large sardines, scaled and gutted*

1 lemon, cut into wedges

## DIRECTIONS

**1.** Preheat a grill to 450°F.

**2.** In a large skillet, heat the oil over medium-high heat. Add the onion and bell peppers. Season with a big pinch of salt and sauté until tender, about 2 minutes. Add the chilies and garlic, continuing to cook for another 2 minutes until fragrant and tender. Sprinkle in the breadcrumbs, tossing to coat and stirring frequently with a wooden spoon until the breadcrumbs are toasted and crispy.

**3.** Remove from the heat and season the mixture with the lemon zest, parsley, salt, and pepper. Stuff a few spoonfuls of breadcrumb mixture into each sardine.

**4.** Drizzle the sardines with olive oil and season with salt and pepper. Carefully place the stuffed sardines into a grill basket and grill over medium-high heat until the skin starts to crisp and the sardines are cooked through, about 2 to 3 minutes on each side.**

**5.** Serve the grilled sardines warm with lemon wedges. Garnish with any remaining breadcrumbs.

*Any petite fish (about 6 inches long) that can be stuffed can be substituted for sardines.*

**For best results, use a fish grilling basket or soaked skewers to hold the sardines together. In lieu of grilling altogether, use a cast-iron pan and sear the sardines until crisp.*

# PORTUGUESE PORCO À ALENTEJANA

## WITH BLISTERED CHERRY TOMATOES

**YIELDS:** 4-6 SERVINGS

½ pound peewee potatoes

1 pound Iberico pork secreto or kurobuta pork chops, thinly sliced into strips

Kosher salt

1 tablespoon extra-virgin olive oil, plus more as needed

8 ounces hard chorizo, cut in ¼-inch rounds

3 shallots, thinly sliced, about ¾ cup

2 garlic cloves, finely minced

2 Fresno chili peppers, seeded and thinly sliced

2 red bell peppers, seeded and thinly sliced

2 cups cherry tomatoes

2 cups dry white wine, divided

1 cup tomato puree

1 pound littleneck clams, scrubbed

1 tablespoon fresh thyme leaves

¾ cup fish stock

Freshly ground black pepper

4 tablespoons unsalted butter

1 lemon, zested

Toasted baguette, for serving

### DIRECTIONS

**1.** Place the potatoes in a large pot and fill with water, enough to cover the potatoes by ½ inch. Bring the water to a boil and cook until the potatoes are fork-tender, about 10 minutes. Drain the potatoes. When cool enough to handle, cut the potatoes in half. Set aside.

**2.** Generously season the pork with salt. Heat a Dutch oven over medium-high heat. Once hot, drizzle with 1 tablespoon of olive oil. Working in batches, add the pork to the pot and sear until the fat renders slightly. Remove the pork and set aside. Repeat with the chorizo, cooking until it becomes golden brown and crispy, about 5 to 7 minutes. Remove the chorizo and set aside.

**3.** Add the shallots to the Dutch oven, adding more olive oil if necessary, and sauté with a pinch of salt. Sweat until tender, about 3 to 5 minutes.

**4.** Add the garlic, chilies, and bell peppers to the Dutch oven, cooking until fragrant, about 2 to 3 minutes. Toss in the cherry tomatoes and allow to them to blister and burst. Pour in 1 cup of the white wine and simmer until it has reduced by half and the tomatoes become slightly "jammy," scraping the bottom of the Dutch oven to release all the caramelized bits. Pour in the tomato puree and simmer as the flavors meld, 10 to 15 minutes.

**5.** Add the remaining 1 cup of white wine, clams, thyme, and fish stock. Cover and simmer until the clams open, about 3 to 5 minutes. Discard any clams that do not open on their own. Return the pork and chorizo to the Dutch oven. Add the potatoes and season with salt and pepper. Add the butter and continue to cook to reduce the sauce as needed. Garnish with the lemon zest and serve with a toasted baguette.

CHAPTER 14

# THE MAINE INGREDIENT

Along Maine's rugged shoreline, the coastal
state's identity is inextricably linked to its wealth
of natural resources

Dusk falls along Maine's rocky coastline at the Marshall Point Lighthouse in Port Clyde.

Gordon gathers
fresh shellfish in
Rockland, Maine.

**K**NOWN WORLDWIDE FOR ITS ROCKY COASTLINE and inland waterways, Maine is home to some of the most famed seafood in the world. The colder waters and nutrients brought north by the Gulf Stream are optimal for shellfish and smaller baitfish, which in turn, draw larger fish. Another reason seafood is so good here is that the fishery is so close to shore. Dayboat fleets can bring the fresh catch back and transfer it quickly to markets and restaurants. ¶ The state's identity is not only tied to the abundance provided by the ocean, but also to a wealth of land-based fresh ingredients, no matter the season. The lush landscape provides ideal grazing areas for cows, which produce incredible dairy products—from butter to cheese to ice cream. In the wild, there are fiddleheads, ramps, and blueberries to pick. Maine produces nearly 500,000 gallons (1.9 million L) of maple syrup per year, and during

Fresh bounty scavenged from the waves

## NAVIGATOR

### THE SPOT

It's no surprise that the ocean is the prize of Maine. On its coastline, I revel in the state's robust, fresh seafood— and fine rich gems from the land, too.

### THE GEOGRAPHY

The biggest state in New England, Maine is bordered by Canada to the north and east, New Hampshire to the west, and the Atlantic Ocean to the south. The cold waters are part of the reason seafood thrives here.

### FOOD FACT

Maine is one of the largest producers of lobster, bringing in nearly 100 million pounds (45.4 million kg) of lobster per year.

# The ocean-to-table movement is the foundation of coastal communities everywhere.

peak season, from late February through mid-April, it's a serious 24-hour operation.

"Mainers are hard-core, salt of the earth," two-time James Beard Award–winning chef Melissa Kelly told me when we foraged for seaweed in the state's chilly water. Mainers also happen to be pretty tolerant of the cold. The proprietor and executive chef of Primo, in mid-coast Maine, Melissa told me that a lot of chefs and young farmers have relocated to Maine in the past 15 years, lured by its abundance of natural ingredients. They've joined more long-lived Mainers in raising the bar for the local food scene.

The ocean-to-table movement is the foundation of coastal communities everywhere, especially in Maine, where lobster is a way of life. Maine holds the title of Lobster Capital of the World because the crustaceans thrive in the cold, clean waters off the coastline, where the temperatures keep salt from entering the meat of the shellfish, which results in a sweeter taste. Lobsters here are bigger, with larger claws, and grow at a slower rate than elsewhere—and they gather in numbers so plentiful that the state's waters account for 80 percent of the lobster population in the United States.

Maine lobster wasn't considered a delicacy until the 19th century. Before then, lobsters washed up on Maine's beaches in such large numbers they were considered a poor man's or prisoner's staple. Residents have had many years of practice incorporating lobster into all manner of dishes, from bisque to roll to thermidor. People have deep allegiances to Maine's lobster rolls—a center-cut hot-dog roll that's buttered and toasted and filled with big chunks of cold lobster meat tossed with mayonnaise.

Most lobster fishers set traps from June to October,

## A FAMILY AFFAIR

Thousands of years ago, Maine's first inhabitants ate oysters and clams—a practice that continues to this day. At the head of a tidal inlet on North Haven Island, Adam Campbell and his son Zebadiah run the North Haven Oyster Company. Their oysters have a rich, briny taste and are grown on the ocean floor, where cold salt water rushes over them on an incoming tide and brackish water shoots past them on an outgoing tide. Market

**Adam Campbell (right) and his son, Zeb, in front of their seafood shop**

oysters are enjoyed on the half shell, but some of their oysters are brined overnight, smoked for 24 hours, and packed in virgin olive oil.

**COASTAL PARADISE**
Clockwise from top left: Chef Melissa Kelly selects the finest pieces of bladderwrack seaweed; nothing beats a sunset sail; the Big Cook features bluefin tuna seared on hot rocks.

# FARM TO TABLE WITH CHEF MELISSA KELLY

Chef Melissa Kelly received some of her earliest cooking lessons from her Italian grandmother. Born on Long Island, New York, Melissa studied at the Culinary Institute of America before working in Japan, France, California, and New York. She settled in Maine a little more than 20 years ago. She bought a 4.5-acre (1.8 ha) piece of property across from Penobscot Bay, put up a greenhouse, started a garden, added some bees and farm animals, and opened her restaurant, Primo, in 2000. With a menu that changes daily, she makes sure that the highest-quality ingredients are being served, fully embodying the concept of "farm to table."

"I always wanted to cook close to land and product," Melissa said. "It's really the dream way to cook." About 80 percent of her restaurant's ingredients are sourced from her farm in peak season. The farm may have started small, but it's evolved to include two greenhouses, more farm animals, and more seats in the restaurant—from 50 to 150. The full-circle relationship between the farm and restaurant also allows kitchen waste to be recycled. The two-time James Beard Award winner has since opened two other outposts of Primo in Orlando and Tucson, which follow her farm-to-table philosophy.

**Chef Melissa Kelly and Gordon put the finishing touches on their dishes while cooking outside.**

when the shellfish are closer to shore and more plentiful, but there still happen to be a hardy few who brave the winter's freezing temperatures and rough offshore waters to bring in a day's catch. Working on a lobster boat, even in summer, is tough work. You need to work quickly to haul the lobster pot out of the water, grab the catch, measure lobsters and band their claws, store them, bait the crate, close it, and toss it back in the water without getting tangled in the line.

Long fingers of land on the state's coast form estuaries where freshwater from inland rivers combines with Atlantic salt water. These jagged fingers are home to tidal coves that are ideal for oysters and clams. The shellfish are longtime Mainers, evidenced by their presence in prehistoric waste heaps dotting some of the region's riverbanks.

The brininess of a Maine oyster can vary greatly, depending on tidal flow, water brackishness, and proximity to the ocean. As with lobsters here, oysters grow slower in the cold waters, allowing them to develop a greater depth of flavor in the three to four years it takes for them to reach market size. Maine clams come in two varieties: hard and soft shell. Soft shell clams are generally thinner and more brittle, and they're extremely popular in the restaurant industry, either steamed or shucked. Hard shell clams feature a hard, thick shell,

Maine isn't home solely to abundant seafood. The open farmland and fresh, clean air make for happy cows—and delicious butter and cream.

and their sizes vary. Gigantic Atlantic surf clams (also known as hen clams) can weigh more than a pound, while mahogany clams (also known as ocean quahogs) are much smaller with a saltier flavor profile. They're also among the longest-lived marine organisms in the world and can live longer than 200 years.

Even seaweed and marine microalgae are part of the ocean harvest. There are 250 different species of sea vegetable in the Gulf of Maine, only 11 of which are commercially harvested. In recent history, Mainers have shifted from collecting wild seaweed to farmed varieties, and annual harvests are getting larger. Some of those farmers are lobster fishers who grow kelp during their off-season. Mineral-rich seaweed such as dulse, bladderwrack, Irish moss, fingered kelp, and sugar kelp produce a briny umami flavor optimal for fish and shellfish dishes.

Dairy products have long been staples produced in Maine, too. Hundreds of thousands of acres of open farmland and small woodlands in the fresh air are prime grazing areas for cows, sheep, and goats, yielding milk for delicious butter, cream, yogurt, cheese, and ice cream. The state has 196 dairy farms, 99 percent of which are family owned and operated. With more than 28,000 cows making 70 million gallons of milk per year, that's more than enough butter for lobster. While there are creameries making dairy products on a commodity and artisanal scale, some dairy farmers—like Swallowtail Farm and Creamery, where I churned my own cultured butter for the Big Cook—craft their own products on-site.

Maine's diverse fisheries make the state one of the best seafood destinations anywhere on this planet. From the important element of the state's nutrient-rich, cold water to fishing dayboats bringing back the absolute freshest catch, it's no surprise that water will always get the glory here. But when you combine Maine's treasure from the ocean with its riches from the land, the ingredients work hand in glove to blow your mind.

INSIDER KNOWLEDGE

## TIMBER LAND

**M**ostly covered by extensive forests, Maine is known as the Pine Tree State and has a rich history of logging—with origins credited to English explorers first cutting trees on Monhegan Island in the 17th century. Because cedar can add a smoky-savory flavor to fish and meat, I wanted to get my hands on some, and "Timber" Tina Scheer showed me how to cut my own in true lumberjack fashion. She grew up logrolling, chopping, sawing, ax throwing, and speed climbing with her family. Now, she hosts the Great Maine Lumberjack Show in her own logging sports facility.

"Timber" Tina Scheer shows Gordon the finer points of ax wielding.

# GRILLED TUNA DECONSTRUCTED BLT

## WITH POACHED OYSTER AIOLI, NASTURTIUM, AND OPAL BASIL

*Recipe provided by Melissa Kelly*

**YIELDS:** 4 SERVINGS

### POACHED OYSTERS

1 cup white wine

10 oysters, shucked, reserve 4 shells for plating

### AIOLI

8 large egg yolks

6 poached oysters (from above)

2 garlic cloves

¼ cup fresh-squeezed lemon juice

¼ cup cold water

1 cup extra-virgin olive oil

Ground white pepper

### TUNA

1 pound bluefin tuna steak

2 tablespoons extra-virgin olive oil

1 tablespoon kosher salt

2 teaspoons freshly ground black pepper

### FOR SERVING

1 pound thick-cut bacon, cooked until crispy

1 pound heirloom tomatoes, sliced

1 pound cherry tomatoes, cut in half

4 heads little gem lettuce, washed and roots removed

Nasturtium

Opal basil

### DIRECTIONS

**1.** Make the **poached oysters:** In a small saucepan, bring the white wine to a boil over medium-high heat. Once boiling, place the oysters in the liquid and let simmer until the edges of the oysters begin to curl, about 1 to 2 minutes. Remove the oysters from the liquid and let cool completely.

**2.** Make the **aioli:** In a blender, combine the egg yolks, 6 of the poached oysters, garlic, lemon juice, and water. Blend until the mixture is combined. With the blender running on low speed, slowly drizzle in the olive oil until smooth. Season with a pinch of white pepper.

**3.** Grill the **tuna:** Preheat a grill to 400°F. Brush the tuna steak with the olive oil and season all over with the salt and pepper. Place the tuna on the preheated grill and sear just until the tuna begins to caramelize, about 1 minute. Flip and continue grilling until the other side just begins to brown, about 1 more minute. Remove the tuna and place on a cutting board. Let it rest for 5 minutes, then slice against the grain.

**4.** To serve, pour the aioli on a large serving plate and spread to cover the bottom of the plate. Arrange the tuna, bacon, tomatoes, lettuce, and remaining 4 poached oysters in the reserved oyster shells on the platter. Garnish with the nasturtium and opal basil.

# OYSTERS ROCKEFELLER

## WITH CREAMED SPINACH AND BREADCRUMBS

**YIELDS:** 4 SERVINGS

### CREAMED SPINACH

**3 cups spinach**

**2 tablespoons unsalted butter**

**1 shallot, finely chopped**

**1 garlic clove, minced**

**½ teaspoon freshly ground nutmeg**

**Chili flakes**

**½ cup heavy cream**

**2 ounces cream cheese, softened**

**1 lemon, zested**

**¼ cup grated Parmesan cheese**

### BREADCRUMBS

**1 tablespoon olive oil**

**1 garlic clove, finely minced**

**½ cup panko breadcrumbs**

**Pinch of kosher salt**

### OYSTERS

**12 oysters on the half shell**

**Rock salt or seaweed, optional**

**1 lemon, cut into wedges**

### DIRECTIONS

**1.** Make the **creamed spinach:** Bring a large pot of salted water to a boil, then blanch the spinach for about 30 seconds. Remove from the water. Once the spinach is cool enough to handle, drain as much water as possible from the spinach and set aside.

**2.** Heat a large, high-walled skillet over medium heat. Add the butter, then the shallot, and cook until soft and translucent, about 2 minutes. Add the garlic, nutmeg, and a pinch of chili flakes and stir to combine. Add the heavy cream and cream cheese, stirring until melted and incorporated. Let the mixture simmer for a moment or so to thicken the heavy cream, then add the drained spinach back to the pan. Stir to incorporate and add the lemon zest and Parmesan cheese. Set aside.

**3.** Make the **breadcrumbs:** In a small bowl, combine all breadcrumb ingredients and mix with your fingers to incorporate everything evenly. Set aside.

**4.** Cook the **oysters:** Preheat a grill or oven to 450°F. Place the oysters on a small baking tray lined with rock salt or seaweed, or crumple aluminum foil lightly on top of a sheet tray and place the oysters on top so they don't fall over.

**5.** Top each oyster with a heaping tablespoon of the creamed spinach, followed by a generous spoonful of the breadcrumbs. Place on the hot grill or in the oven and cook until the spinach bubbles and the breadcrumbs are golden brown and crispy, about 5 to 8 minutes.

**6.** Serve with lemon wedges.

# LOBSTER AND CLAM BOUILLABAISSE

**YIELDS:** 6 SERVINGS

1 whole lobster, about 1½ pounds

¼ cup olive oil

1 yellow onion, thinly sliced

3 garlic cloves, thinly sliced

1 pound heirloom cherry tomatoes

1 pound peewee potatoes

4 sprigs thyme, picked

1 teaspoon chili flakes

1 saffron thread, optional

Kosher salt

¼ cup tomato paste

½ cup white wine

4 cups seafood stock

2 pounds clams, cleaned

1 lemon, halved

Parsley leaves, chopped

Fennel fronds, chopped

Crusty bread, for serving

## DIRECTIONS

**1.** Bring a large pot of heavily salted water to a boil. Add the whole lobster to the boiling water and blanch for 2 to 3 minutes. Remove the lobster from the water and place in an ice-water bath to cool. Drain the lobster. When cool enough to handle, cut in half and clean. Remove all the meat from the lobster, reserving the meat and shells for later. Cut the meat into 1-inch pieces. Store in the refrigerator until ready to use.

**2.** Heat a large, heavy-bottomed stockpot over medium heat and add the olive oil. Once the oil is hot, add the onion and sauté until tender, about 2 to 3 minutes. Add the garlic and cherry tomatoes, letting them blister and break down, about 2 to 3 more minutes. Add the potatoes, thyme, chili flakes, and saffron, if using, then season with a large pinch of salt and stir to combine. Let cook for about 1 minute.

**3.** Push the ingredients to the sides of the pot and add the tomato paste to the empty center. Stir the tomato paste to caramelize, about 1 minute. Add the wine to deglaze the pot, using a wooden spoon to scrape up any browned bits from the bottom. Add the seafood stock and lobster shells and bring to a simmer. Let simmer for about 30 minutes.

**4.** Taste for seasoning and adjust as needed. Remove and discard the lobster shells.

**5.** Add the clams to the pot, stir to incorporate, and place a lid over the stew so the clams will steam and open.* Discard any clams that do not open on their own. When the clams have opened, add the reserved lobster meat and stir to combine. Add a squeeze of lemon juice, if needed.

**6.** Divide among bowls and top with parsley leaves and fennel fronds. Serve with crusty bread.

*Instead of steaming the clams, you can grill them over an open fire or on a grill like I did in Maine, then add them to the stew when you add your lobster meat.*

# LOBSTER THERMIDOR

## WITH GRILLED CORN AND RED CABBAGE SLAW

**YIELDS:** 2 SERVINGS

### SEAWEED BUTTER

½ cup unsalted butter, room temperature

2 tablespoons edible seaweed, such as red wakame or dulse, roughly chopped

2 tablespoons tarragon leaves, finely chopped

1 lemon, zested

1 garlic clove, minced

1 teaspoon smoked paprika

¼ teaspoon kosher salt

### PARMESAN BREADCRUMBS

1 tablespoon olive oil

1 garlic clove, minced

½ cup panko breadcrumbs

¼ cup grated Parmesan cheese

Pinch of kosher salt

### CABBAGE SLAW

½ small red cabbage, core removed, thinly sliced

1 teaspoon salt

2 tablespoons apple cider vinegar

1 tablespoon mayonnaise or whole-fat yogurt

1 teaspoon honey, plus more if needed

½ lemon, zested and juiced

1 teaspoon freshly ground black pepper

### GRILLED CORN

2 ears corn, shucked

Extra-virgin olive oil

Kosher salt

1 tablespoon seaweed butter (from above)

### LOBSTER THERMIDOR

1 whole lobster, about 1½ pounds

1 tablespoon olive oil

1 shallot, minced

1 garlic clove, minced

Kosher salt

Dry sherry or white wine

2 tablespoons seaweed butter (from above), divided

1 tablespoon all-purpose flour

1 cup heavy cream

Freshly ground black pepper

2 tablespoons tarragon, finely chopped

Fresh lemon juice

Parmesan breadcrumbs (from above)

### DIRECTIONS

**1.** Make the **seaweed butter:** In a medium bowl, combine all the ingredients until smooth and incorporated. Taste and adjust seasoning as needed. Set aside.

**2.** Make the **Parmesan breadcrumbs:** In a small bowl, combine all the ingredients and mix with your fingers to incorporate everything evenly. Set aside.

**3.** Make the **cabbage slaw:** Place the cabbage in a large bowl and sprinkle with the salt, then use your hands to massage briefly. In a medium bowl, combine the other slaw ingredients and whisk until smooth. Transfer the cabbage to the bowl with the dressing, leaving behind any liquid released from the cabbage, and toss to combine. Taste and adjust seasoning. Set aside.

**4.** Make the **grilled corn:** Preheat a grill to 400°F or heat a cast-iron grill pan over medium-high heat. Brush the corn all over with oil, sprinkle with salt, and place directly onto the hot grill or pan. Turn occasionally to get color on all sides, then remove from grill once cooked through and nicely charred. Brush with the seaweed butter and set aside to keep warm.

any browned bits at the bottom of the pan.

**8.** Add 1 tablespoon of the seaweed butter, letting it melt, and then add the flour, whisking to combine. Let the mixture cook until fragrant, about 30 seconds. Slowly pour in the cream and whisk to incorporate. Let this mixture simmer and thicken for a few minutes, until it's thick enough to coat the back of a spoon.

**9.** Add the lobster meat and remaining 1 tablespoon of seaweed butter. Season to taste with salt and pepper if needed, and let the mixture return to a simmer to heat the lobster meat through, about 3 to 5 minutes. Add the tarragon and a squeeze of lemon juice.

**10.** Place the lobster shells on a baking sheet. Divide the filling evenly between the two shells, top with the breadcrumbs, and place in the oven. When the mixture is bubbling and the breadcrumbs are golden brown, remove from the oven.

**11.** To serve, place the filled lobster shells on a platter with the corn and serve the cabbage slaw on the side.

*\* Instead of boiling the lobster whole, you can slice it in half lengthwise and grill it over an open fire, like I did in Maine.*

**5.** Make the **lobster thermidor:** Bring a large pot of water to a boil. Add the whole lobster and boil for 8 minutes.\* Remove from the water and when cool enough to handle, cut in half and clean.

**6.** Remove all the meat from the lobster, reserving the shell. Cut the meat into ½-inch pieces.

**7.** Set a large skillet over medium heat and add the oil. Once hot, add the shallot and sauté until tender, about 2 to 3 minutes. Add the garlic and season with a large pinch of salt and cook for about 1 more minute until the garlic is fragrant. Add a splash of sherry and stir to deglaze, scraping up

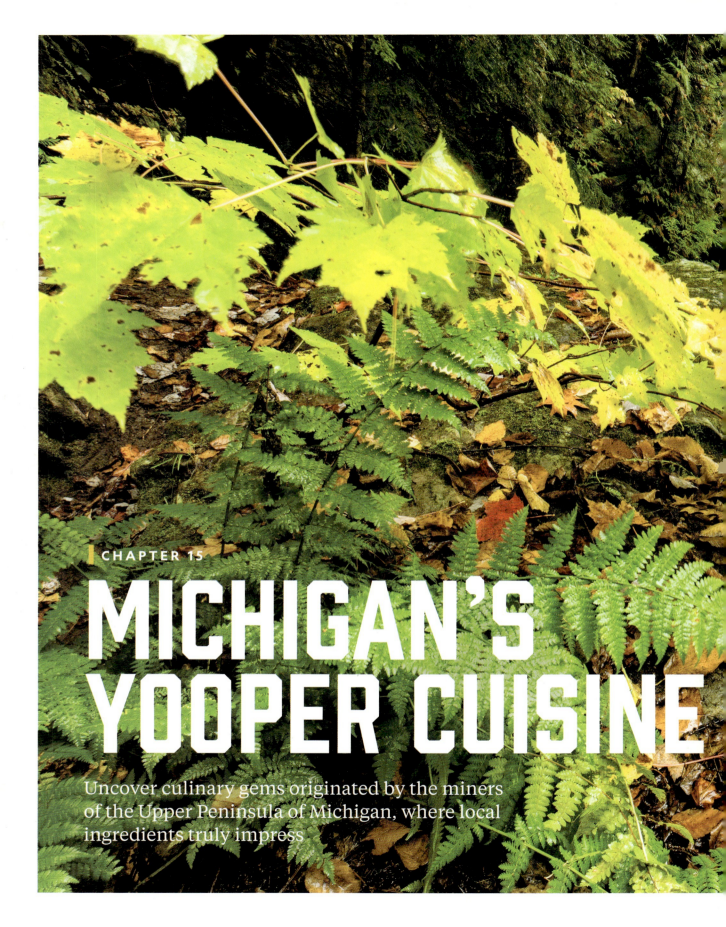

# CHAPTER 15

# MICHIGAN'S YOOPER CUISINE

Uncover culinary gems originated by the miners of the Upper Peninsula of Michigan, where local ingredients truly impress

A lush canopy of ferns and vines drapes Hungarian Falls in Michigan's Keweenaw Peninsula.

A quiet moment on Lake Fanny Hooe near Copper Harbor, Michigan

**I**N THE HEART OF THE GREAT LAKES, the remote Upper Peninsula (UP) of Michigan is blessed with natural beauty. Here residents rely on hard work to enjoy the area's best ingredients. Bounded on three sides by lakes—Lake Superior to the north, Lake Michigan to the south, and Lake Huron to the east—the UP has a sense of solitude. It was only in 1957 that the two peninsulas, Upper and Lower, were connected by the Mackinac Bridge. Considering the peninsula accounts for 28 percent of Michigan's landmass yet only about 3 percent of its population, residents have deep experience with self-sufficiency. ¶ The mountainous, isolated peninsula has a rich mining heritage that has influenced the regional cuisine—from easy-to-pack foods for taking into the mines to seasonal delicacies that are foraged, fished, or hunted despite the weather's temperament. Comfort

## NAVIGATOR

### THE STOP

In the Upper Peninsula (UP) of Michigan, there are lessons to be learned from watching the weather and from deep roots in the region's mining history.

### THE GEOGRAPHY

The heavily forested UP of Michigan—on the border of Ontario, Canada—is bounded by three of the Great Lakes and has nearly 4,300 inland lakes.

### FOOD FACT

Pasties, or meat pies, were typical miner's food, used as an easy lunch to be heated over a lantern's flame.

Erik Strazzinski introduces Gordon to his assistant for the day's hunt: Chip, a Llewellin setter.

## Yoopers are proud of their resilience in the face of the natural elements and their rugged life.

foods eaten back in mining days still inspire the cuisine here. And "Yoopers" (the self-proclaimed nickname of UP residents) are proud of their resilience in the face of the natural elements and their rugged life among the UP woodlands, waterfalls, and icy trout streams.

"Being in the UP makes you in tune with nature," said chef James Rigato as we sat around a campfire near an abandoned copper mine in the Keweenaw

TRAVEL 101

## MEAT-AND-BEER KIND OF STATE

**M**ichigan ranks sixth in the United States in breweries, microbreweries, and brewpubs, with nearly 400 throughout the state. Be sure to try some of the Great Lakes State's amazing variety of brews and discover why the Michigan Brewers Guild calls it the "Great Beer State." If your travels include the Upper Peninsula, don't miss a chance to taste a pasty, which are similar to ones we have in Cornwall. These savory meat pies are not only absolutely delicious; they also happen to go really well with beer. See whether your allegiance aligns best with those who prefer gravy or ketchup with their pasties.

Peninsula, the northernmost part of Michigan's UP. The Michigan native, James Beard Award semifinalist, and owner of Mabel Gray restaurant in Hazel Park admitted that the best meals eaten in the region are likely to be outdoors, over a campfire. "You're paying attention to the weather and seasons. That's what I love about it—listening to Mother Nature, which is harder and harder to tap into in the modern world," James said.

The fall and winter storms that lash Lake Superior bring not only intense weather but also significant wave height on the lake. Being in tune with nature and weather conditions is essential for living and finding food here.

The largest of the Great Lakes and the world's largest body of freshwater (by surface area), Lake Superior is home to more than 80 fish species, luring anglers from around the country. Lake trout is among the most popular catch, along with steelhead, brown trout, brook trout, and splake (a cross between brook and lake trout)—but salmon, whitefish, walleye, northern pike, and smallmouth bass are also on anglers' lists.

With a reputation of being a trash fish, the burbot (also known as eelpout) is widely misunderstood; it's common in some places for burbot to be caught and discarded on the ice by ice fishers. But the fish is the only freshwater member of the cod family, and despite its less-than-beautiful appearance, when boiled and dipped in butter it's supposed to taste like lobster, earning the nickname "poor man's lobster."

Smoked fish is a staple of roadside stands in the UP, and if you're lucky, you'll get a whiff of that fish smoking as you pull up. Many Yoopers prefer a

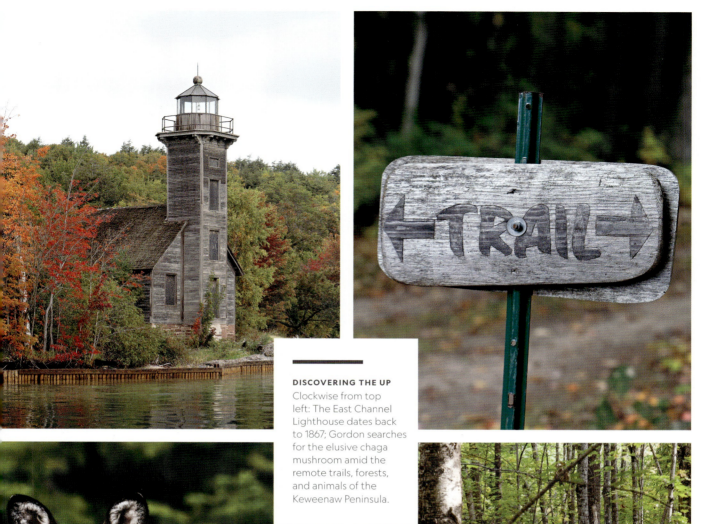

**DISCOVERING THE UP**
Clockwise from top left: The East Channel Lighthouse dates back to 1867; Gordon searches for the elusive chaga mushroom amid the remote trails, forests, and animals of the Keweenaw Peninsula.

# PRESERVING THE LORD'S WORK

Father Ephrem and his fellow monks at the Holy Protection Monastery produce Poorrock Abbey preserves made from wild berries picked on-site on the Keweenaw Peninsula, the northernmost part of Michigan's UP. The Jampot, run by the monastery, also sells candies, chocolates, cookies, fruitcakes, and muffins. One of the standout products is their thimbleberry preserves, with a delicious tart-sweet flavor and beautiful colors. "Thimbleberry season is about six weeks if you're lucky," Father Ephrem told me, and I'm glad the monks are out there doing the Lord's work every thimbleberry season.

The monastery that Father Ephrem calls home produces a unique jam made from local thimbleberries.

Gordon and Father Ephrem share jam and tea made during thimbleberry season.

waterside picnic of freshly smoked whitefish straight from its wrapping paper and a stack of saltines. Others enjoy smoked fish dip, or even fish sliced thinly with red onion and cream cheese on a bagel. Different fisheries have signature tastes that depend on the fish, seasonings, the type of wood used in smoking, and whether they've hot- or cold-smoked the catch. Food truck owner and chef Cap'n Ron told me he used "Cap'n Ron's flavor"—whatever that is, it worked wonderfully.

On land, the tiny, quail-size woodcock is a member of the shorebird family that has adapted to live in upland forests. More woodcocks nest and hatch in Michigan than in any other state in the United States. Along with grouse, woodcock is a preferred choice on hunters' lists in the UP, but the flavor is distinctly

different. A dark-meat bird, it has a strong, rich taste that is reminiscent of waterfowl.

The original fast food of UP miners is the pasty, a savory meat pie. Pasties were brought over more than 150 years ago by British miners from Cornwall. They taste of history in a pastry shell filled with varied ingredients—potato, onion, rutabaga, and beef. Pasties were carried into the mine and reheated on a shovel over

---

## INSIDER KNOWLEDGE

# CAP'N RON

Ron Matson, known to most Yoopers as Cap'n Ron, is a fifth-generation commercial fisherman who has worked on Lake Superior since he was 11 years old. By the time Ron was 18, he was the captain of his own boat, and he has been sailing on Lake Superior for more than 50 years. Ron's great-great grandfather started Matson's Fisheries in Munising in 1898, with one of the first commercial fishing licenses in Michigan. The family, tribal fishers for generations before that, comes from the Grand Island Band in the Sault Ste. Marie Tribe of Chippewa Indians.

Like his ancestors who smoked fish to preserve food, Cap'n Ron has perfected his practice of smoking fresh whitefish and lake trout. He started the Cap'n Ron's Fish & Chips food truck to

Cap'n Ron demonstrates sausage stuffing.

sell smoked fish dip, fried fish baskets, fish sandwiches, and smoked fish sausages—all his own recipes. Ron told me that he'd put his smoked fish sausage up against anyone else's, and now that I've tasted it, I understand why. The spice is perfect, and the smoke gives it such incredible flavor.

lantern candles. The practical dish with working-class roots generally isn't seasoned with anything but salt and pepper, and the combination of protein and complex carbohydrates is all about sustenance. A long-standing debate exists between serving pasties with gravy or ketchup (but not both), and it's a tension that families grow up with and that fuels strong opinions.

Small, delicate thimbleberries grow wild in the UP, and like that of raspberries, their tart flavor is used in beloved local jams and jellies. The bright-red fruit has a hollow core, making the berries easy to fit on the tip of your finger like a thimble. Thimbleberries are smaller and softer than raspberries, and the sweet-tart taste is wonderful when you can just pop them in your mouth after picking, but they're also ideal in preserves, smoothies, and baked goods like cookies and scones.

Chaga mushrooms look more like clumps of dirt than traditional mushrooms, but this nutrient-dense superfood that grows on birch trees is packed with vitamins and is beloved by foragers. Many people drink tea made from chaga, and the deep floral, earthy flavor is actually quite delicious. After foraging in the UP forest, I tasted chaga tea with orange and honey, which tasted almost like a nonalcoholic deep-woods cocktail. Brewed chaga can be added to the dough or batter of cookies and cakes, to stock in soups and sauces, and even mixed into coffee.

Here in the Upper Peninsula, it took the resourcefulness and long experience of living among the natural elements to determine the true flavor of the region. In this wonderfully remote place where residents call Michiganders living south of them "trolls," the cuisine is some of the most delicious comfort food out there.

# SMOKED WHITEFISH CROSTINI
## WITH FENNEL CONFIT AND CUDIGHI SAUSAGE

**YIELDS:** 6 SERVINGS

### FENNEL CONFIT

1½ cups blended oil*

1 fennel bulb, trimmed and sliced in half lengthwise

1 lemon, peeled with a peeler

### SMOKED WHITEFISH SPREAD

2 tablespoons shallots, finely minced

2 ounces capers, rinsed and chopped

½ lemon, zested and juiced

3 ounces crème fraîche

8 ounces smoked whitefish, flaked

3 sprigs fresh dill, finely chopped

Kosher salt

Freshly ground black pepper

### FOR SERVING

Crusty baguette

Extra-virgin olive oil

½ lemon, plus 1 lemon cut into wedges

Fresh picked dill, chopped

1 link grilled cudighi sausage, sliced

## DIRECTIONS

**1.** Make the **fennel confit:** Bring the oil to a light simmer in a medium pot, then add the fennel and lemon peel and simmer until the fennel is tender, about 45 to 60 minutes. Remove the fennel from the pot and let cool on a cutting board. Discard the oil and lemon peel. After the fennel is completely cool, dice it into small pieces.

**2.** Make the **smoked whitefish spread:** In a medium bowl, mix the shallots, capers, lemon zest and juice, and crème fraîche until incorporated. Fold in the smoked whitefish, dill, and fennel confit. Season with salt and pepper.

**3.** Slice the baguette into 1-inch-thick pieces, brush with olive oil, and toast both sides under a broiler or in a grill pan.

**4.** To serve, place a heaping spoonful of the whitefish spread on each baguette slice and finish with a big squeeze of lemon. Garnish with dill and top with a slice of grilled sausage. Serve with lemon wedges.

*Blended oil can be bought or made easily at home. I recommend a 75 percent olive oil and 25 percent vegetable oil blend for a flavorful yet not overpowering oil that has a higher smoke point.*

# PAN-SEARED LAKE TROUT
## WITH GRILLED SUCCOTASH AND CREAMY CELERIAC AND CARROT PUREE

**YIELDS:** 2 SERVINGS

### CREAMY CELERIAC AND CARROT PUREE

**1 pound celeriac root, peeled and roughly chopped**

**3 carrots, peeled and roughly chopped**

**4 tablespoons unsalted butter, divided**

**2 cups whole milk**

**Kosher salt**

**Freshly ground black pepper**

### GRILLED CORN AND BELL PEPPER SUCCOTASH

**2 red bell peppers**

**Extra-virgin olive oil**

**2 ears corn, shucked**

**½ cup finely diced red onion**

**1 garlic clove, finely minced**

**Kosher salt**

**Freshly ground black pepper**

**1 lime, halved**

**2 tablespoons fresh cilantro, minced**

### PAN-SEARED LAKE TROUT

**2 5-ounce trout fillets, pin bones removed**

**Extra-virgin olive oil**

**Kosher salt**

**Freshly ground black pepper**

**2 tablespoons unsalted butter**

**2 sprigs fresh thyme**

**2 garlic cloves, smashed**

## ▌ DIRECTIONS

**1.** Make the **puree:** In a medium pan, sauté the celeriac and carrot in 1 tablespoon of the butter over medium-high heat until caramelized. Add the milk and remaining butter. Reduce the heat to medium-low and cover. Cook until the vegetables are extremely tender. Puree in a blender or food processor until smooth. Season with salt and pepper to taste.

**2.** Make the **succotash:** Set the broiler to high. Coat the bell peppers with oil and spread them in a single layer on a sheet pan. Broil in the oven, frequently turning the peppers until they are charred on all sides. Remove and set aside to cool. Once cool enough to handle, peel the peppers, remove the stems and seeds, and dice the peppers into small pieces. Brush the corn with olive oil and place on a sheet pan. Broil the corn, rotating it until it is charred on all sides. Once cool enough to handle, slice the kernels off the cob. Drizzle a large nonstick pan with more olive oil and sauté the onion until tender. Add the garlic, diced peppers, and corn kernels and toss to coat. Season with salt, pepper, and a squeeze of lime juice. Remove from the heat and stir in the cilantro.

**3.** Make the **lake trout:** Using a sharp paring knife, score the skin side of each trout fillet by making 3 incisions about 2 inches long and ½ inch apart. Brush with olive oil and season with salt and pepper on each side.

**4.** Heat a large sauté pan over high heat, drizzle lightly with olive oil, and carefully place each fillet in the pan. Allow the skin to crisp and become golden brown, about 2 minutes. Add the butter to the pan, reduce the heat slightly, and melt the butter until it's "foamy." Add the thyme and garlic to the pan. Baste the flesh of the fish with the melted butter until cooked through.

**5.** Remove from the heat and serve immediately over the warm puree, crispy-skin side up. Garnish with the succotash.

# MAPLE CHAGA–GLAZED CORNISH HENS

## WITH RED WINE RASPBERRY–BRAISED ROOT VEGETABLES

**YIELDS:** 4 SERVINGS

MAPLE-CHAGA GLAZE

½ cup pure maple syrup

3 tablespoons chaga mushroom powder*

CORNISH HENS

4 Cornish game hens or California baby quail, quartered

Kosher salt

Freshly ground black pepper

RED WINE RASPBERRY–BRAISED VEGETABLES

5 baby Japanese, or Tokyo, turnips, sliced in half

Kosher salt

Freshly ground pepper

8 baby carrots, trimmed and sliced in half lengthwise

¼ cup finely diced red onion

3 garlic cloves, finely minced

1 cup red wine, such as a red Burgundy or pinot

2 cups chicken stock

½ cup fresh raspberries

2 tablespoons fresh local raspberry jam

2 cups mixed beet and turnip greens, trimmed and sliced into ½-inch strips

## ▌ DIRECTIONS

**1.** Make the **maple-chaga glaze:** Whisk together the maple syrup and chaga mushroom powder until smooth. Set aside, reserving half for serving.

**2.** Preheat your oven to 375°F. Place a sheet pan rack on top of a baking sheet and set aside.

**3.** Make the **Cornish hens:** Season the hen quarters liberally with salt and pepper. Heat a Dutch oven over medium-high heat and sear the hens skin side down until the skin is golden brown and starts to crisp and render. Remove from the pot and set the pot aside (do not clean) and place the hens on the baking sheet rack, skin side up. Brush with the maple-chaga glaze and roast in the oven until cooked through, about 20 minutes, basting frequently throughout.

**4.** Make the **braised vegetables:** In the same pot used for the hens, sear the turnips cut side down in the rendered hen fat and cook over medium heat until golden brown. Season with salt and pepper and remove from the pot. Add the carrots and sear until golden and cook until caramelized and tender, then set aside with the turnips. Sauté the onion until caramelized and tender, about 5 to 7 minutes, then add the garlic and cook until fragrant, about 30 seconds.

**5.** Deglaze the pot with the red wine, scraping up any caramelized bits, and pour in the chicken stock and simmer until thickened and reduced by half. Stir in the raspberries and raspberry jam, mashing the raspberries slightly. Season with salt and pepper to taste. Add the veggies back to the pot, stirring to coat with sauce. Just before serving, stir in the beet and turnip greens, tossing to coat until slightly wilted.

**6.** To serve, place a heaping spoonful of the braised vegetables on a platter and top with the glazed Cornish hen. Surround with the greens. Serve the remaining maple-chaga glaze on the side.

*Chaga mushroom powder can be found at many supermarkets and in vitamin shops.*

The wilds of the Great Smoky Mountains are home to a cuisine as diverse and historic as the landscape.

# CHAPTER 16

# THE GREAT SMOKY MOUNTAINS

A harrowing and treacherous quest to
unearth the most delicious ingredients in this
magnificent mountain range

Deep Creek Trail in
Great Smoky Mountains
National Park

T

**HE HERITAGE OF THE GREAT SMOKY MOUNTAINS** traces back thousands of years to when Indigenous peoples hunted, fished, and gathered their food here. The inventive practices of early inhabitants—from native Cherokee to formerly enslaved people to European immigrants—created a melting pot of food traditions with a strong sense of place. Even today, many residents here take pride in living like their ancestors and are fiercely tied to their land and what grows and thrives on it. ¶ Generations of mountain wisdom came from independence and resourcefulness: learning to work with the short growing season, practicing food preservation, and finding ingredients through foraging in the most biologically and botanically diverse foodshed in North America. Because of the care that has been taken over the years—through the practices of people who continue the legacy of seed saving, foraging, and

**NAVIGATOR**

**THE STOP**

Moonshine, foraged mushrooms, trout, and pig are just a few of the secret ingredients behind the sauce of the Great Smoky Mountains' food scene.

**THE GEOGRAPHY**

The Great Smoky Mountains are part of the Appalachian chain. Within Great Smoky Mountains National Park, peaks reach more than 5,000 feet (1,520 m) tall.

**FOOD FACT**

America's first legal moonshine distillery, Piedmont Distillers out of Madison, North Carolina, opened in 2005.

Gordon pours a water-corn mixture into a moonshine still deep in the woods.

> ## "The Smoky Mountain region is one of the most biodiverse places on the planet."
>
> —Chef William Dissen

hunting in the Smoky Mountains—traditions endure even while culinary methods evolve.

"It's like a little 'foodtopia,'" chef William Dissen told me after I rappelled down a 50-foot (15 m) waterfall to meet him for some fly-fishing. The award-winning chef, who is the owner and executive chef of The Market Place in Asheville, North Carolina, works with a network of local farmers, fishers, and artisan producers to create dishes from some of the best products in the area. "The Smoky Mountain region is one of the most biodiverse places on the planet," he said. "It's likely one of the reasons the Cherokee

people settled here so long ago. There are four very temperate seasons, clear water, fertile soil, wild fish in the streams, wild game in the forest, and edible and medicinal plants growing everywhere."

Learning to live with the land, native Cherokee used dried maize to make hominy. Soaking the corn kernels over heat in an alkaline substrate made from water and the lye in hardwood ash is a process called nixtamalization, which produces a number of changes in the corn—the most significant being that it heightens humans' ability to digest and absorb its inherent nutrients, such as lysine, tryptophan amino

---

LOCAL FLAVOR

## MAKING THE MOST OF LIVERMUSH

**M**att Helms, head butcher and co-owner of the Chop Shop Butchery in Asheville, showed me how to make livermush—an Appalachian staple. The savory sliced loaf is made from pork liver, scrap meat, spices, and cornmeal. "It's the Southern cousin of pâté," Matt said. "But instead of having a panade in it, it's got cornmeal as a binder." While livermush is popular in breakfast dishes, it is also paired with grilled onions in sandwiches and used as a pizza topping. The affordable dish is a good example of using all the parts of an animal without letting anything go to waste.

**Matt Helms and Gordon whip up a batch of livermush.**

**ADVENTURE AWAITS**
Clockwise from top left: Bacon sizzles on an outdoor grill; Gordon rappels down the side of a waterfall; mushroom-crusted trees stand tall in the forest; Gordon fly-fishes with local legend William Dissen.

# HOMINY HISTORY WITH MALIA CROWE

The land once inhabited by Malia Crowe's ancestors was vast, spreading from North Carolina through Alabama, Georgia, Kentucky, South Carolina, Tennessee, Virginia, and West Virginia. Malia lives in the Qualla Boundary in North Carolina, a small piece of that original territory, inhabited by the AniKituhwa, the preferred term for the Cherokee people. Corn has a prominent role among the AniKituhwa where *selu* is both the word for "corn" in the Tsalagi (Cherokee) language and the name of the Corn Mother, who gave of herself so the people would have sustenance in the matrilineal society. Selu is deeply rooted in the culture's ceremonies, beliefs, and economy.

Hominy is used in several sweet and savory dishes in the AniKituhwa community, from being ground into cornmeal to make bread and dumplings to being used whole in soups and stews that often also include beans. "The three sisters—corn, beans, and squash—are planted together so the corn gives the beans a stalk to climb and grow, beans give the roots of the corn and squash nitrogen to keep the soil healthy, and spiny squash leaves protect the plants and roots," Malia said. "That shows our strong belief in *gadugi*—everyone helping each other and being community-minded."

**Malia Crowe teaches Gordon how to prepare hominy.**

**THE BIG COOK**
The table is set—with
an incredible view—and
ready for guests to judge
the meals.

acids, and niacin. It also loosens the hulls from the kernels and softens the corn. After it's rinsed, the clean hominy can be prepared for a meal or dried for later use because nixtamalization keeps the corn from sprouting and allows dried hominy to be stored for long periods of time.

The range of climates and elevations, old-growth forests, and protected lands in these mountains allow for many wild, edible mushrooms to thrive. I was lucky to have expert forager Alan Muskat along with me in the woods so I didn't wind up with a deadly mushroom by accident. The pale, tan hen-of-the-woods (also known as maitake) mushroom grows on the bases of trees in shelflike clusters that resemble the tail feathers of a sitting hen. We found a prize specimen that looked like a beautiful work of art—and was ultimately one of the best-tasting mushrooms I've ever had. There's no way I was going to pass up using it in one of my dishes for the Big Cook.

Fly-fishing is allowed year-round in the Smoky Mountains, and there are plenty of clear, quiet streams to find trout (wild brook, brown, and rainbow varieties). Trout has kept mountain people alive for generations. The versatile ingredient—whether grilled, smoked, or pan-fried—pairs well with a variety of seasonal produce.

Turn over a rock in most North Carolina streams in summer, and you're likely to spy a crayfish darting backward to get away. The common freshwater crustacean is found throughout the entire state. North Carolina is home to more than 40 species of freshwater crayfish, many of which are found nowhere else on earth. The number of crayfish you find in a waterway is often a good indicator of that waterway's health. Using a little bit of bacon and the ingenuity of a simple six-dollar trap that includes an empty cheese ball container and a Gatorade bottle, kayaker Keith Sprinkle showed me how he catches crayfish. We caught plenty with those low-tech traps.

North Carolina is the second largest producer of hogs in the United States, so pork finds its way into more than a few dishes here. A breakfast staple in the western part of the state, livermush is a puree of pig's liver and spices bound with cornmeal to make it moldable and sliceable—like pâté. While store-bought versions are typically fully cooked, slices are often seared in a cast-iron skillet before they are used to top a biscuit, tucked between toast slices, or eaten with a side of eggs. The ready-made food was an easy choice for those who needed an affordable, filling, and tasty start to their day. And despite the unappetizing name, livermush is truly delicious.

Moonshine—illegal, untaxed whiskey—has been part of North Carolina lore for centuries; however, it became a big business after 1908, when the state adopted the prohibition of alcohol a decade before the rest of the United States. NASCAR has its roots in moonshine—distillers enhanced their stock cars to boost their smuggling and driving performance and speed in order to outrun the law. Nowadays, there is a growing legal moonshine industry, with the number of craft distillers increasing each year. One of those distillers showed me how it was made back in the day, with no shortcuts. After grinding corn, we drove through the snaking backroads to his still's hidden location in the woods, where we cooked the mash and then distilled it. The result was a 100-proof whiskey that made me feel like a flamethrower.

Every layer I peeled away in the Great Smoky Mountains was fascinating, and the ingredients found there are among the best-kept culinary secrets in the world. The land still provides here, thanks to those who've practiced and advanced food traditions for many generations. I've only scratched the surface of the biodiverse region's incredible food history, and I know there's much more I can learn.

INSIDER KNOWLEDGE

## APPALACHIAN ROOTS

Chef William Dissen's childhood spent in the Appalachian Mountains of West Virginia has always been a major influence on his life. Just as his grandmother's garden-to-table meals were, his approach to food has been inspired by the region's dedication to sustainable agriculture and local cuisine and its celebration of beloved flavors and customs. After graduating from the Culinary Institute of America, William worked in kitchens in West Virginia, California, and South Carolina before heading to Asheville, North Carolina. He is the owner and executive

**Chef William Dissen explains the preparation of an aged country ham.**

chef of The Market Place, where he continues to focus on sustainable, farm-fresh, and locally sourced ingredients.

# LIVERMUSH BISCUITS
## WITH PICKLED ONIONS AND MUSHROOMS

**YIELDS:** 6 SERVINGS

### PICKLED ONIONS AND MUSHROOMS

1 red onion, thinly sliced

1 cup shimeji mushrooms

2 cups champagne vinegar

½ cup granulated sugar

### LIVERMUSH BISCUITS

3 tablespoons blended oil, divided*

8 ounces livermush or pâté or country terrine

3 biscuits, cut in half

6 fresh quail eggs

1 teaspoon kosher salt

1 teaspoon freshly ground black pepper

2 tablespoons whole-grain mustard

Flat-leaf parsley, chopped

### DIRECTIONS

**1.** Make the **pickled onions and mushrooms:** Combine the onions and mushrooms in a medium bowl. In a small pot over medium heat, add the vinegar and sugar and bring the mixture to a boil.

**2.** Once the sugar has dissolved, pour the mixture over the onions and mushrooms and let sit at room temperature until cooled. Refrigerate until ready to use.

**3.** Make the **livermush biscuits:** In a large sauté pan over medium-high heat, add 1 tablespoon of the blended oil.

**4.** Slice the livermush into ½-inch pieces and place in the pan. Sear both sides until crispy, about 2 to 3 minutes per side. Remove the livermush from the pan and set aside. Do not drain the fat from the pan.

**5.** In the same pan, toast the biscuits, cut side down, in the remaining fat. Remove the biscuits from the pan.

**6.** Add the remaining 2 tablespoons of oil and crack each quail egg into the pan. Fry the eggs and season with the salt and pepper.

**7.** To serve, spread mustard on each biscuit and layer with the seared livermush, fried egg, and pickled onions and mushrooms. Garnish with parsley.

*\* Blended oil can be bought or made easily at home. I recommend a 75 percent olive oil and 25 percent vegetable oil blend for a flavorful yet not overpowering oil that has a higher smoke point.*

# BUTTERED CRAWFISH
## WITH CHEDDAR CHEESE GRITS

**YIELDS:** 2 SERVINGS

CHEDDAR CHEESE GRITS

2  cups unsalted seafood stock*

1  cup stone-ground grits, white or yellow

1  cup heavy cream

1  cup shredded sharp cheddar cheese

Kosher salt

Freshly ground black pepper

BUTTERED CRAWFISH

3  tablespoons unsalted butter

1  shallot, finely minced

1  garlic clove, minced

2  cups picked crawfish meat, fresh or frozen and defrosted

Apple moonshine or apple brandy

½  lemon, zested and juiced

1  scallion, thinly sliced

## DIRECTIONS

**1.** To make the **cheddar cheese grits:** In a medium pot, bring the seafood stock to a boil over high heat. Whisk in the grits and reduce the heat to low. Cover and simmer for 20 minutes, whisking frequently to prevent clumping and scorching. Whisk in the cream. Continue to cook until the grits are tender, about 5 to 10 minutes more. Remove from the heat and sprinkle in the cheddar cheese. Taste and season with salt and pepper, as needed.

**2.** Make the **buttered crawfish:** Heat a large skillet over medium-high heat. Add the butter to the pan and melt. Add the shallot and garlic, cooking until tender and fragrant. Add the crawfish and toss to coat. Deglaze the pan with a couple of splashes of apple moonshine, scraping up any brown bits from the bottom. Simmer until the liquid is glossy, about 3 to 5 minutes. Remove from the heat and stir in the lemon zest and juice.

**3.** To serve, ladle the grits into two bowls and top with the buttered crawfish. Garnish with the sliced scallion.

*Seafood stock tends to be a bit on the saltier side, so be sure to taste before seasoning with salt, especially with the addition of heavy cream and cheddar, which can also be salty.*

# HONEY-ROASTED HEIRLOOM SQUASH
## WITH BROWN BUTTER MUSHROOMS

**YIELDS:** 2–4 SERVINGS

### HONEY-ROASTED HEIRLOOM SQUASH

1  heirloom squash, such as Silver Moon or red kuri, sliced in half and seeds removed*

Kosher salt

Freshly ground black pepper

3  tablespoons local honey, divided

Extra-virgin olive oil

Chili flakes, optional

2  tablespoons white wine vinegar

### BROWN BUTTER MUSHROOMS

1  pound assorted mushrooms, such as hen-of-the-woods, chicken-of-the-woods, or trumpet, trimmed and cleaned

Extra-virgin olive oil

Kosher salt

Freshly ground black pepper

8  tablespoons (1 stick) unsalted butter, divided

2  shallots, finely diced

2  garlic cloves, minced

1  Fresno chili pepper, seeded and thinly sliced

2  sprigs fresh sage

1  small bunch chives, thinly sliced

### DIRECTIONS

**1.** Make the **heirloom squash:** Preheat your oven to 400°F. Line a baking sheet with foil and set aside.

**2.** Prepare the squash by slicing it lengthwise into 1-inch-thick strips. Toss the squash slices into a bowl and season generously with salt and pepper. Drizzle with 2 tablespoons of the honey and 1 or 2 tablespoons of olive oil, enough to lightly coat the squash. Sprinkle with a pinch of chili flakes, if using, and scatter on the prepared baking sheet in a single layer.

**3.** Roast the squash for 20 to 30 minutes, until caramelized and tender, turning halfway through. Remove from the oven and drizzle the squash slices with the white wine vinegar and remaining 1 tablespoon of honey. Set aside.

**4.** Make the **brown butter mushrooms:** Break the mushrooms into 1-inch pieces with your hands. Toss together with about 2 tablespoons olive oil, enough to lightly coat. Season with salt and pepper and set aside. Heat a skillet over medium-high heat and add 2 tablespoons of the butter. Once the butter is melted, add the shallots and garlic and sauté until fragrant and tender. Add the mushrooms to the skillet along with the chili pepper and continue to cook until the mushrooms are tender and begin to brown, about 3 to 5 minutes per side. Remove the mushroom mixture from the skillet and set aside.

**5.** Reduce the heat to medium and add the remaining 6 table-spoons of butter and the sage sprigs to the skillet. To brown the butter, continually stir, scraping the bottom of the pan with a wooden spoon to scrape up the brown bits. Keep stirring until the butter begins to foam and sizzle around the edges, about 5 to 8 minutes. Set aside to let cool slightly. Remove and discard the sage sprigs and skim off any white film that rises to the top.

**6.** Add the mushrooms and squash to the skillet and toss to coat.

**7.** Serve family style, garnished with the chives.

*\* Butternut, acorn, or kabocha squash may be used instead.*

# HOMINY AND PINTO BEAN STEW
## WITH SMOKED HAM HOCK

**YIELDS:** 6 SERVINGS

½ **pound thick-cut bacon, cut into lardons**

1 **yellow onion, diced small**

2 **carrots, peeled and diced small**

2 **stalks of celery, diced small**

1 **leek, cleaned and diced small**

2 **garlic cloves, minced**

2 **ounces tomato paste**

4 **cups dried pinto beans, soaked overnight and drained**

2 **cups canned hominy, drained and rinsed**

**Kosher salt**

**Freshly ground black pepper**

1½ **cups red wine**

1 **smoked ham hock***

4 **cups chicken stock**

3–4 **fresh thyme sprigs**

1 **fresh bay leaf**

2–4 **tablespoons apple cider vinegar**

**Scallions, thinly sliced**

**DIRECTIONS**

**1.** Heat a large stockpot over medium-high heat. Add the bacon and render until it starts to brown. Add the onion, carrots, celery, leek, and garlic to the pot, stirring to coat with bacon fat. Sauté until tender and caramelized, about 5 minutes.

**2.** Stir in the tomato paste and scrape the bottom of the pot with a wooden spoon to release all of the brown bits. Cook until the tomato paste is lightly brown and toasted, about 2 to 3 minutes.

**3.** Add the pinto beans and hominy to the pot. Season with salt and pepper and stir to coat.

**4.** Add the red wine to deglaze the pot, scraping the bottom with a wooden spoon to release all of the brown bits. Heat to a simmer and cook until the liquid is reduced by half. Add the ham hock to the pot, followed by the stock, thyme sprigs, and bay leaf. Cover and simmer for about 1 hour or until the beans are tender and the liquid has thickened into a stew. Add the apple cider vinegar, to taste.

**5.** Remove the ham hock from the pot and transfer to a cutting board. Once cool enough to handle, remove the meat from the bone and cut into bite-size pieces, discarding the bone, fat, skin, and cartilage. Add the meat back to the pot and stir to combine. Remove and discard the bay leaf and thyme sprigs.

**6.** Ladle the stew into bowls and garnish with scallions. Serve warm.

*\* If you can't find ham hocks at your local grocery store, opt for ½ pound of smoked bacon instead.*

Gordon checks out the view during the Big Cook in the heart of South Central Texas.

# CHAPTER 17

# TEXAS THROWDOWN

Herding cattle, catching rattlesnakes, and hunting feral hogs
give new meaning to "Texas tough" in the Lone Star State

Longhorn cattle
catch the sunrise
from the field.

**T**EXANS HAVE A REPUTATION for having big and bold attitudes, a reflection of the state's gargantuan size (it has the largest landmass in the continental United States). With Texas's varied and sometimes challenging terrain, which includes everything from plains to rolling hill country, combined with its unforgiving climate, the state's culture has always been about roughing it to some degree. But scratch the surface a little and there's much more here than appearances might suggest. Experiencing true Texas flavor requires digging deeply into a history that spans a variety of cultures, and it is a more diverse culinary destination than its reputation might lead you to believe. ¶ The influences of Indigenous peoples, settlers, and immigrants have shaped the food we think of as Texan. Tex-Mex food reflects Tejano cooking from Native American, Spanish, and Mexican peoples. Cajun cuisine is

Justin Yu instructs Gordon on the finer points of cutting mesquite.

## NAVIGATOR

### THE STOP

Everything is bigger in Texas—from the beef and pork to the wild ingredients that can be foraged.

### THE GEOGRAPHY

Home to a diverse ecosystem, Texas boasts sweeping plains of thorny shrubs as well as subtropical woodlands in the Rio Grande Valley in the southern part of the state.

### FOOD FACT

A wide range of cultures have influenced Texas barbecue, including African Americans in the South and immigrants from Germany.

from Acadians who immigrated from French Canada to the coasts and bayous of Louisiana and Texas. The Creole influence on Texas came from Louisiana ranchers who brought with them the food traditions of France, Spain, the Caribbean, and parts of Africa. Waves of German, Czech, and Polish immigrants settled in the center of the state and have influenced the state's barbecue. Other culinary influences came from the American South. And then there's the cowboy, raising and driving cattle across the plains—the inspiration for chuck wagon fare. It took all these cultures together to create Texan cuisine over the centuries—a unique blend from a wealth of backgrounds and experiences.

"There's a definite toughness to Texas that makes you build a level of character," said chef Justin Yu as we sat down to a bowl of his venison chili after chopping up some mesquite for firewood. The Texas native, James Beard Award winner, and chef and owner of Theodore Rex in Houston showed me that despite the tough exterior, there's room for interpretation in Texan cuisine. He's living proof, having made a popular signature chili with venison instead of beef from the state's famed cattle country.

Beef is a staple in the Texas diet. Texas cattle culture goes back to Spanish Mexico, when cattle ranching spread north into the land now known as Texas in the 16th and 17th centuries, and the earliest ranches were those of Spanish missionaries. While I certainly won't be hired on to wrangle cattle for Clint Radley, visiting his ranch helped me get a sense of the entire process and how involved his ranchers need to be to produce some of the best beef in the Lone Star State. While barbecue steak and brisket are stars on a menu in Texas, beef also shows up in a variety of Tex-Mex dishes (such as fajitas, machacado, rolled enchiladas, and tacos) that are a combination of Indigenous American and

---

INSIDER KNOWLEDGE

## NOT YOUR MAMA'S HUNT

Chef Ric Rosser is passionate about hunting, fishing, and the great outdoors—something that's added depth to his hyperlocal cuisine at Spread Oaks Ranch in Markham, Texas. He sources most of the lodge kitchen ingredients right from his ranch and is constantly on the lookout for wild seasonal foods to forage. To aid our hunt of invasive feral hogs that tear up acres of farmland, he sprayed me with an all-natural ingredient to keep mosquitoes at bay, cover up my human scent, and attract the animals. He called it "Mama's Recipe," but it smelled distinctly of hog piss.

A javelina pauses in the dry grass.

**TASTE OF TEXAS**
Gordon explores the well-guarded fruits of the prickly pear cactus (below left), known as tunas. The paddles are also edible and taste similar to green beans.

# TEXAS TOUGH WITH CHEF JUSTIN YU

**A** native Houstonian, chef Justin Yu was reared on backyard Texan classics and sharpened his skills in Michelin-starred kitchens in California and Europe before returning to his roots in the Lone Star State. The James Beard Award–winning chef rose to global acclaim with his previous restaurant, Oxheart, which he closed in 2017 and reopened six months later as Theodore Rex (known to many as T-Rex). Yu, also the chef and owner of Better Luck Tomorrow and Squable, is constantly ahead of the culinary curve, innovating relentlessly to help propel Houston to be the country's breakout dining destination.

"You have to be tough to make it in Texas," Justin said. "It's really hot down here and there are a lot of ingredients that can be tough to work with, but there are beautiful flavors and a lot of depth that you can't find in the same way anywhere else in the world."

He enjoys building on the bare-bones basics of cooking, starting with the ingredients first and building a dish around them. And he'll always root for Texas. "There's a lot of diversity in this big state, and all the flavors and layers of culture are really what makes Texas cuisine special," he said.

**Chef Justin Yu and Gordon game-plan for their cook-off at the end of the week.**

Spanish food traditions that came together in a distinct new cuisine.

Traditional corn tortillas made from hand-ground masa are essential to Tex-Mex food. Corn tortillas form the basis for many Tex-Mex dishes, from tacos to quesadillas and tostadas to chilaquiles. Masa, a dough made from corn, is prepared by soaking dried corn kernels in an alkali solution, grinding them, and then forming dough balls that most people place into a tortilla press. The tortilla press helps ensure even pressure so the tortilla turns out beautiful and round before it's cooked briefly to a light toast.

Modern Texas barbecue was influenced by southern African American cooking customs and German meat markets, as well as by Spanish *barbacoa*—a cooking method used in South Texas that involves wrapping meat and cooking it in a pit of coals. Aside from beef, a favorite local barbecue protein is pork, and

Texans' mouths will start to water when you mention barbecued ribs or smoked pulled pork. The state has more than 4 million free-ranging wild boars, which are in direct competition for resources and habitats against agriculture and native wildlife, including some endangered species. Hunters pursue invasive feral hogs to help keep their numbers under control.

Despite playing a key role in the regional ecosystem, the Western diamondback rattlesnake is often considered a pest because of its dangerous venom. Each year, thousands of the snakes are killed and thrown away when their paths cross that of humans. But with

## The influences of Indigenous peoples, settlers, and immigrants have shaped the food we think of as Texan.

its light, delicate flavor, its meat is also a food source in Texas for those who can catch one safely. I learned how to cook rattlesnake in the field, Texas style, by tucking the meat into the middle of a cactus paddle and burying it in campfire ashes—what an amazing natural way to steam a wild bite.

Harvesting parts of a prickly pear cactus can result in getting edible paddles (nopales) that taste like green beans and pink fruit called tunas that have a flavor reminiscent of pomegranate. The bounty of the land also shows in foraging for wild ingredients, such as petite native pecans that have a slightly tannic flavor with a buttery sweetness perfect for pralines or pecan pie. The pecan tree is Texas's state tree and is typically found along the banks of rivers and streams as well as in fertile bottomlands. The pecan is the only commercially grown nut in Texas, although I preferred to find my own through foraging. Foragers also hunt for wild onion, with its tiny flowers and sweet bulb that can be enjoyed raw or cooked as seasoning.

Before embarking on my quest to find out whether everything is truly bigger in Texas, I knew Texans were a breed of their own. But never in my wildest dreams did I know that they possess that much grit. With the wealth of ingredients from the land, many cultures have come together to make a cuisine that is unique to the region and is the basis of a strong sense of pride and love. I'm glad I messed with Texas enough to discover a deeper understanding of what it means to be a Texan.

### LOCAL FLAVOR
## HEIRLOOM TRADITIONS

After migrating with his family from Mexico to Houston at nine years old, Emmanuel Chavez accompanied his parents to their workplaces in restaurants, developing a curiosity for the industry. When he moved to Seattle for a few years, there weren't many Mexican restaurants in his neighborhood. So to find a taste of home, he immersed himself in nixtamalization—the process of adding an alkali solution to dried corn kernels to transform them into nixtamal, a product that releases essential nutrients. In Mexican food, nixtamalization is the foundation of everything. When Emmanuel returned to Houston, he founded his business, Tatemó, to showcase the diversity of heirloom corn.

**Emmanuel Chavez gives Gordon a lesson on how to make the perfect masa.**

# COFFEE AND
# ANCHO CHILI–RUBBED RIB EYE
## WITH NOPALES CHIMICHURRI
## AND CRISPY POTATOES

## COFFEE AND ANCHO CHILI-RUBBED RIB EYE

**2 tablespoons finely ground coffee or espresso**

**1 tablespoon ancho chili powder**

**2 teaspoons smoked paprika**

**3 tablespoons brown sugar**

**1 teaspoon mustard powder**

**2 tablespoons Aleppo pepper**

**1 teaspoon dried ginger**

**1 teaspoon kosher salt**

**1 teaspoon freshly ground black pepper**

**2 16- to 20-ounce bone-in rib eye steaks, 1½–2 inches thick**

**Extra-virgin olive oil**

## CRISPY POTATOES

**1 pound fingerling potatoes**

**Kosher salt**

**Extra-virgin olive oil**

## NOPALES CHIMICHURRI

**Vegetable oil**

**2 fresh nopales (cactus paddles)***

**½ cup finely chopped cilantro**

**½ cup finely chopped parsley**

**⅓ cup green onion, thinly sliced**

**2 garlic cloves, minced**

**1 lemon, zested and juiced**

**⅓ cup extra-virgin olive oil**

**Kosher salt**

**Freshly ground black pepper**

## DIRECTIONS

**1.** Marinate the **rib eyes:** In a small bowl, combine all the rub ingredients. Liberally season the rib eyes with 2 to 3 tablespoons each of rub and set aside to marinate at room temperature for 30 minutes to 1 hour, or up to 3 hours in the refrigerator.

**2.** Prepare the **crispy potatoes:** Place the potatoes in a large pot and cover with cool water. Season generously with salt and bring to a boil. Reduce to a simmer and cook until the potatoes are fork-tender, about 15 to 20 minutes. Drain the water and set the potatoes aside to cool on a baking sheet. Once the potatoes are cool to the touch, lightly smash them using the palm of your hand so they break open slightly. You can also use a large spoon or the bottom of a cup or mug instead. Set the potatoes aside.

**3.** Make the **nopales chimichurri:** Preheat a grill to high heat, about 400–450°F, and brush the grill lightly with vegetable oil. Place the nopales on the grill and cook until tender, turning occasionally to ensure even charring, about 5 minutes total. Set the nopales aside to cool, then chop them into small dice.

**4.** In a medium bowl, combine the chopped nopales with the cilantro, parsley, green onion, garlic, lemon zest and juice, and olive oil. Season with salt and pepper to taste.

**5.** Grill the rib eyes: Drizzle the rib eyes lightly with olive oil and grill until caramelized, about 3 to 5 minutes. Flip the rib eyes and grill for another 3 to 5 minutes or until desired temperature is reached (135°F for medium rare). Transfer the rib eyes to a plate to rest for 5 minutes before slicing off the bone and against the grain in 1-inch strips.

**6.** Cook the crispy potatoes: While the rib eyes cook, heat a heavy-duty skillet over medium-high heat and drizzle with enough olive oil to coat the bottom of the pan. Working in batches, add the potatoes and fry until golden brown and crispy, turning once. Season with a big pinch of salt.

**7.** To serve, place the sliced rib eye on plates with a heaping spoonful of crispy potatoes and top with a hefty drizzle of the nopales chimichurri.

*Jarred nopales can be used if fresh nopales are not available.*

# COFFEE AND ANCHO CHILI–RUBBED BABY BACK RIBS

## WITH TANGY YOGURT COLESLAW AND CLASSIC BARBECUE SAUCE

**YIELDS: 4 SERVINGS**

COFFEE AND ANCHO CHILI-
RUBBED BABY BACK RIBS

**2 tablespoons finely
ground coffee or
espresso**

**1 tablespoon ancho
chili powder**

**2 teaspoons smoked
paprika**

**3 tablespoons
brown sugar**

**1 teaspoon
mustard powder**

**2 tablespoons
Aleppo pepper flakes**

**1 teaspoon dried ginger**

**1 teaspoon kosher salt**

**1 teaspoon freshly
ground black pepper**

**1 rack baby back ribs
(about 3 pounds)**

CLASSIC BARBECUE SAUCE

**1 tablespoon extra-
virgin olive oil**

**1 white onion,
finely chopped**

**3 garlic cloves,
finely chopped**

**Kosher salt**

**Freshly ground black
pepper**

**2 tablespoons
brown sugar**

**1 teaspoon smoked
paprika**

**¼ cup apple cider
vinegar**

**¾ cup ketchup**

**1–2 teaspoons
Worcestershire sauce**

TANGY YOGURT
COLESLAW

**½ cup plain yogurt**

**1 tablespoon honey**

**3–4 tablespoons
apple cider vinegar**

**4–5 cups shredded
green or red cabbage
or both**

**2 green onions,
thinly sliced**

**½ cup grated apple**

**1 red onion,
thinly sliced**

**1 carrot, peeled and
shredded**

**Kosher salt**

**Freshly ground black
pepper**

**¼ cup chopped pecans,
toasted**

## DIRECTIONS

**1.** Prepare a charcoal grill for indirect grilling by lighting coals and pushing them to one side once the coals appear mostly gray.

**2.** Marinate the **ribs:** In a small bowl, combine all the rub ingredients. Generously season the ribs with rub on both sides. Set the ribs aside to marinate at room temperature for 1 hour.

**3.** Make the **barbecue sauce:** In a medium pan over medium-high heat, add the olive oil and sauté the onion and garlic until softened and just starting to caramelize. Season with salt and pepper and sprinkle with the brown sugar. Cook for about 3 minutes until the onion is caramelized and tender. Add the smoked paprika and pour in the apple cider vinegar and bring to a simmer. Cook until the liquid has reduced by half. Stir in the ketchup and Worcestershire sauce, cooking for another 2 to 3 minutes or until the sauce thickens to desired consistency. Remove the pan from the heat.

**4.** Grill the ribs: Wrap the ribs in foil and place them on the grill farthest from the coals. Cover the grill and cook for 2 to 3 hours at 250°F until ribs are tender, adding charcoal as needed to maintain the heat.

**5.** Once the ribs are tender, remove and discard the foil and return the ribs to the grill. Brush with barbecue sauce, reserving half for serving, and continue to cook for another 35 to 45 minutes, flipping occasionally and brushing with more barbecue sauce, until caramelized. Remove the ribs from the grill and let cool slightly before slicing.

**6.** Make the **coleslaw:** While the ribs cook, in a large bowl, whisk together the yogurt, honey, and apple cider vinegar until smooth. Add the cabbage, green onions, apple, red onion, and carrot and toss to combine. Season with salt and pepper.

**7.** To serve, divide the ribs between four plates and sprinkle with toasted pecans. Portion out the coleslaw and remaining barbecue sauce.

# CHAPTER 18

# LUSH & WILD PUERTO RICO

From the bright blue sea to the lush mountains of its interior, the island offers culinary riches and a new food identity

The inlets and coves of Puerto Rico's turquoise waters and white sand beaches

Gordon and shrimper Jorge experience the rainy season firsthand as they cross a narrow bridge on their way to catch shrimp in the racing river below.

**F**ROM PUERTO RICO'S MOUNTAINOUS INTERIOR to its coastal lowlands and surrounding waters, the possibilities for showcasing the island's cuisine are nearly endless. But Puerto Rico's rich variety of ingredients hasn't always been top of mind. Despite a climate that allows farmers to grow food year-round, the island imports nearly 85 percent of its food. That trend is starting to change. A renewed focus on what the land and sea provide has launched a movement of self-sustainability pioneered by food entrepreneurs who are helping to create a new culinary identity on the archipelago. ¶ Puerto Rico was a Spanish colony for more than 400 years, during which native farming traditions were overtaken by plantations of sugar and coffee, products that were mostly shipped to Europe. As fewer people were able to farm the

Tampico Beach in Culebra

## NAVIGATOR

### THE STOP

In Puerto Rico, a new movement toward food sovereignty is inspiring local flavors and new agriculture.

### THE GEOGRAPHY

The main island of Puerto Rico is just 111 miles (179 km) long and 39 miles (63 km) wide and boasts rainforest, dry forest, rivers, and waterfalls.

### FOOD FACT

Sancocho has roots in much of Latin America. Along with being a favorite in Puerto Rico, it is a national dish of the Dominican Republic.

A renewed focus on what the land and sea provide has launched a movement of self-sustainability.

land using traditional practices, more food products were imported, and the products that Puerto Ricans traditionally consumed were no longer harvested on a scale that could support the population. That colonial history established a system in which people were forced to work for someone else and were unable to become entrepreneurs.

Slavery was abolished in Puerto Rico in 1873, and the country became a U.S. territory in 1917. A cen-

tury later, Puerto Rico is still working to reinvent its food system and return to its native roots. "When you stop importing, you're creating jobs," said chef José Enrique as we made some delicious snapper ceviche on stunning Flamenco Beach on the small island of Culebra. The Puerto Rico native and chef and owner of his eponymous restaurant in San Juan is a strong believer in sustainability and utilizing what the island offers, allowing for more fresh, local ingredients to come directly from the land and surrounding waters. "You're creating passion for the land and a pride in what we can create for ourselves. After Hurricane Maria, local farming is coming back with a vengeance," he said.

Just a short distance from Puerto Rico's capital, San Juan, the Atlantic Ocean reaches its deepest point, and some of the most sought-after seafood is easily accessible from the island's shores. Because Puerto Rico doesn't have a large fishing industry, much of the local seafood is caught by independent fishers using small boats, something I learned when spearfishing for snapper in the beautiful waters off Culebra. The diversity of sea life is astounding, and local anglers have plenty to choose from. Offshore beasts like tuna, wahoo, and mahi-mahi abound at different times throughout the year. Caribbean conch, octopus, and shrimp can be found closer to shore among seagrass and reef ecosystems. Even the tiny, transparent fish known as cetí that shelter in rivers and estuaries and run from midsummer through December are part of the seafood diet in Puerto Rico.

The interior mountain rivers foster the ideal habitat for chágara, a large-clawed crayfish-like freshwater shrimp. The small edible crustacean measures about

# THE FRUITS OF LOCAL LABOR

One of the joys of traveling is getting a deeper sense of a place by enjoying the food from the destination rather than the same dishes and ingredients you can get back home. Puerto Rico has some fantastic local products that you won't easily forget, and tasting the abundance of amazing fruits—from tamarind to chironja—may very well change your life. Liquid delights abound in Puerto Rico, too. The island's volcanic soil supports delicious single-origin coffee, while Puerto Rico's rum-making tradition dates back centuries to when sugarcane production began here. If that weren't enough, a boom in craft brewing is also turning out high-quality beer.

**NATURE CALLING**
From iguanas to chágaras (river shrimp), the diversity of Puerto Rico's wildlife is just as astounding as its beauty.

## SPOTLIGHT

# LA COPA DE LA VIDA WITH DRACO ROSA

**D**raco Rosa found international fame as a teenager in the 1980s boy band Menudo. He pivoted to a successful solo career and co-wrote and produced songs for band member and friend Ricky Martin, including "Livin' la Vida Loca." Draco was diagnosed with non-Hodgkin's lymphoma in 2011 and had two stem-cell transplants. He credits changing his diet and retreating to his sanctuary, Monte Sagrado Reserve, for his recovery after cancer treatment. The experience changed his life in many ways. After nearly a decade since his last original record, he released his album *Monte Sagrado* in 2018, which won the Latin Grammy Award for Best Rock Album the next year.

Draco's Monte Sagrado Reserve in the mountains of Utuado is a 100-acre (40 ha) working coffee plantation and ecolodge retreat. Here, at more than 2,000 feet (610 m) above sea level, the temperatures are ideal for coffee growing. The organic Arabica coffee beans are harvested at the height of ripeness, dried in the sun, and roasted, making a delicious coffee that carries the terroir of the most mountainous area of Puerto Rico. Draco seems to have found the perfect place to drink from "La Copa de la Vida," celebrate health, and live in the moment.

**Draco Rosa leads Gordon through the process of separating coffee beans from their skins.**

two inches (5 cm) long and lives in ponds and rapids along rivers. They play an important role in aquatic ecosystems as part of the food chain and in recycling organic matter from plants. It's a laborious process to keep your balance in the river and hold a small net while lifting river rocks to expose the shrimp, and it can be easy to lose track of time while focusing on the next best place to search. Those fishing at rivers deep in canyons must pay special attention during the rainy season because precipitation here comes fast and hard, bringing the continual threat of mudslides and flooding.

On land, small-scale sustainable farming is driving a resurgence in locally grown produce that is helping to revitalize the local economy and improve food sovereignty. The historical reliance on food imports puts places like Puerto Rico in the position of being cut off from external resources after disastrous events, which is what happened after Hurricane Maria, when the island's ports were damaged so badly that ships couldn't dock. Farms produce organic fruit and vegetables such as okra and cassava, and farmers who maintain traditional techniques often bounce back more quickly after natural disasters.

Viandas (starchy root vegetables) and tubers such as yuca (cassava), batata (sweet potato), ñame (yam), and yautía (taro) are a big part of Puerto Rican cuisine and culture. Yuca, the root of the native cassava plant, was the principal food of the Indigenous Taíno people.

Among its many preparations, boiled yuca is mixed with escabeche sauce (a mixture of oil and vinegar) or garlicky citrus mojo dressing, and is included with other root vegetables in sancocho, a hearty beef stew.

Tropical fruits abound in Puerto Rico. Aside from the most popular and well-known fruits, such as mango, papaya, lime, and tamarind, lesser known fruits are more than worth trying. José introduced me to the chironja, a hybrid citrus that combines the flavors of orange and grapefruit. There's also the quenepa, also known as Spanish lime, with a yellow tart and tangy pulp surrounded by a tight green skin. The caimito is a purple- or green-skinned fruit with sweet, white, juicy flesh that some people know as star apple, because when it's cut in half, you see the shape of a star.

Coffee has a long history in Puerto Rico, beginning with its introduction in 1736 when the archipelago was a Spanish colony. Puerto Rico's volcanic soil coupled with shade-growing techniques at altitudes as high as 3,500 feet (1,070 m) above sea level result in extraordi-

nary flavors, especially at the tranquil Monte Sagrado Reserve. Here, Draco Rosa, a founding member of the 1980s boy band Menudo, farms his coffee in between studio sessions. The movement of self-sustainability in food touches coffee as well. Puerto Rico has struggled to produce enough coffee to keep up with local consumption and imports coffee to make up the difference in supply. But more farmers, like Draco, are focusing on high-quality, single-origin coffee, which they believe is the future of their industry.

The spirit of resilience has helped shape the cuisine of Puerto Rico, and the reinvention of its food system with the movement to increase family farming has planted the seeds of food sovereignty. Despite much of this change stemming from the trauma of devastating natural disasters, seeing people taking pride in growing, cultivating, and fishing in ways that are self-sustaining is inspirational. From what I've seen and tasted, along with its blend of cultural history with innovation, Puerto Rico is well on its way.

## HOMEGROWN SUCCESS

Food was part of everything during chef José Enrique's childhood in Puerto Rico, and spending time in the kitchen while his grandmother cooked for the family helped inspire him to be a chef. After graduating from the Culinary Institute of America, José worked in kitchens in New York, Florida, and Louisiana before returning to his home in Puerto Rico. Since his eponymous restaurant opened in 2007, it has become the island's most lauded restaurant and he has become Puerto Rico's most decorated chef—he was nominated for a James Beard Award

**Chef José Enrique and Gordon high-five after completing their Big Cook right on the beach.**

every year from 2013 to 2020 and was a semifinalist in three of those years.

# RED SNAPPER CEVICHE
## WITH AVOCADO

**YIELDS:** 2 SERVINGS

⅓ cup finely diced red onion

1 garlic clove, finely minced

2 limes, zested and juiced

1 orange, zested and juiced

½ cup diced mango

8 ounces skinless fresh red snapper, cut into ¼-inch dice

Kosher salt

1 tablespoon extra-virgin olive oil

1 avocado, pitted and diced small

2 tablespoons fresh cilantro, finely chopped, plus more for garnish

**DIRECTIONS**

**1.** In a medium bowl, combine the onion, garlic, lime and orange zest and juice, mango, and snapper. Season with salt and toss gently to coat. Refrigerate for 20 to 30 minutes.

**2.** Before serving, gently fold in the olive oil, avocado, and cilantro. Serve the ceviche on its own or pair with plantain or tortilla chips.

# COFFEE-SPICED PORK SHOULDER
## WITH SWEET POTATO AND YUCA

**YIELDS:** 4 SERVINGS

### COFFEE-SPICED PORK SHOULDER

**2 teaspoons ground cumin**

**2 teaspoons sweet paprika**

**1 tablespoon kosher salt**

**1 tablespoon finely ground coffee**

**1 tablespoon granulated sugar**

**¼ teaspoon chili flakes, or more to taste**

**2 teaspoons annatto seeds, finely ground***

**½ boneless pork shoulder (about 3 pounds)**

**Extra-virgin olive oil**

### SWEET POTATO AND YUCA

**1 red onion, diced into ½-inch pieces**

**1 star anise**

**3 garlic cloves, crushed**

**Kosher salt**

**1 sweet potato, peeled and diced into 1-inch pieces**

**1 yuca, peeled and diced into 1-inch pieces**

**1 cup dark rum**

**3–4 cups chicken stock**

## ▍ DIRECTIONS

**1.** Prepare the **pork shoulder:** In a small bowl, combine the cumin, paprika, salt, coffee, sugar, chili flakes, and annatto.

**2.** Season the pork shoulder with the rub, rubbing it in with your hands to coat evenly. Set the pork shoulder aside to marinate at room temperature for at least 30 minutes.

**3.** Heat a large Dutch oven over high heat and drizzle the pork with olive oil. Place the pork shoulder in the pot and sear on all sides until caramelized and golden brown. Remove the pork from the pot and set aside.

**4.** Make the **sweet potato and yuca:** To the pot, add the onion, star anise, and garlic. Season with salt. Cook until all the ingredients begin to caramelize and the anise is aromatic, about 7 to 10 minutes. Add the sweet potato and yuca and sauté for 5 minutes longer, until they start to brown. Add the rum to deglaze the pot, scraping the bottom with a wooden spoon to release all of the brown bits. Simmer until the rum is reduced by half.

**5.** Finish the pork shoulder: Return the pork to the pot and pour in the chicken stock, making sure the stock comes halfway up the side of the pork, adding more liquid if needed. Bring to a boil, then cover and reduce to a simmer, cooking for about 2 hours or until the pork easily breaks apart with a fork. Remove the vegetables with a slotted spoon.

**6.** Once the pork is tender, remove it from the pot and set it on a large plate or cutting board. Pull the pork into large pieces using two forks.

**7.** Reduce the cooking liquid that remains in the pot by half until slightly thickened.

**8.** To serve, plate the pork and vegetables on a serving platter and drizzle cooking liquid over top.

*\* If you can't find annatto seeds, you can substitute with 2 teaspoons achiote paste.*

# WHOLE GRILLED RED SNAPPER

## WITH PUERTO RICAN—INSPIRED MOJO ROJO

PUERTO RICAN–INSPIRED
MOJO ROJO

**1–2 tablespoons extra-virgin olive oil, plus ¾ cup**

**1 yellow onion, chopped**

**Kosher salt**

**2 cups cherry tomatoes**

**2 garlic cloves, smashed**

**2 roasted bell peppers (jarred or homemade), cleaned, seeded, and chopped**

**1 Scotch bonnet pepper, minced and seeds removed**

**1 cup vegetable stock**

**1 lemon, juiced**

GRILLED RED SNAPPER

**1 whole large red snapper (about 3 pounds), gutted, scaled, and cleaned***

**Kosher salt**

**4 garlic cloves, sliced**

**1 lemon, sliced into ¼-inch rounds**

**¼ yellow onion, cut into ¼-inch-thick slices**

**Extra-virgin olive oil**

SAUTÉED EGGPLANT, PEPPERS, AND ONION

**2–3 small Japanese eggplants, sliced into ¼-inch-thick pieces**

**Extra-virgin olive oil**

**Kosher salt**

**Freshly ground black pepper**

**2 red bell peppers, seeded and sliced into ½-inch-thick strips**

**¼ yellow onion, cut into ¼-inch-thick slices**

**5 scallions, roots trimmed**

**½ lemon, plus 1 lemon cut into wedges**

## DIRECTIONS

**1.** Make the **mojo rojo:** In a large skillet over medium-high heat, drizzle 1 to 2 tablespoons of the olive oil. Add the onion and a pinch of salt and sauté until translucent. Add the cherry tomatoes and garlic and cook until the tomatoes blister and begin to break down. Add the bell peppers and Scotch bonnet, cooking for another 5 minutes until tender.

**2.** Add the vegetable stock to the skillet and continue to cook for 5 to 7 minutes, until the liquid reduces

slightly. Remove the skillet from the heat and season the mixture with salt. Let the mixture cool a bit, then pour into a blender and blend on high until smooth, pouring in the remaining ¾ cup olive oil to thicken and emulsify the mojo rojo. Add the lemon juice. Set aside, reserving half for serving.

**3.** Make the **grilled red snapper:** Preheat a grill to 400°F. Rinse the snapper thoroughly and pat dry with paper towels. Score each side of the fish by making shallow incisions along each fillet side, about 1 inch apart. Rub with salt, making sure to season inside the cavity of the fish as well. Stuff the garlic, lemon slices, and the onion slices inside the snapper.

**4.** Drizzle the fish with olive oil and carefully place it on the preheated grill. Cook for about 10 to 12 minutes. Gently flip the fish, then brush with mojo rojo, cooking for another 10 to 12 minutes.

**5.** Make the **eggplant, peppers, and onion:** In a medium bowl, add the eggplant and a large drizzle of olive oil and season generously with salt and pepper. Heat a skillet over high heat and sear the eggplant until golden brown and tender, turning once. Remove the eggplant from the skillet and set aside in a medium bowl. Add a large drizzle of olive oil and the peppers and onion. Sauté until the peppers have blistered and the vegetables are tender. Add the vegetables to the bowl with the eggplant. Toss to combine.

**6.** In the same skillet, wilt the scallions quickly until charred, then add them to the bowl with the other vegetables. Squeeze the lemon half over the vegetables and season with salt and pepper, if needed.

**7.** To serve, place the grilled snapper on a platter and surround with the sautéed vegetables. Top with extra mojo rojo and serve with lemon wedges.

*\* Two smaller snappers (1 to 2 pounds each) can be substituted if a large snapper is unavailable.*

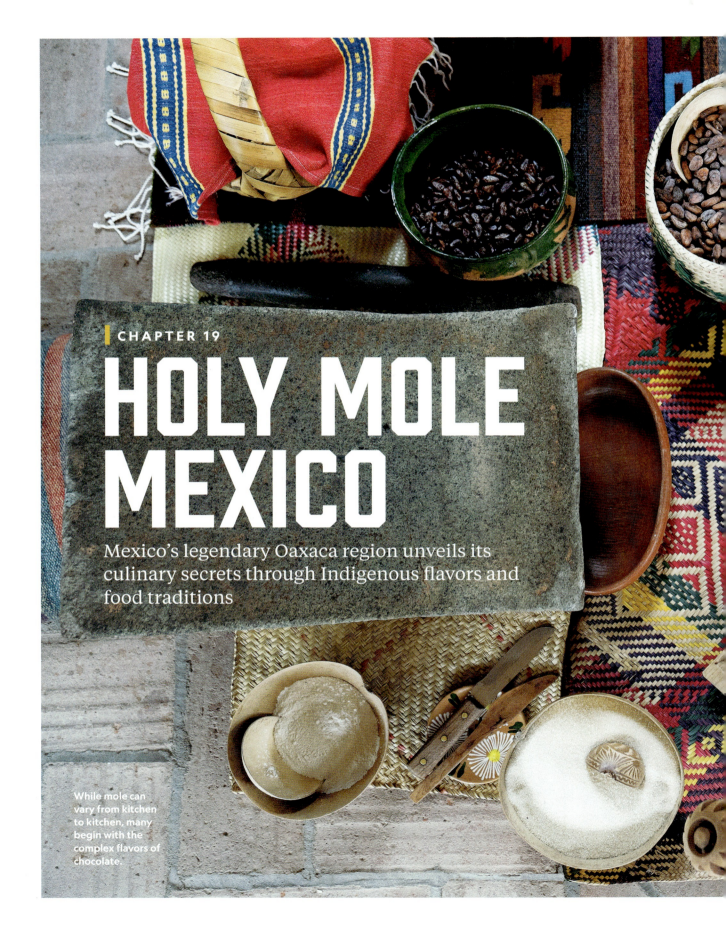

# CHAPTER 19

# HOLY MOLE MEXICO

Mexico's legendary Oaxaca region unveils its culinary secrets through Indigenous flavors and food traditions

While mole can vary from kitchen to kitchen, many begin with the complex flavors of chocolate.

Farmland near
the village of
Totontepec Villa
de Morelos, northeast
of Oaxaca City

**W**ITH THE LARGEST PERCENTAGE of Indigenous people in Mexico representing a cultural heritage spanning thousands of years, Oaxaca is known as the culinary capital of Mexico. These pre-Hispanic communities have survived successive generations and still thrive, proud of their cultural roots that have influenced the region—from the incorporation of traditional ingredients to the use of ancient cooking techniques. Of Mexico's 68 recognized Indigenous groups, 16 are based in Oaxaca—some of whose foodways remain untouched by the European ingredients that have found their way into some of Mexico's cuisine. ¶ The abundant microclimates and rich biodiversity in Oaxaca are home to wild herbs and produce that are everyday staples for those who continue in the footsteps of their ancestors. With many dishes relying on

## NAVIGATOR

### THE STOP

In "the land of seven moles," flavor and culinary traditions abound, making Oaxaca one of my favorite *Uncharted* destinations.

### THE GEOGRAPHY

Oaxaca is the fifth largest region in Mexico. The southeast part of the country borders the Pacific Ocean to the south.

### FOOD FACT

Every mole is unique—with regional and familial varieties that all boast bold flavors and spices.

Made from the agave plant, mezcal has a smoky-sweet flavor all its own.

# Oaxaca's diversity is born of its terrain—a rugged landscape of ravines, caverns, and sheer jungle ascents.

chilies, corn, greens, and herbs found only in one particular area of Oaxaca, the region's cuisine is the apex of local and regional flavor. Relying on native grains and plants made the Indigenous peoples here creative and resourceful, as they use every part of a plant and rely on useful proteins.

Oaxaca's diversity is born of its terrain—a rugged landscape of ravines, caverns, and sheer jungle ascents with varied microclimates—and the result is a combination of colors, flavors, and aromas found nowhere else.

"In Mexico, everybody's proud of Oaxaca," chef Gabriela Cámara told me when we met in an outdoor kitchen to roast and grind cacao. One of Mexico's most well-known and influential chefs, she showed me from the beginning that Mexican cuisine is far more than the simple, rustic food many people believe it to be. "The region is so complex, culturally, and the food is as complex as the Oaxacan culture," Gabriela said.

Spicy and sweet, mole is as diverse as Oaxaca. The region is famously called "the land of seven moles," and while chocolaty mole negro is perhaps the most emblematic version of the dish, the other six—amarillo, chichilo, coloradito, manchamanteles, rojo, and verde—are all just as beloved. But there are far more than seven versions of this pre-Hispanic dish, which has a base of dried or fresh chilies, especially with the wide diversity of chilies found in Oaxaca. No two moles are alike, and many regional (as well as familial) variations abound with potentially dozens of ingredients. It's a complex and elaborate dish generally saved for festive occasions and is intended to be the star of the meal.

Mole is generally some combination of chilies, nuts, seeds, spices, vegetables, and other ingredients like chocolate and dried fruits—all ground together and served with a protein or an *antojito* (snack or appetizer). Through the grinding of the ingredients on a *metate*, the smoke of the *comal,* and the heat of the fire, all the ingredients blend together—with none standing out on its own. Because there are so many varieties of mole, everyone has a different expectation and definition. Instead of being the land of seven moles, Oaxaca is more like the land of thousands of moles.

Maize is the source of life in Oaxaca. To allow people to grind fresh nixtamal (the result of an ancient

## TRAVEL 101
# SUNSET VIEWS

Food everywhere in Oaxaca is extraordinary. It's worth an extended trip just to sample some of the best, especially in some of the rural villages where the default style includes earthenware cooking vessels and a wood fire. One of my favorite places to grab a drink or snack and watch the sunset is from a rooftop restaurant (such as Pitiona) in Oaxaca City's zocalo. This main square is surrounded by cafés and restaurants and bounded by the Templo de Santo Domingo de Guzmán on one side. It's one of the best views in the city.

**IN THE DETAILS**
Clockwise from top left: *Gusano* (worms) are good sources of protein; Gordon searches for honey ants; agave plants are the main ingredient of mezcal.

Gordon is engrossed in the mole-making process.

# A FAMILY AFFAIR WITH CHEF JORGE LEÓN

**S**ince the age of 14, Jorge León has been cooking mole every day, on a quest to master the art of creating the perfect version. The obsession, considering that he grew up in Oaxaca—first in the village of Santo Domingo Nundó and then in the small town of San Juan Bautista la Raya—makes perfect sense. He obtained the nickname "El Mole" while working for years in the kitchens of Oaxaca and Mexico City. Jorge returned home to open Alfonsina, a restaurant in his family's rustic compound. His mother, Elvia León Hernández, had already been selling tortillas and *comida corrida* (an affordable set-price meal) out of her home for 15 years.

Alfonsina combines their experiences—from serving comida corrida to offering tasting menus inspired by the day's fresh offerings at the market. They focus on heirloom ingredients that are grown within Oaxaca's variety of microclimates and have been used for generations. Elsewhere, due to the easy access to cheaper commercial products, the traditional items are beginning to be forgotten or replaced. That family attention, back to the roots of Oaxacan culture, keeps a living, breathing tradition alive by reinterpreting native flavors that have always been here.

**Top: Chef Jorge León's mother, Elvia León Hernández, explains how to make homemade tortillas. Bottom: Jorge guides Gordon in fire-roasting chili seeds on a *comal*.**

No two moles are alike, and variations abound with potentially dozens of ingredients.

process by which dried corn is transformed by soaking and cooking it in an alkaline solution) for their home kitchens, community grinders exist in both city and rural locations. Many people also grind it at home with their metates. The resulting masa is then formed into thin discs and cooked on a comal. Tortillas here can be small and thick to make memelas (fried or toasted masa cakes, similar to sopes), the size of a dinner plate for tlayudas (large corn tortillas smothered in refried beans and other toppings), or a happy medium for a wide variety of dishes.

Because ancient Mesoamericans had to be creative and resourceful with the land to survive, lean protein-rich insects figure into Oaxaca's gastronomy—from grasshoppers to worms to wasp larvae to honey ants. These wild, sustainable ingredients can be foraged or found in open-air markets, either plain or dried. I don't have a great history with worms, and even cooking them on a comal instead of eating them raw didn't quite do it for me. But knowing when and where to collect different insects was once essential for survival. Today, local delicacies such as chapulines (grasshoppers) find their way into tacos and quesadillas, as well as tasty bar snacks. Chicatanas (leafcutter ants) are harvested annually after the rains, toasted on a comal, and added to salsa chicatana. Even ant larvae (escamoles) are served fried in tortillas or with scrambled eggs.

Tequila, a type of mezcal, can be made from only one agave plant (*Agave tequilana,* blue Weber variety) and is produced only in approved regions. Mezcal, an agave-based liquor similar to tequila, can be made from more than 30 varieties of agave. Once considered a poor substitute for tequila, mezcal has become one of Oaxaca's largest industries. Agave plants can take at least 10 years to mature and are hand harvested, by shearing off the spiny, fleshy leaves *(pencas)* to get to the *piña*—the heart of the agave, which looks like a pineapple. Traditional mezcal is produced with the help of native yeasts, and the spirit's smoky flavor comes from cooking the piña in earthen pits lined with lava rocks and filled with wood and charcoal. The piña is shredded and crushed to extract its juice, which is then fermented before being distilled in copper, clay, or stainless-steel stills.

Mezcal is distilled according to the maker's taste, often a reflection of generations of *mezcaleros* before them, as well as the culture of their community. The diversity of mezcal offers a wide variety of flavors from different terroirs in Oaxaca—from earthy to floral, herbal to peppery, and astringent to mineral. And because of the time it takes for an agave to mature, mezcal follows a different rhythm and is generally made by small producers. The spirit has a double function: It plays an important cultural role in holidays and rituals and it is a source of economic sustenance for those who make its production a way of life.

Oaxaca opened my eyes up to why the region reigns supreme as the beloved culinary capital of Mexico. The complex flavors and the rich history are why this has been one of my favorite *Uncharted* destinations yet.

---

**INSIDER KNOWLEDGE**

## AN APPETITE FOR FLAVOR

I n 1998, chef Gabriela Cámara opened Contramar in Mexico City to re-create the feel of the beachside restaurants she loved as a child. Now, the internationally acclaimed chef is the owner of four restaurants (Contramar, Entremar, Caracol de Mar, and Itacate del Mar) and an appointee to Mexico's Council of Cultural Diplomacy. "The common thread in my food has to do with caring about each part of what I do," Gabriela said. "It's the care in what ingredient you choose. It's the care in how you treat it. It's the care in how it's presented. It's what really matters to me."

**Chef Gabriela Cámara**

# BRAISED PORK AND MOLE–STUFFED CHILES RELLENOS

## BRAISED PORK

2 pounds boneless pork shoulder

Kosher salt

Freshly ground black pepper

Vegetable oil

1 yellow onion, diced into ¼-inch pieces

1 celery stalk, diced into ¼-inch pieces

3 garlic cloves, crushed

2 Roma tomatoes, quartered

2 sprigs thyme

1 tablespoon Mexican oregano

1 cup Mexican lager

½ cup mezcal, optional

4 cups chicken stock

2 cups mole coloradito (recipe on page 317)

1 cup Oaxaca cheese, shredded

## CHILES RELLENOS

10 poblano peppers

6 eggs, separated

Kosher salt

2 cups all-purpose flour

Blended oil*

½ cup queso fresco, crumbled

Fresh cilantro, chopped

## DIRECTIONS

**1.** Make the **braised pork:** Season the pork generously with salt and pepper and set aside to marinate at room temperature for 30 minutes. Heat a Dutch oven over high heat. Once hot, add a large drizzle of oil to the pot, then add the pork and sear until golden brown and caramelized on all sides. Remove the pork from the pot and set aside.

**2.** Add the onion, celery, and garlic to the pot and cook until tender and caramelized, about 3 to 5 minutes. Add the tomatoes and cook for an additional 3 minutes, until the skin blisters slightly.

**3.** Return the pork to the pot and add the thyme and oregano. Pour in the beer and mezcal, if using, and bring the mixture to a boil. Immediately lower to a simmer and cook until the liquid is reduced by half. Pour in the chicken stock and bring to a boil, then

cover and simmer until the meat is very tender, about 2 hours. Remove the pot from the heat.

**4.** Once cool enough to handle, set the pork on a large cutting board. Pull the pork into bite-size pieces. In a large bowl, add the pulled pork and mole coloradito and toss until evenly coated. Stir in the cheese.

**5.** Make the **chiles rellenos:** Roast the peppers whole over an open flame, turning frequently, until blackened and the skin blisters, about 20 to 30 minutes. Once finished, place the peppers in a bowl and cover with plastic wrap. Once the peppers are cool enough to handle, use your hands to remove the charred skin. Slice the top off of each pepper and scoop out and discard the seeds.

**6.** Stuff each pepper with pulled pork until the pepper is full but not overflowing.

**7.** In a medium bowl, whisk the egg yolks until smooth and season with a pinch of salt. In a separate bowl, whisk the egg whites until they form stiff peaks, then gently fold in the yolks. Combine the flour and 1 teaspoon of salt in a separate medium-size shallow dish.

**8.** Heat a large pan over medium-high heat and add ½ inch oil. Line a baking sheet with paper towels.

**9.** Gently roll each pepper in the seasoned flour until coated all over, shaking off any excess flour before carefully dipping into the egg batter.

**10.** Place the peppers into the hot frying oil and fry until golden brown on both sides, about 7 to 10 minutes. Transfer to the paper towel–lined baking sheet.

**11.** To serve, ladle the mole coloradito onto a plate and top with the chiles rellenos. Garnish with the queso fresco and cilantro.

*Blended oil can be bought or made easily at home. I recommend a 75 percent olive oil and 25 percent vegetable oil blend for a flavorful yet not overpowering oil that has a higher smoke point.*

# MOLE COLORADITO

**YIELDS:** 2 CUPS

3  Roma tomatoes

2  tablespoons vegetable oil, divided

Kosher salt

3  dried ancho chilies, seeds and stems removed

2  dried guajillo chilies, seeds and stems removed

⅓  cup sesame seeds

5  black peppercorns

4  cloves

1½  teaspoons ground cinnamon

1½  teaspoons dried Mexican oregano

1  white onion, quartered

3  garlic cloves, chopped

2  teaspoons raisins

¼  cup white vinegar

½  cup whole almonds

½  cup dark chocolate, at least 85% cocoa, chopped

## DIRECTIONS

**1.** Preheat your oven to 400°F. Brush the tomatoes with 1 tablespoon of the oil and sprinkle all over with salt. Place on a baking sheet in a single layer. Roast in the oven until caramelized and tender, about 20 to 30 minutes. Set aside to cool.

**2.** Heat a cast-iron skillet over medium heat and add the ancho and guajillo chilies and cook until puffed and toasted on both sides, about 3 to 5 minutes. Remove the peppers from the heat and place them in a medium-size bowl. Pour enough hot (but not boiling) water over top to cover the peppers. Set aside to soak until tender, about 30 minutes.

**3.** In the same skillet, add the sesame seeds, peppercorns, and cloves and toast until fragrant and the sesame seeds are golden, about 2 to 3 minutes. Transfer the spice blend to a small bowl. Add the ground cinnamon and oregano and stir to mix well.

**4.** Drizzle 1 tablespoon of oil into the pan. Add the onion and garlic and sauté until tender, about 10 minutes. Remove from the heat and transfer the onion and garlic to a small bowl.

**5.** Place the raisins in another small bowl. Wipe the pan clean, then return to medium heat. Pour in the vinegar and bring to a simmer. Remove from the heat and pour the vinegar over the raisins to rehydrate and soften them. Let soak at least 10 minutes.

**6.** Drain the chilies that were soaking and reserve the water.

**7.** In a high-power blender, add the tomatoes, chilies, spices, onion, garlic, raisins (and raisin-soaking liquid), and almonds and blend on high until the mixture is smooth, adding reserved chili-soaking water if needed for a smoother texture.

**8.** Pour the mixture into a medium saucepan and heat over medium-low heat to bring to a simmer. Whisk in the chocolate and continue to simmer for 20 minutes, stirring frequently, until the sauce turns a deep red-brown color.

**9.** Serve the mole coloradito over enchiladas, eggs, or roasted meat such as chicken or turkey.

# SHRIMP MOLE VERDE TOSTADAS

## WITH QUICK PICKLED ONIONS AND FRESNO CHILIES

**YIELDS: 4 SERVINGS**

QUICK PICKLED ONIONS
AND FRESNO CHILIES

**1 cup white vinegar**

**2 tablespoons
granulated sugar**

**1 small red onion,
thinly sliced**

**2 Fresno chili peppers,
sliced, seeds intact**

MOLE VERDE

**1 jalapeño**

**8 tomatillos, husked
and rinsed**

**1 tablespoon blended
oil, plus ⅓ cup***

**½ cup chopped white
onion**

**2 garlic cloves,
roughly chopped**

**Kosher salt**

**3 hoja santa leaves,
spines removed and
roughly chopped**

**¼ cup raw pepitas
(pumpkin seeds)**

**¾ cup fresh cilantro,
roughly chopped**

**¼ cup fresh lime juice,
plus more as needed**

SHRIMP TOSTADAS

**Extra-virgin olive oil**

**½ cup finely diced
white onion**

**2 garlic cloves, finely
minced**

**12 medium shrimp,
shelled and deveined**

**4 ounces mezcal**

**Kosher salt**

**Freshly ground black
pepper**

**1 lime, zested and juiced,
plus more for serving**

FOR SERVING

**4 crispy tostada shells**

**1 avocado, pitted and
sliced**

**Fresh cilantro,
chopped**

## DIRECTIONS

**1.** Make the **pickled onions and chilies:** In a small saucepan, add the vinegar and sugar and bring to a boil, just until the sugar dissolves. Place the onion and chilies in a heatproof jar with a lid and pour in the liquid. Set aside to cool to room temperature for at least 10 minutes, allowing the onion and chilies to "pickle" before serving. You can refrigerate for up to a month.

**2.** Make the **mole verde:** In a heavy-duty skillet over high heat, add the jalapeño and tomatillos and cook until charred and tender, about 3 to 5 minutes (alternatively, you can use a comal or an open flame). Remove the vegetables from the skillet. Slice and reserve 3 tomatillos for tostada assembly later. Slice off the stem of the jalapeño and discard it along with the seeds. Set aside.

**3.** Add 1 tablespoon of the oil to the skillet and heat over high heat. Add the onion, garlic, and a big pinch of salt and sauté for 2 minutes. Add the hoja santa leaves and pepitas and toast until fragrant and the leaves are wilted. Set aside to cool slightly.

**4.** Place the ingredients from the skillet, except for the 3 reserved tomatillos, in a high-speed blender and add the cilantro, lime juice, and remaining ⅓ cup of oil. Blend on high and adjust consistency until smooth by adding more oil as needed. Season to taste, adding more salt or lime juice if necessary. The mole should be a vibrant green color.

**5.** Make the **shrimp tostadas:** Heat a skillet over medium-high heat. Once hot, add a large drizzle of oil, and sauté the onion and garlic until tender and fragrant, about 10 minutes. Add the shrimp to the skillet and cook just until caramelized on one side, about 2 to 3 minutes. Flip the shrimp and add the mezcal to deglaze the pan, scraping the bottom to release all of the brown bits. Simmer until the mezcal is reduced by half, then remove the skillet from the heat. Season the shrimp with salt, pepper, and lime zest and juice.

**6.** To serve, spread a heaping spoonful of mole verde on each tostada shell and top with 3 sautéed shrimp on each, followed by sliced avocado, sliced tomatillos, a pinch of salt, and a squeeze of lime. Garnish with the pickled onions and chilies and fresh cilantro.

*\* Blended oil can be bought or made easily at home. I recommend a 75 percent olive oil and 25 percent vegetable oil blend for a flavorful yet not overpowering oil that has a higher smoke point.*

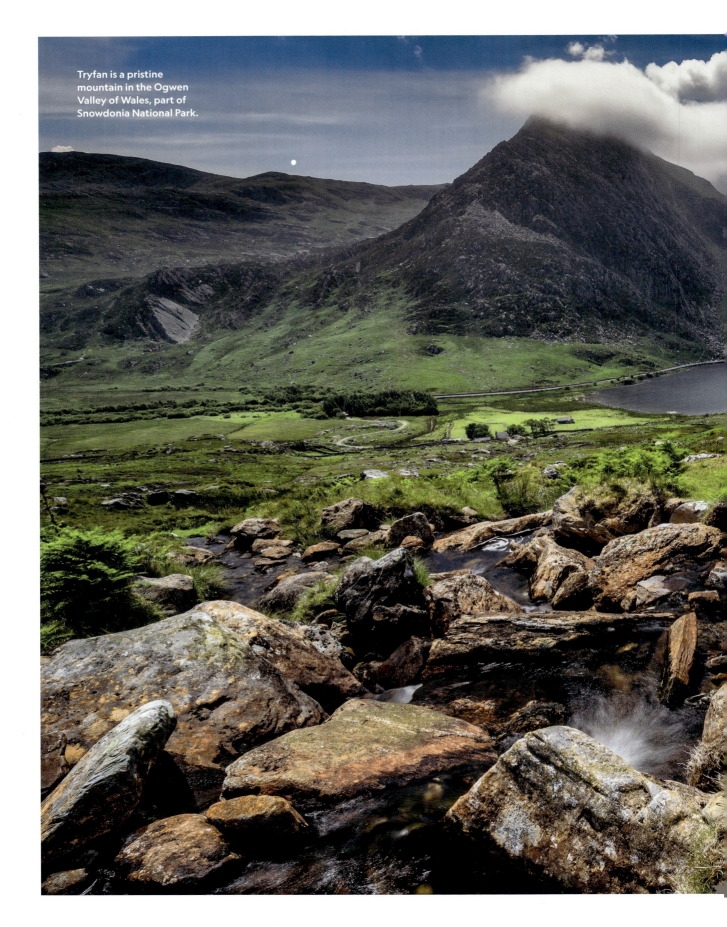
Tryfan is a pristine mountain in the Ogwen Valley of Wales, part of Snowdonia National Park.

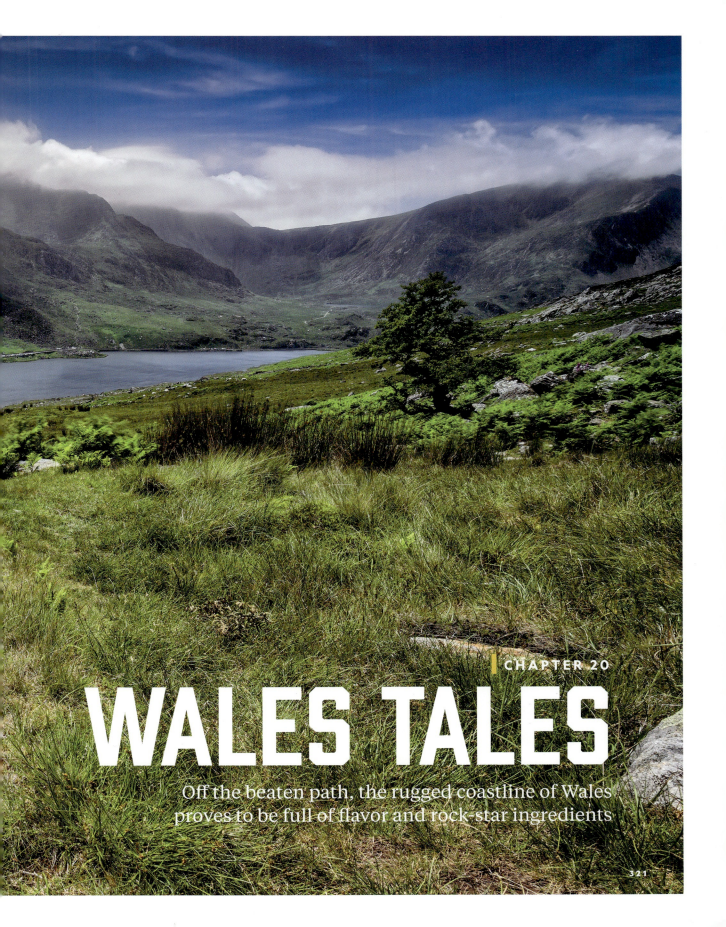

# CHAPTER 20

# WALES TALES

Off the beaten path, the rugged coastline of Wales
proves to be full of flavor and rock-star ingredients

Gordon holds a coracle, a traditional, lightweight Welsh boat, on his way to the river to catch sewin (sea trout).

**W**ALES, ON THE WILD, western edge of Great Britain, is a place of stunning beauty. Bordered by the Irish Sea and England, this land of mountainous national parks, rugged coastline, and rolling countryside often flies under the radar compared with its British neighbors. You must look beyond the fact that there are three times more sheep than people here to understand how its rural history and the practice of living off the land and sea make Wales uniquely positioned to be a gastronomic leader. ¶ Simple, rustic culinary traditions were born out of working-class necessity and continue today. While these rituals are still celebrated locally, many remain largely unknown to the outside world. But with the farm-to-table movement, a new generation of Welsh chefs is weaving together Wales's working-class past and world-class ingredients to create a

**NAVIGATOR**

**THE STOP**

In Wales, I dive deeply into the country's past—including Celtic culture and historical farm-to-table practices.

**THE GEOGRAPHY**

Known for its mountains and rugged coastline, Wales, a part of the United Kingdom, is bordered by England to the east, the Irish Sea to the north, and the Bristol Channel to the south.

**FOOD FACT**

Cockles, also known as heart clams, are served for breakfast with fried eggs and laverbread.

A road leading into the misty mountains of Snowdonia National Park

cuisine that is quietly catching the culinary world's attention.

The Welsh motto, "*Cymru am byth*—Wales forever," illustrates the proud Celtic heritage at play in everyday life in a place that has a strong influence on its residents. In recent years, the number of Welsh speakers has surged, and the Welsh Parliament has set a goal of 1 million speakers by 2050 (among a total population of 3.1 million).

The word *hiraeth* doesn't easily translate into English, but it loosely represents a wistful but unrealizable longing for home. The pull of the Welsh homeland is strong. Chef Matt Waldron started his career in a country house hotel, the Glen-Yr-Afon in Usk, and completed his degree at the University of West London. After working under my protégé Angela Hartnett, he returned to Wales to be a champion of the country's exciting local ingredients.

"There's always one underlying constant in Wales with regard to our gastronomy," Matt, now head chef at the Stackpole Inn, said. "It's working with the best produce we can get in the region—whether it goes into traditional working-class comfort food or dishes where we're pushing the envelope and getting more creative because we have such excellent ingredients. Because of the wealth of choices locally, we have little need to source elsewhere." Food traditions of Wales have historically reflected a skill for making something memorable from meager ingredients, but Welsh ingredients are finally getting the recognition they deserve. Wales's rainy winter conditions result in an expansive carpet of lush green countryside across a rugged land of mountains and valleys. As the summer progresses, lambs eat the grasses, heather, herbs, and sage as they progress up the mountainsides, resulting in some of the best tasting lamb in the U.K.

Salt marsh lamb, which graze in coastal areas that are often waterlogged by seawater, have a free-range roaming habit that keeps them a little leaner than their slightly more fenced-in brethren. They also graze almost equally on grass and samphire—a succulent, salt-tolerant plant with vibrant green stalks that has a

## FARMING THE FUTURE

On Wales's southwest coast, Rosie Rees and her father, Steve, are part of Câr-Y-Môr (For the Love of the Sea), a community-owned project that started the first commercial seaweed and shellfish farm in Wales. This coastline is known for its pristine waters, and zero-input farming—requiring no freshwater, land, or fertilizer—sequesters carbon, helps rebuild reef ecosystems, and serves as food, fertilizer, and animal feed. Rosie showed me how to harvest sweet sugar kelp and salty, dense

Harvesting sugar kelp and oarweed

oarweed—she also smacked me in the face with a piece of kelp. She blamed the wind, but I'm not so sure.

**HISTORY
IN THE MAKING**
Clockwise from top:
Wildflowers blanket
the windswept cliffs
of Snowdonia National
Park; Gordon tries
his hand at sheep-
herding; the historic
Dolbadarn Castle
ruins.

# HOME IS WHERE THE KITCHEN IS FOR CHEF MATT WALDRON

Chef Matt Waldron learned to cook in the Welsh mining town of Usk before earning his stripes in top London kitchens. I met him years ago when he worked under my protégé, Michelin-starred chef Angela Hartnett. Eventually, home beckoned, and Matt returned to Wales to celebrate the exciting, robust local ingredients his country has to offer. "There's no room to cut corners and now, more than ever, the provenance has become more important," he said. "With a basis of the best simple ingredients, it's possible to become more creative with flavors, spicing, and cooking methods to really bring out the best and develop Wales's identity as a culinary destination."

As head chef at the Stackpole Inn in Pembrokeshire, Matt creates dishes that showcase the country's amazing produce using traditional methods, something that's great to see in a rapidly changing world. "In this troubled financial time, people are still happy to come out and eat good food as long as they feel like they have had an experience," he said. "This experience can be in the shape of the ambience of the restaurant, service, ingredients, techniques, and menu creation, resulting in new and exciting dishes they wouldn't find at home."

**Chef Matt Waldron and Gordon discuss Welsh cooking over breakfast.**

crisp and salty taste. The lambs' diet gives their meat a tender sweetness and an almost buttery texture.

The lush green grass in Wales is also ideal for grazing herds, leading to more than 100 kinds of cheese. I followed Richard Newton-Jones of the Snowdonia Cheese Company into the Llechwedd Slate Caverns to taste the company's Rock Star, a vintage cave-aged cheddar. Aging cheese in caves is something that's been done for hundreds of years, due to the consistent cool temperature and lower barometric pressure, which give the cheese a firm texture. The Rock Star cheese is creamy and rich and has sweet, nutty notes, making it ideal for many dishes. I used it in a rarebit, a traditional cheese-on-toast sandwich that has thousands of variations, but usually includes mustard, beer, Worcestershire sauce, flour, butter, cream, and cheddar cheese.

Traditional coracle fishing in Wales, a coastal region with loads of waterways, dates back to pre-Roman times. It's done in a small basket-looking boat, made

of ash and willow with a waterproof covering, that's steered through the water with a single-handed sculling method. Coracle fishing for sewin—migratory sea trout that can live in both freshwater and salt water—can only be done legally on the Taf, Tywi, and Teifi Rivers in western Wales.

Malcom Rees is an eighth-generation fisherman who's been fishing the River Tywi (Towy in English) since he was a boy. He taught me the finer points of coracle fishing, beginning with carrying a craft that looks like an industrial-size wok on my back to the river, which made me feel like an escargot crossed with a middle-age Teenage Mutant Ninja Turtle. The

## LOCAL FLAVOR

# THE COCKLE HARVEST

Rob Griffiths shows Gordon the art of gathering cockles.

Cockle gatherer Rob Griffiths is among the people upholding a Welsh tradition that goes back centuries. One of the only year-round cockle-harvesting locations in Wales is the Burry Inlet in Carmarthen Bay, and it can take years to get a license. Because the backbreaking work is dependent on the short window of time when the tide is low, gatherers like Rob must be skilled in flicking the cockles out of the sand while keeping an eye out for the rising tide. It's a delicate dance to get the technique right and work smartly for this delicious reward.

paddle technique consists of swirling the blade in a figure eight in the water to move sideways. Deploying the net is harder than it looks; it felt like stretching a tennis net across the river with one hand while trying to steer the coracle with the other. The whole thing felt very unstable. It takes a lot of practice to do it well and, no surprise, I fell out. But the efforts are worth it: When cooked, sewin has a buttery taste with nutty undertones.

Wales's coastline is essential to the country's gastronomy. A proper Welsh breakfast includes two seafood items: cockles and laverbread. Cockles, small bivalves that are sweeter and less briny than clams, are gathered from the sand at low tide. Archaeological evidence suggests that Penclawdd cockles have been found in Wales's Burry Inlet estuary since Roman times. For breakfast, cockles are cooked in bacon fat

## The pull of the Welsh homeland is strong.

and served alongside fried eggs and laverbread. Laverbread isn't bread at all but rather a dark green puree made from slow-cooked laver, a type of seaweed that has been harvested for centuries in Wales.

Wales may have a working-class, coal-mining background, but you can't simply buy that Welsh spirit. I have a newfound respect for the country's absolute goldmine of world-class ingredients, as well as for those who are working to shine the light on this incredible fresh cuisine with its deep sense of place.

# BRAISED LEG OF LAMB
## WITH FINGERLING POTATOES AND CARROTS

**YIELDS:** 6–8 SERVINGS

1 boneless leg of lamb
(about 6–7 pounds),
cleaned and trussed

3 tablespoons olive oil, divided

1 tablespoon kosher salt

½ teaspoon freshly ground black
pepper

10 ounces fingerling potatoes,
cut in half

1 bunch small carrots,
cut into 3-inch pieces

2 small yellow onions,
chopped

4 garlic cloves, chopped

3–4 sprigs fresh rosemary

3–4 sprigs fresh thyme

2 tablespoons tomato paste

3 cups hearty red wine,
divided

3 cups veal or chicken stock

## DIRECTIONS

**1.** Preheat your oven to 325°F.

**2.** Season the lamb all over with 1 tablespoon of the olive oil and the salt and pepper.

**3.** Heat a large Dutch oven or roasting pan over high heat and add the lamb, searing on all sides until caramelized. Remove from the pot and set aside.

**4.** Drizzle the remaining 2 tablespoons of olive oil into the pot. Add the potatoes and carrots and quickly sear the vegetables until caramelized, about 5 minutes. Remove the vegetables from the pot and set aside. Add the onions and sauté until they begin to caramelize, about 3 to 5 minutes. Add the garlic, rosemary, and thyme and cook for 1 minute until fragrant. Stir in the tomato paste and toast until it darkens slightly, about 2 minutes.

**5.** Add 1½ cups of the red wine to deglaze the pot, scraping the bottom to release all of the brown bits. Simmer until the wine is reduced by half. Return the lamb to the pot, fat side up, along with the potatoes and carrots. Pour in enough stock to cover the lamb halfway and bring to a simmer. Cover, transfer the pot to the oven, and braise the lamb until tender when pierced with a paring knife, about 3½ to 4 hours, turning the lamb in the pot halfway through.

**6.** To finish the lamb, once it is tender, strain the braising liquid into a large pan and add the remaining 1½ cups of wine. Bring to a simmer and reduce until the sauce is thickened. Transfer the lamb to a cutting board and slice or shred the meat. Add the meat to the pan with the braising liquid and toss to coat evenly.

**7.** To serve, arrange the lamb on a large serving platter with the potatoes and carrots and top with the braising liquid. Serve alongside cauliflower gratin (recipe on page 335).

# COCKLES WITH CRAB, PRAWNS, AND GRILLED BREAD

**YIELDS:** 4–6 SERVINGS

### SEAWEED BUTTER

½ cup (1 stick) unsalted butter, softened

3 tablespoons finely chopped edible seaweed, such as dulse, wakame, or nori

### COCKLES

2 tablespoons extra-virgin olive oil

1 fennel bulb, finely diced

1 shallot, finely diced

2 garlic cloves, minced

2 pounds cockles, scrubbed

½ cup seafood stock

½ pound lump crab meat

½ pound jumbo prawns, peeled and deveined

2 lemons, zested and juiced

### GRILLED BREAD

6 slices hearty bread

Extra-virgin olive oil

Kosher salt

## DIRECTIONS

**1.** Make the **seaweed butter:** In a small bowl, combine the butter and seaweed until smooth and incorporated.

**2.** Make the **cockles:** In a large skillet over medium-high heat, add the olive oil. Once the oil is shimmering, add the fennel, shallot, and garlic and cook until softened, about 2 minutes.

**3.** Add the cockles to the skillet and continue cooking until they begin to open. Add the seafood stock and seaweed butter and stir to combine. Place a lid on the skillet and continue cooking until all cockles have opened, about 5 to 10 minutes. Discard any cockles that do not open on their own.

**4.** Remove the lid and add the crab meat and prawns. Continue cooking until the sauce has reduced slightly and the prawns begin to turn opaque, about 2 minutes.

**5.** Add the lemon zest and juice and stir to combine.

**6.** Grill the **bread:** Heat a cast-iron pan or grill over medium-high heat. Brush the bread on both sides with olive oil and sprinkle with a pinch of salt. Grill 1 to 2 minutes per side until crispy and just starting to char on the edges.

**7.** Serve the seafood in the skillet with the grilled bread on the side.

# CAST-IRON CAULIFLOWER GRATIN

**YIELDS:** 6-8 SERVINGS

2-3 tablespoons olive oil

1 medium head of cauliflower, cut into florets

½ cup yellow onion, diced

2 garlic cloves, minced

Kosher salt

Freshly ground black pepper

4 tablespoons unsalted butter

2 tablespoons all-purpose flour

½ teaspoon nutmeg, freshly ground

2 cups whole milk

2 cups aged English cheddar cheese, grated, divided

½ cup breadcrumbs

Fresh parsley, chopped, optional

**DIRECTIONS**

**1.** Preheat your oven to 400°F or set the broiler to high.

**2.** Heat a large cast-iron skillet over medium heat and drizzle with the oil. Add the cauliflower and sauté until it just begins to caramelize, about 5 minutes. Add the onion and garlic and cook for another 2 to 3 minutes. Season with salt and pepper and remove the vegetables from the skillet. Set aside.

**3.** Add the butter to the skillet and let melt. Once the butter is bubbling, sprinkle in the flour and nutmeg and cook, stirring constantly for 1 to 2 minutes. Pour in the milk and whisk to incorporate. Return the vegetables to the skillet and bring to a simmer on low heat until the sauce is creamy and the cauliflower is tender, about 5 to 7 minutes.

**4.** Remove from the heat and stir in 1½ cups of the cheese and then sprinkle with the breadcrumbs and the remaining cheese. Place the skillet in the oven or toast under the broiler until the cheese is golden brown and bubbly. Garnish with parsley, if desired. Serve in the skillet.

# CHAPTER 21

# ENGLAND'S JURASSIC COAST

A wealth of amazing regional ingredients—from buffalo mozzarella to world-class seafood—awaits in my own backyard

The incredible chalk formations of Old Harry Rocks are part of the Jurassic Coast, a UNESCO World Heritage site.

Gordon takes
in the coastline
just outside
Cornwall.

**S**OUTHWEST ENGLAND'S JURASSIC COAST stretches for more than 95 miles (150 km) through Dorset and East Devon. Around 200 million years ago, this jagged coastline was entirely submerged under a tropical sea. Embedded in the cliffs, coastal stacks, and barrier beaches lie the remains of creatures that once swam in that sea. The region's wild moorland, picturesque fishing villages, and towering white cliffs above the crashing sea are the most spectacular highlights, but look closer and you'll find much more. ¶ The varied landscape here and in neighboring Cornwall is teeming with culinary delights. People here work hard to farm, fish, and forage, and their simple yet beautifully crafted dishes focus on the incredible flavor of the ingredients. Those in the local food industry have developed a collaborative and supportive community with a passion for seeking new combinations using local produce as the seasons change.

Trevose Head Lighthouse near Padstow, Cornwall

## NAVIGATOR

### THE STOP

On an exploration of England's Jurassic Coast, I am reminded of the riches available on and off this rugged coastline.

### THE GEOGRAPHY

On the southwestern peninsula of England lie secluded marshland, woodland, and river valleys, along with a rugged and extreme coastline.

### FOOD FACT

Buffalo mozzarella is made with milk from, of course, buffalo. The milk has twice as much fat as cow milk.

# The varied landscape here and in neighboring Cornwall is teeming with culinary delights.

I was excited to explore my backyard in greater detail. The Jurassic Coast has some of the best seafood anywhere in Europe, thanks to its coastline and rich varieties of fish and shellfish, amounting to more than 40 different species—from oysters and mussels to crab and lobster to Dover sole, sea bass, and mackerel. Chef Paul Ainsworth grew up just down the coast in Southampton, but after working in London kitchens for many years (including six with Restaurant Gordon Ramsay), he moved to Cornwall to start his own restaurant empire.

"The world-class seafood in Cornwall and the Jurassic Coast is phenomenal," said the Michelin-starred chef and proprietor of Paul Ainsworth at No6, the Mariners Public House, Caffè Rojano by Paul Ainsworth, and Padstow Townhouse. "Southwest England's warmer climate and the perfect natural connection of the soil and water make this location one of the best in the world. It's no wonder many of us have such a passion for these ingredients."

Location is indeed a gift in southwest England—and that mix of climate, land, and water produces ingredients it's easy to be passionate about. The broad Camel Estuary in Cornwall is home to Porthilly Shellfish, where Tim Marshall of Porthilly Oysters produces a year-round supply of Pacific oysters. The fifth-generation oyster farmer grows them from "seed" at a young age in mesh bags on the estuary, where

## COASTEERING FOR SEAWEED

Adventurer Dan Scott is inspired by the landscape of Dorset and the Jurassic Coast, from its spectacular coastline to the heathlands and woodlands of the interior. He and his wife, Jade, founded Fore/Adventure to provide tailor-made outdoor experiences using adventure as a means by which to forage. On a coasteering tour at the Dancing Ledge, a remote cliff face packed with fossils dating back to the Jurassic period, Dan encouraged chef Paul Ainsworth and me to jump off the cliffs to forage local seaweed such as gutweed and pepper

Forager Dan Scott

dulse, often called the "truffle of the sea" for its powerful umami flavor.

**THE BEST COAST**
The Jurassic Coast stretches down the coast of southern England from East Devon (home to the spectacular Powderham Castle, at top) to Studland's isolated dunes (bottom left).

# JURASSIC FLAVORS WITH CHEF PAUL AINSWORTH

**G**rowing up in his parents' guesthouse in Southampton, chef Paul Ainsworth was part of the hospitality industry from an early age. A passionate supporter of Cornish farmers, fishers, and artisanal producers, Paul worked for Restaurant Gordon Ramsay for six years before leading the kitchen at No6 in Padstow. Soon enough, he became chef-owner, relaunching the restaurant as Paul Ainsworth at No6 and winning a Michelin star in 2013. He has since added the Mariners Public House, Caffè Rojano by Paul Ainsworth, and Padstow Townhouse—a boutique hotel.

"With the ingredients we have in Cornwall and the Jurassic Coast, you can't go wrong," he said. "Our diverse ecosystem all boils down to the mild climate and terroir. With the interaction of the land and sea and the constant coastal breeze, grazing animals don't have to go indoors in the winter, and dishes can incorporate more ocean-based ingredients. In the past 10 to 12 years, everyone has gone to the next level with what they're producing."

Paul's talent and determination from his days as a young chef have really paid off. Even though he poked at me for being well seasoned, I'm proud of him and happy he shared these delicious ingredients with me.

**Chef Paul Ainsworth puts the finishing touches on a lobster claw and fried Porthilly mussel salad during the Big Cook.**

**ROOM FOR DESSERT**
Gordon visits with
Fosse Farmhouse's Caron
Cooper to sample
traditional lardy cake.

twice-daily tidal patterns alternately immerse them in freshwater and salt water. The oysters are harvested when they reach a size that's ready for consumption—a process that can take 16 to 24 months.

Paul and I shook the bags of oysters and flipped them while the tide was out to help develop the round pocket in the shell. Without that work, the oysters' shells would be flat. Paul had fun pointing out that my shucking skills might be a little rusty when I got a small cut while shucking some oysters to taste. I thought it was important to remind him that his first time opening an oyster was when he worked for me at Restaurant Gordon Ramsay on Royal Hospital Road in London. But what's most important is that the oysters were absolutely delicious.

The long coastline gives foragers along the Jurassic

Coast access to a wide variety of edible seaweeds, sea vegetables, and other wild plants. Gutweed has great flavor when it is dried or deep-fried, and it can also be sprinkled as a seasoning on dishes. Pepper dulse has a peppery or garlicky flavor when fresh, but once it is dried it develops a deeper umami flavor and is known among chefs as the "truffle of the sea." To me, it tastes like lightly salted and peppery wasabi with some sweet elements.

# The time I spent in Cornwall and the Jurassic Coast served as a stern reminder of just how good the United Kingdom's artisan purveyors are in producing high-quality, amazing ingredients.

This rugged coast may have amazing seaweed, but it's almost impossible to bring a boat close enough to harvest it, so we went "coasteering" (swimming and walking the intertidal zone), which entailed jumping off a massive, slippery cliff called Dancing Ledge. The clear, shallower waters close to the cliffs along the Jurassic Coast are also where the best Dorset lobsters are found. To get closer to the coastline, fishers take a kayak out to bait and retrieve lobster traps. It's definitely challenging to keep your balance while doing all that, but it makes success that much sweeter.

Traditional dishes, such as rich lardy cake, are still served in places like the Fosse Farmhouse, a bed-and-breakfast in the heart of southwest England. Made with lard, butter, olive oil, flour, sugar, spices, currants, and raisins, it was considered a poor man's cake because it was so inexpensive to make. It's served as part of a classic English afternoon tea and has a unique taste that is like a super-rich croissant.

The buffalo mozzarella made in Somerset by Buffalicious, a family farm with a herd of 250 water buffalo, takes advantage of the lush local grass that helps them produce milk that's the perfect consistency for mozzarella. Buffalo milk has double the fat content of cow milk, which is better for mozzarella. While I was lucky to milk a buffalo for about a second, tasting the delicious cheese was a huge personal highlight.

Although we have a lot of spirits to choose from here in the United Kingdom, I especially enjoyed tasting the hand-crafted gin from Cornwall's Wrecking Coast Distillery, which is made with some surprising ingredients. The distillery produces a navy-strength (57 percent alcohol by volume) gin using scurvy grass, which has a mustard, peppery flavor when it's in full bloom. For me, the most surprising was its aptly named Clotted Cream Gin, a clear gin that tastes like alcoholic clotted cream in liquid form.

The time I spent in Cornwall and the Jurassic Coast served as a stern reminder of just how good the United Kingdom's artisan purveyors are in producing high-quality, amazing ingredients. It can be easy to forget about the incredible ingredients that are close to home, and I loved discovering so many new things right here in my own backyard. It's an experience I'll never forget.

## TRAVEL 101

# FEATHERED FRIENDS

England lives up to its reputation of having unpredictable weather, and the southwest corner of the country is no exception. Even in the summer, there will likely be a rain shower around the corner, so make sure you pack a rain jacket and waterproof shoes. The long stretch of coastline and varied landscape along Cornwall and the Jurassic Coast is incredible for bird-watchers in fall and winter months, with plenty of seabirds, rarities, and migrating birds stopping by along their journey. Even if you don't keep a life list, bring along some binoculars to join in the fun.

# GIN-POACHED OYSTERS
## WITH SEAWEED TAGLIATELLE TOPPED WITH CAVIAR

**YIELDS:** 2 SERVINGS

TAGLIATELLE

**2 cups all-purpose flour, plus more as needed**

**1 teaspoon kosher salt**

**2 large eggs**

**½ cup fresh seaweed, minced, blanched, shocked, and completely dried**

**Kosher salt**

GIN BEURRE BLANC

**½ cup gin**

**1 shallot, minced**

**2 sprigs thyme, picked**

**½ cup (1 stick) unsalted butter, cubed**

**1 teaspoon kosher salt**

GIN-POACHED OYSTERS

**1 cup gin**

**2 tablespoons salted butter**

**1 piece lemon peel, about 1 inch**

**½ teaspoon kosher salt**

**6 oysters, shucked, with shells kept and cleaned**

**1 cup rock salt**

**1 ounce caviar**

## ▌ DIRECTIONS

**1.** Prepare the dough for the **tagliatelle:** In a medium bowl, combine the flour and salt and mix well. Pour the flour mixture onto a clean, flat surface and make a well in the middle.

**2.** Carefully crack the eggs into the center of the well and use a fork to gently beat them and gradually begin mixing the eggs into the flour.

**3.** Once a dough forms, add the seaweed and begin to knead the dough. Continue kneading until the dough is smooth and elastic, about 10 minutes. If the dough is still too wet, add more flour as needed. Shape the dough into a ball and cover with plastic and refrigerate for 20 minutes.

**4.** Make the **gin beurre blanc:** In a large skillet over medium heat, add the gin, shallot, and thyme and bring to a boil. Reduce to a simmer and cook until the liquid is reduced by half.

**5.** Reduce the heat to low and gradually add the butter, swirling the pan constantly to melt the butter completely. Season the sauce with the salt and keep warm.

**6.** Roll out and cook the tagliatelle: Bring a large pot of water to a boil. Season liberally with salt.

**7.** Place the dough on a lightly floured surface and use a rolling pin to roll it out to be ¼-inch thick, making sure to dust the surface with flour as needed to prevent the dough from sticking. Cut the dough into strips that are ¼-inch wide.

**8.** Drop the pasta into the boiling water and cook until al dente, about 45 to 60 seconds. Remove the pasta from the water and add to the pan with the beurre blanc. Toss the pasta to coat evenly.

**9.** Make the **gin-poached oysters:** In a small pot over medium-high heat, add the gin and bring to a boil. Add the butter, lemon peel, and salt. Once the butter is melted, reduce to a simmer over medium-low heat.

**10.** Add the oysters to the simmering liquid and cook until firm, about 30 to 45 seconds.

**11.** To serve, place 6 small mounds of rock salt on a platter. Place the 6 cleaned oyster shells on the salt mounds to secure them.

**12.** Use a pasta fork to twist the tagliatelle into a small nest and place in a cleaned oyster shell. Place a poached oyster on top. Repeat with the remaining pasta and oysters. Finish the oysters with a dollop of caviar.

# POACHED LOBSTER

## WITH BROWN BEURRE BLANC, ROASTED FINGERLING POTATOES, AND PICKLED VEGETABLES

**YIELDS:** 2–4 SERVINGS

### PICKLED VEGETABLES

3 tablespoons kosher salt, divided

10 sugar snap peas

10 Thumbelina carrots

1 head Romanesco, cut into florets

2 cups champagne vinegar

4 sprigs dill

½ cup granulated sugar

1 teaspoon whole black peppercorns

### ROASTED FINGERLING POTATOES

2 cups fingerling potatoes

2–4 tablespoons extra-virgin olive oil

2 tablespoons minced garlic

1 tablespoon kosher salt

1 teaspoon freshly ground black pepper

### POACHED LOBSTER

½ cup kosher salt

1 lemon, cut in half

2 sprigs thyme

2 sprigs parsley

2 sprigs tarragon

1 whole lobster, about 1½ pounds

### BROWN BEURRE BLANC

1 cup white wine

1 shallot, sliced

4 tablespoons unsalted butter, cubed

2 tablespoons brown butter

1 sprig tarragon, minced

1 teaspoon kosher salt

## DIRECTIONS

**1.** Make the **pickled vegetables:** Have a large bowl of ice water standing by. In a large pot over medium-high heat, bring about 4 quarts of water to a boil. Season the water with 2 tablespoons of the salt.

**2.** Add the snap peas, carrots, and Romanesco florets. Let the vegetables cook until bright and crispy, about 2 minutes. Remove the vegetables from the water and immediately put them into the ice water bath to shock them and stop them from cooking further. Once cooled, drain the vegetables and place them in a bowl or jar.

**3.** In a small pot over medium-high heat, bring 2 cups water, the vinegar, dill, sugar, remaining 1 tablespoon of salt, and peppercorns to a boil until the sugar is dissolved in the liquid. Allow the liquid to cool, then pour it over the vegetables. Allow to marinate at least 30 minutes.

**4.** Make the **fingerling potatoes:** Preheat your oven to 350°F.

**5.** In a bowl, combine all the potato ingredients and toss to coat the potatoes completely.

**6.** Spread the potatoes on a baking sheet in a single layer and roast in the oven until fork-tender, about 45 minutes.

**7.** Increase the heat to 400°F and continue cooking until crispy, about 15 minutes.

**8.** Poach the **lobster:** Have a large bowl of ice water standing by. In a large pot over medium-high heat, bring about 4 quarts of water to a boil. Add the salt, lemon halves, thyme, parsley, and tarragon.

**9.** Lower the lobster into the pot and cook until the meat turns pink, about 8 to 9 minutes. (To check the meat, use a sharp knife to split the shell where the tail meets the body.)

**10.** Remove the lobster and shock it in ice water for 5 minutes.

**11.** Remove the lobster from the ice water and use kitchen shears to cut along the claw line to remove the meat. Twist and remove the tail from the body, wrap it in a towel, and press into the curves of the tail to loosen the meat. If needed, cut down the middle of the tail with the shears to break the meat loose. Set the meat aside and discard the shell.

**12.** Make the **beurre blanc:** In a small saucepan over medium heat, add the white wine and shallot and bring to a boil. Reduce the liquid to 3 tablespoons, about 10 to 15 minutes. Strain the shallot and discard. Keep the reduction warm over low heat.

**13.** Gradually add the cubed butter, swirling the pan constantly to melt butter completely. Add in the brown butter and continue swirling the pan until it's fully incorporated. Stir in the tarragon and salt.

**14.** To serve, place the lobster meat on a platter and drizzle the beurre blanc over top. Cut the potatoes in half and serve on the side along with the pickled vegetables.

# GRILLED CORNISH GAME HEN

## WITH SEAWEED PESTO
## AND WHIPPED MOZZARELLA

**YIELDS:** 2 SERVINGS

### SEAWEED PESTO

½ cup fresh seaweed, blanched and shocked

¼ cup basil leaves

¼ cup flat-leaf parsley

¼ cup grated Parmesan cheese

1 garlic clove

½ lemon, zested and juiced

1 teaspoon kosher salt

1 cup extra-virgin olive oil

### TOMATO OIL

1 cup extra-virgin olive oil

2 garlic cloves

6 cherry tomatoes

2 sprigs thyme

### GAME HENS

2 Cornish hens*

2 tablespoons seaweed pesto (from above)

1 cup tomato oil (from above)

Kosher salt

Freshly ground black pepper

### WHIPPED MOZZARELLA

2 balls fresh mozzarella

½ lemon, zested

2 tablespoons mascarpone

1 teaspoon kosher salt

1 tablespoon extra-virgin olive oil

## DIRECTIONS

**1.** Make the **seaweed pesto:** In a food processor, combine all the pesto ingredients and blend until smooth. Add more salt or lemon juice as needed.

Reserve half of the pesto for grilling and set aside the remaining half to serve with the Cornish hens.

**2.** Make the **tomato oil:** In a room-temperature saucepan, combine the tomato oil ingredients and heat over medium heat. Do not bring the mixture to a boil or cook over high heat, because it will fry the ingredients. Cook until the garlic is soft, about 2 to 3 minutes, then turn the heat off and let the mixture cool. Strain the oil and set aside.

**3.** Prepare the **game hens:** Preheat a grill to 400°F. Stuff the seaweed pesto under the skin of the game hens and spread the pesto to coat evenly. Brush the hens with the tomato oil and season with salt and pepper.

**4.** Place the hens in a grill basket and set it on the grill, being cautious of hot spots on the grill to avoid burning the hens. Continue to brush tomato oil on the hens while they cook to get the skin extra crispy.

**5.** Make the **whipped mozzarella:** In a food processor, combine the mozzarella ingredients and blend until smooth. Add more salt and lemon zest as needed. If the whipped mozzarella is too thick, add a touch of water or milk to thin it out.

**6.** Quarter the hens and serve on a platter alongside the whipped mozzarella and the remaining pesto.

*When purchasing Cornish hens, ask your local butcher to spatchcock them by removing the backbone and ribs.*

## ACKNOWLEDGMENTS

The adventures I've had with the *Uncharted* series to learn about the ingredients, flavors, dishes, and cultures around the world have been life changing. The gastronomy and how ingredients fit into the overall puzzle of a culture give us a greater understanding of a place. I'm so grateful to everyone who has worked on this book, and I hope it inspires your future travels and meals.

Thanks so much to the amazing people who make my path easier to navigate—from Rachel Ferguson, who keeps me on track every day; to Justin Mandel, whose photography and insight into the show are invaluable; to Codii Lopez, whose brilliant work on the recipes keeps everything moving forward.

Thank you to National Geographic and the production team of the *Uncharted* series. You all have been an essential part of this wild journey, particularly Jon Kroll, Neil DeGroot, and Tara Williams for working your magic and keeping chaos under control, and Gary and Dennis for saving my life a number of times.

The chefs on my team, especially Alex and Jocky Petrie, as well as the chefs and dedicated cultural and culinary experts I met while filming *Uncharted*, have been incredible. A huge thank-you to everyone who stepped out of their kitchens and embarked on these amazing culinary adventures with me.

Thank you also to the mighty team at National Geographic Books for putting their heart into this book— an *Uncharted* experience itself. Particular thanks go to my co-author, Jill K. Robinson, who has also joined me on set a few times; senior editor at the helm of this book Allyson Johnson; designer Jerry Sealy and senior photo editor Jill Foley for the stunning pages; editorial director Lisa Thomas; creative director Elisa Gibson; director of photography Adrian Coakley; project editor Ashley Leath; senior production editor Michael O'Connor; production editor Becca Saltzman; and copy editor Jenny Miyasaki.

Finally, thank you to my wonderful family, who keep me going and inspire me to give my best in all circumstances: my wonderful wife, Tana, and our five children, Megan, Holly, Jack, Tilly, and Oscar. You lot are the motivation for everything I do and my journey is much better because of you.

# ILLUSTRATIONS CREDITS

*Some recipes are inspired by the Big Cook on* Uncharted *and have been adapted for home kitchens. Imagery may differ from finished recipe.*

NG = National Geographic; HPRL = Humble Pie Rights Limited

Cover, Photo illustration by NG with background by Henryk Welle/Getty Images; back cover: (UP LE), NG/Justin Mandel; (UP RT and CTR LO), HPRL/Justin Mandel; (CTR UP), NG/Lisa Corson; (LO), NG/Ritam Banerjee; 2–3, NG/Ernesto Benavides; 4, NG/Lisa Corson; 6–7, HPRL/Justin Mandel; 9 (UP), Moreno Geremetta/mauritius images GmbH/Alamy Stock Photo; 9 (LO), NG/Mark Johnson; 10–13, HPRL/Justin Mandel; 14–5, NG/Ritam Banerjee; 16–7, NG/Justin Mandel; 18–9, NG/Camilla Rutherford; 20–1, HPRL/Justin Mandel; 22–3, NG/Mark Johnson; 24–5, NG/Ernesto Benavides; 26, Jason Edwards/NG Image Collection; 27, Patrick_Gijsbers/Getty Images; 29 (UP LE and CTR RT), NG/Ernesto Benavides; 29 (UP RT), Edward Viljoen/EyeEm/Getty Images; 29 (CTR LE), Elizabeth Beard/Getty Images; 29 (LO LE and LO RT), HPRL/Justin Mandel; 30–1, NG/Ernesto Benavides; 32, wayfarerlife photography/Getty Images; 33, HPRL/Justin Mandel; 34–5, Alec Jacobson; 36, NG/Lisa Corson; 38, NG/Ernesto Benavides; 40–1, NG/Mark Johnson; 42, Starcevic/Getty Images; 43, NG/Mark Johnson; 45, Leonid Andronov/Shutterstock; 46–7, HPRL/Justin Mandel; 48 (UP), Japhotos/Alamy Stock Photo; 48 (LO LE), alessandro0770/Getty Images; 48 (LO RT), Chris Griffiths/Getty Images; 49, HPRL/Justin Mandel; 50–3, NG/Mark Johnson; 54, HPRL/Justin Mandel; 56–7, Mlenny/Getty Images; 58, NG/Jock Montgomery; 59, NG/Jock Montgomery; 61–2 (UP LE), NG/Jock Montgomery; 62 (UP RT), travelstock44.de/Juergen Held/Alamy Stock Photo; 62 (LO), NG; 63–5, HPRL/Justin Mandel; 66, NG/Lisa Corson; 68, HPRL/Justin Mandel; 70–1, NG/Camilla Rutherford; 72, Lans Hansen/Getty Images; 73, Jon Kroll; 74, HPRL/Justin Mandel; 75, Nigel Killeen/Getty Images; 76–8, HPRL/Justin Mandel; 79, NG/Camilla Rutherford; 80, NG/Lisa Corson; 82–4, HPRL/Justin Mandel; 86–7, Christian Heeb; 88, NG/Michael Muller; 89, Ron Dahlquist/robertharding; 90, HPRL/Justin Mandel; 91, NG; 92–3, NG/Michael Muller; 94 (UP LE), Douglas Peebles/Getty Images; 94 (UP RT), Greg Vaughn/Alamy Stock Photo; 94 (LO LE), Christian Heeb; 94 (LO RT), elena_suvorova/Adobe Stock; 95, © StockFood/Laurange; 96–8, HPRL/Justin Mandel; 102–3, Beverly Joubert/NG Image Collection; 104, HPRL/Justin Mandel; 105, Hayden Elliott/500px/Getty Images; 107, Brenda Lindon/Getty Images; 108–10, HPRL/Justin Mandel; 111 (UP LE), Shannon Wild/NG Image Collection; 111 (UP RT), Brand SA/Greatstock/Alamy Stock Photo; 111 (LO LE), Angela Bax/EyeEm/Getty Images; 111 (LO RT), Lindokuhle Dlamini/Getty Images; 112, NG/Jon Kroll; 114, NG; 116, NG/Jon Kroll; 118–9, Pablo Joanidopoulos/Shutterstock; 120, Mark Bridger/Getty Images; 121, Marius Dobilas/Shutterstock; 123, NG/Jon Kroll; 124–5, NG/Justin Mandel; 126 (UP LE and LO RT), HPRL/Justin Mandel; 126 (UP RT and LO LE), NG/Justin Mandel; 127–8, HPRL/Justin Mandel; 130, NG/Justin Mandel; 132, HPRL/Justin Mandel; 134–5, Posnov/Getty Images; 136, Jonathan Ayres/Alamy Stock Photo; 137, blickwinkel/AGAMI/G. Steytler/Alamy Stock Photo; 138, HPRL/Justin Mandel; 139–41, NG/Justin Mandel; 142–4, HPRL/Justin Mandel; 146 (UP), NG/Justin Mandel; 146 (LO), HPRL/Justin Mandel; 148–9, HPRL/Justin Mandel; 150, NG/Justin Mandel; 151, Adrian Catalin Lazar/Getty Images; 153, Anton Jankovoy/Getty Images; 154–6 (LE), NG/Justin Mandel; 156 (RT), Franck Guiziou/hemis.fr/Alamy Stock Photo; 157, NG/Ritam Banerjee; 158, NG/Justin Mandel; 160, HPRL/Justin Mandel; 162–4, Virginia Hanusik; 165–6, NG/Rush Jagoe; 167, JT Blatty/Alamy Stock Photo; 168–9, NG/Rush Jagoe; 170 (UP), Matthew D. White; 170 (LO LE and LO RT), HPRL/Justin Mandel; 171, HPRL/Justin Mandel; 172–4, NG/Rush Jagoe; 176, HPRL/Justin Mandel; 178–9, John Bragg/Alamy Stock Photo; 180, Westend61/Thomas Haupt/Getty Images; 181–2, NG/Justin Mandel; 183, Frank Fell/Alamy Stock Photo; 184–5, NG/Justin Mandel; 187 (UP LE and LO RT), HPRL/Justin Mandel; 187 (UP RT), Slaven Sarkanovic/EyeEm/Getty Images; 187 (LO LE), zlatkozalec/Shutterstock; 188, HPRL/Justin Mandel; 190, NG/Justin Mandel; 192–3, RnDmS/Getty Images; 194, anyaberkut/Getty Images; 195–6, HPRL/Justin Mandel; 197 (UP LE), Thomas P. Peschak/NG Image Collection; 197 (UP RT), HPRL/Justin Mandel; 197 (LO), Michael Melford/NG Image Collection; 198–9, NG/Justin Mandel; 200, Mike Schirf/Cavan Images; 201–2, HPRL/Justin Mandel; 204–6, NG/Justin Mandel; 208–9, Artur Carvalho/Getty Images; 210–16, HPRL/Justin Mandel; 217, Classic Image/Alamy Stock Photo; 218–20, NG/Justin Mandel; 222–3, Deb Snelson/Getty Images; 224, NG/Justin Mandel; 225–7 (UP LE), HPRL/Justin Mandel; 227 (UP RT), Remo Nonaz/Shutterstock; 227 (LO), HPRL/Justin Mandel; 228–9, NG/Justin Mandel; 230, Randy Harris Images/Offset; 231–2, HPRL/Justin Mandel; 234–6, NG/Justin Mandel; 239, HPRL/Justin Mandel; 240–1, Craig Sterken/Getty Images; 242, dszc/Getty Images; 243, NG/Justin Mandel; 245 (UP LE, UP RT, and LO RT), HPRL/Justin Mandel; 245 (LO LE), Christian Raguse/Cavan Images; 246–8, HPRL/Justin Mandel; 249, Chuck Haney/DanitaDelimont/Alamy Stock Photo; 250–4, NG/Justin Mandel; 256–7, WerksMedia/Getty Images; 258, carlosalvarez/Getty Images; 259, NG/Justin Mandel; 260–1 (UP LE), HPRL/Justin Mandel; 261 (UP RT), NG/Justin Mandel; 261 (LO LE and LO RT), HPRL/Justin Mandel; 262–4, HPRL/Justin Mandel; 265–6, NG/Justin Mandel; 268, HPRL/Justin Mandel; 270, NG/Justin Mandel; 272–6, HPRL/Justin Mandel; 277, NG/Justin Mandel; 278, twildlife/Getty Images; 279 (UP), NG/Michael Starghill, Jr.; 279 (LO LE), Candice Estep/EyeEm/Getty Images; 279 (LO RT), Chester Leeds/Getty Images; 280–2, HPRL/Justin Mandel; 283, NG/Justin Mandel; 284, HPRL/Justin Mandel; 286, NG/Justin Mandel; 288–9, Norbert Figueroa/EyeEm/Getty Images; 290, NG/Joelly Rodríguez; 291–3 (UP), shakzu/Getty Images; 293 (LO LE), Laura Hasenmayer/Getty Images; 293 (LO RT), HPRL/Justin Mandel; 294–5, HPRL/Justin Mandel; 296, NG/Justin Mandel; 297, HPRL/Justin Mandel; 298–302, NG/Justin Mandel; 304–5, NG/Justin Mandel; 306–7, Quinn Glabicki; 309 (UP LE), HPRL/Justin Mandel; 309 (UP RT), NG/Justin Mandel; 309 (LO), Bloomberg Creative Photos/Getty Images; 310–1 (UP), HPRL/Justin Mandel; 311 (LO), NG/Justin Mandel; 312, Quinn Glabicki; 313, HPRL/Justin Mandel; 314, NG/Justin Mandel; 316–8, HPRL/Justin Mandel; 320–1, AJE44/Adobe Stock; 322, HPRL/Justin Mandel; 323, Axel Brunst/TandemStock; 324, HPRL/Justin Mandel; 325 (UP), Michael Roberts/Getty Images; 325 (LO LE), Joe Daniel Price/Getty Images; 325 (LO RT), HPRL/Justin Mandel; 326–34, HPRL/Justin Mandel; 336–7, David Photography/500px/Getty Images; 338, HPRL/Justin Mandel; 339, robertharding/Nigel Hicks/Offset; 340, HPRL/Justin Mandel; 341 (UP), Maciej Olszewski/Adobe Stock; 341 (LO LE), Alexander Jung/Shutterstock; 341 (LO RT), HPRL/Justin Mandel; 342–50, HPRL/Justin Mandel.

# INDEX

Boldface indicates illustrations.

## ABOUT THE AUTHOR

Scottish by birth, Gordon Ramsay was brought up in Stratford-upon-Avon, England, and initially aspired to be a professional footballer. However, when an injury prematurely put an end to any hopes of a promising career on the pitch, Ramsay went back to college to complete a course in hotel management. His dedication and natural talent led him to train with some of the world's leading chefs.

Now, internationally renowned and holding seven Michelin stars, Ramsay has opened 34 restaurants globally, including in Europe, the United States, Asia, and the Middle East. He is also an Emmy-nominated television host and star of hit series in both the United States and the United Kingdom, including National Geographic's *Gordon Ramsay: Uncharted*, as well as *Next Level Chef* and *MasterChef*.

A keen triathlete, Ramsay lives with his wife, Tana, and five children, Megan, Jack, Holly, Tilly, and Oscar. He divides his time between London, Los Angeles, and Cornwall.

National Geographic Partners, LLC
1145 17th Street NW
Washington, DC 20036

Library of Congress Cataloging-in-Publication Data

Names: Ramsay, Gordon, author.
Title: Gordon Ramsay's uncharted : a culinary adventure with 60 recipes from around the globe / Gordon Ramsay.
Description: Washington, DC : National Geographic, [2023] | Includes index. | Summary: "Chef Gordon Ramsay travels the world to share mouthwatering recipes and insights into a variety of cultures"--Provided by publisher.
Identifiers: LCCN 2022036830 (print) | LCCN 2022036831 (ebook) | ISBN 9781426222702 (hardcover) | ISBN 9781426223518 (ebook)
Subjects: LCSH: International cooking. | Ramsay, Gordon--Travel.
Classification: LCC TX725.A1 R295 2023  (print) | LCC TX725.A1  (ebook) | DDC 641.59--dc23/eng/20220803
LC record available at https://lccn.loc.gov/2022036830
LC ebook record available at https://lccn.loc.gov/2022036831

Since 1888, the National Geographic Society has funded more than 14,000 research, conservation, education, and storytelling projects around the world. National Geographic Partners distributes a portion of the funds it receives from your purchase to National Geographic Society to support programs including the conservation of animals and their habitats.

Get closer to National Geographic Explorers and photographers, and connect with our global community. Join us today at nationalgeographic.org/joinus

For rights or permissions inquiries, please contact National Geographic Books Subsidiary Rights: bookrights@natgeo.com

Interior design: Jerry Sealy

Printed in South Korea

22/SPSK/1